D0296561

THE VIEW FROM THE KREMLIN

ALSO BY BORIS YELTSIN

Against the Grain

BORIS YELTSIN

THE VIEW FROM THE KREMLIN

Translated by

Catherine A. Fitzpatrick

HarperCollins*Publishers*

HarperCollins*Publishers*
77–85 Fulham Palace Road,
Hammersmith, London W6 8JB

Published by HarperCollins*Publishers* 1994
1 3 5 7 9 8 6 4 2

A catalogue record for this book is
available from the British Library

ISBN 0 00255544 1

Set in New Aster

Printed in Great Britain by
HarperCollinsManufacturing Glasgow

To my mother,
Klavdia Vasilievna Yeltsina

PUBLISHERS' NOTE

This book is Boris Yeltsin's journal. It was written for the most part in the period from August 1991 until October 1993. Whenever possible, the translator and editors have added notes to indicate events that proceeded or followed those in Yeltsin's own account. Because the book was conceived as a journal, the opinions and emotions of the moment have not been altered by the editors to take advantage of hindsight. In chapters 1, 7, and 9, some of the journal entries are dated by Yeltsin. Others have not been. Throughout, he offers some of his most personal thoughts under the heading *After Midnight.*

In a few places, Yeltsin himself has exercised the author's prerogative to amend his observations and place them in perspective. Clearly, *The View from the Kremlin* is not the last word on the events it describes. It is, however, a permanent record of a period of historic upheaval in Russia as seen by the man chosen by his people as their leader.

CONTENTS

LIST OF ILLUSTRATIONS

Section One

Section Two

Pro-Yeltsin soldier on a tank (*Katz Pictures*)
Moscow's barricades (*Frank Spooner Pictures*)

Sixtieth birthday celebrations (*Rex Features*)
At his mother's graveside (*Rex Features*)

With the grandchildren (*Andrew Nurnberg Associates*)
With his daughters (*Andrew Nurnberg Associates*)

Negotiating with striking coalminers (*Frank Spooner Pictures*)
On tour in Siberia (*Rex Features*)

With President Bush (*Katz Pictures*)
With President Clinton (*Katz Pictures*)

Aerial view of G7 summit (*Associated Press/Topham*)
The G7 leaders (*Andrew Nurnberg Associates*)
Testing the wheat crop (*Press Association/AFP*)

Rutskoi (*Frank Spooner Pictures*)
Khasbulatov (*Frank Spooner Pictures*)
The charred White House, October 1993 (*Associated Press/Topham*)

Introducing a new Prime Minister (*Andrew Nurnberg Associates*)

Woman holding up photograph (*Frank Spooner Pictures*)

CHRONOLOGY

December 1985	Yeltsin elected first secretary of the Moscow city party committee.
February 1986	Yeltsin elected candidate member of the politburo.
October 1987	Yeltsin criticizes perestroika and Gorbachev's rule at a central committee plenum and falls from favor.
November 1987	Yeltsin severely censured and removed as first secretary of Moscow.
February 1988	Yeltsin removed from politburo and appointed first deputy chairman of State Construction Trust. Remains member of Central Committee of the party.
March 1989	Yeltsin elected by Moscow to the USSR Congress of People's Deputies, the Soviet legislature.
September 1989	Yeltsin's first visit to the United States.
March 1990	Yeltsin elected by Sverdlovsk as deputy to the Russian Congress of People's Deputies, the national legislature of republic of Russia.
May 1990	Yeltsin elected chairman (speaker) of the Russian Supreme Soviet (standing parliament).
June 1990	Russian Congress adopts a Declaration on the Sovereignty of Russia.
July 1990	Yeltsin quits the Communist party at its 28th Congress.

August 1990	500-Day Program for economic reform is drafted but later rejected by Gorbachev.
January 1991	Soviet troops seize the Vilnius television station, killing fourteen. Yeltsin flies to Tallinn and signs a treaty of cooperation with Baltic republics.
February 1991	Yeltsin calls on television for Gorbachev's resignation.
March 1991	Popular referendum shows majority support for preservation of a renewed Soviet Union but also for popular election of a Russian president.
April 1991	Gorbachev, Yeltsin, and heads of eight other Union republics sign the Novo-Ogaryovo Agreement, which initiates negotiations to replace the Soviet Union with a loose confederation.
June 1991	Yeltsin elected president (and Alexander Rutskoi vice-president) of Russia in a landslide.
August 1991	Reactionary security ministers and their colleagues attempt to depose Gorbachev and take power. Yeltsin leads the resistance to the coup from the Russian White House.
October 1991	Yeltsin becomes prime minister of new Russian government and delegates economic reform to Gennady Burbulis and Yegor Gaidar. Supreme Soviet grants Yeltsin extraordinary powers to rule by decree.
November 1991	Yeltsin issues a decree banning the Communist party of the Soviet Union.
December 1991	Yeltsin and leaders of Belarus and Ukraine sign the Beloverzshy Agreement, effectively dissolving the Soviet Union and creating the Commonwealth of Independent States in its place.
December 1991	Gorbachev resigns and hands over the "nuclear button" and the general secretary's secret archives to Yeltsin. At the Kremlin, the Soviet flag is replaced by the Russian flag.
January 1992	Prices are freed on most goods and privatization begins.
June 1992	Gaidar named acting prime minister of Russia.
December 1992	Viktor Chernomyrdin replaces Gaidar as prime minister.
January 1993	Presidents Yeltsin and Bush sign the START II treaty in Moscow.

March 1993	Yeltsin drafts decree on emergency rule but constitutional court declares it unconstitutional.
March 1993	A parliamentary motion to impeach Yeltsin narrowly fails to receive the necessary majority.
April 1993	Yeltsin receives a clear vote of confidence for himself and his reform policies in a national referendum.
May 1993	Policeman killed and civilians injured during violent May Day demonstration organized by reactionary nationalists and Communists.
September 1993	Yeltsin decrees the dissolution of Russian parliament, but rebel deputies led by Rutskoi and speaker Khasbulatov refuse to leave the White House.
October 1993	Yeltsin orders security ministries to suppress the rebellion of the parliament and its supporters. The official death toll after the storming of the White House is more than a hundred.
December 1993	Elections are held for the new parliament, called the Federal Assembly, consisting of the State Duma and Council of Federation. Gaidar's party, Russia's Choice, does poorly, and extremist Vladimir Zhirinovsky gains a quarter of the vote. A new Russian Constitution is approved.
February 1994	The Russian parliament amnesties the August 1991 coup plotters and the October 1993 rebels. Rutskoi, Khasbulatov and others are released from prison in March.
March 1994	While protesting that the amnesty before trial is unlawful, Yeltsin concedes it in the interests of social peace.

AUTHOR'S NOTE

After I was elected president of Russia, several major international publishers came to me with offers to write a book, but I have always believed that a political figure should not write memoirs while in office; there are other times—like retirement—when such revelations and belated admissions are perfectly appropriate.

Then in August 1991, there was a coup. That event shook the country and apparently the entire world as well. We woke up as usual in one country on August 19, 1991, but by August 21, we found ourselves in completely different terrain. Those three days were a watershed between the past and future. These events first forced me to take up a tape recorder, then to sit down and work on what at the time seemed to be a book about the August 1991 coup. My British friend Andrew Nurnberg, the well-known literary agent who helped me with my autobiography, published in 1991, came to Moscow, and a contract was signed to begin work on a new book. I then dictated several cassettes, filled dozens of pages with thoughts, and asked my wife and children, while their memories were still fresh, to tape their impressions. Later, I was able to work a little on the memoirs during my vacation.

That was almost the end of it. I saw that time was racing forward. In fact, I was the one accelerating events. It was awkward to write about the coup plotters. The Gaidar government started, the USSR was no more and Mikhail Gorbachev had retired. I wasn't able to keep up with developments, let alone find time for the book. I wrote a letter to the publishers, saying that, regrettably, I could not fulfill my obligations. However, if they would be interested in a book sometime in the future, I would like to postpone publication.

Whenever possible I continued to dictate my thoughts, jot down notes, and revise them, usually working at night or on weekends, when there was time off. I felt as if I were writing something people would read sometime in the future, but not soon.

That "future" turned out to be right around the corner. In September and October of 1993, events in Russia forced me to sit down once again with clean sheets of paper; within weeks I had finished the manuscript. I am certain that now is the time—not a year or two hence—when I should tell what happened to our country. August 1991 and October 1993 have merged into one unbroken chain: the empire was destroyed and we witnessed the agonizing and brutal separation from an entire epoch.

As I finish my premature memoirs, I realize perfectly well that the main protagonists of this book are real people. I will have to go on working with them; neither they nor I are going to retire. We will keep meeting and discussing current events and making decisions. Some of them are likely to find my reflections inaccurate; some may have a stronger negative reaction, but that's all as it should be. It would be easier to discuss my colleagues and evaluate events and people from retirement, which is the great advantage of the pensioner who becomes a memoirist. I haven't been so lucky. I am still president, and I still have a lot of work to do. This book is an attempt to explain myself, to try now, rather than in the future, to figure out what happened to Russia, to see where we are headed, and what awaits us all down the road.

I would like to thank several people who provided me a great deal of help in my work on the book. Without their support, publication would not have been possible.

I am grateful to Valentin Yumashev, journalist and deputy editor in chief for the magazine *Ogonyok* (*Little Flame*). We have shared more than fifteen years of collaborative friendship (he helped me with my first book). As I worked on the manuscript throughout the last three years, I knew that he was always close by. Sometimes our conversations took place at night in my Kremlin office; sometimes in an airplane; sometimes in front of the fireplace; but more often we spoke over a Macintosh computer as the most feverish work began on the manuscript. These talks enabled me to keep the outline of my future book constantly in mind. Valentin's discernment and advice were always extremely important to me.

I want to thank Alexander Korzhakov, chief of the presidential security service. His profession is hardly related to book writing, but his job forces him to be near me twenty-four hours a day. Many times I turned to him for help. His sharp observations gave me the opportunity to see familiar situations from a new, unexpected perspective.

I want to say some kind words as well to Viktor Ilyushin, my chief aide. The president's everyday agenda is kept in the memory of the computer on Ilyushin's desk; every hour and minute is filled, both past and future. In Ilyushin's head is an analysis of each day we have lived, and his independent judgments and precise conclusions have been very useful.

I would like to thank Lev Sukhanov, my assistant, who also provided a great deal of help on the book.

My kindest and warmest words are for my family, for their patience, understanding, and support. In those rare moments when we could be together, I had to lock myself in my office to work on the manuscript. They were the first to read these pages and were severe but fair critics; they were the first to hug me when at last I finished the manuscript.

My tremendous thanks to all of you.

As with my first book, I am turning over part of the royalties for this work to charitable projects. I have saved letters from people I do not know—a retired athlete, a disabled teenager, a museum director, a chief physician of a hospital, a farmer, and a mother of a daughter saved—all people who were helped a little with medical treatment and equipment, disposable syringes, wheelchairs, and so on.

I do not want to turn a natural human gesture into a political activity, however; I would be happy if, in giving away royalties for this book, I can help a few people who are in need.

Boris Yeltsin
October 30, 1993

THE VIEW FROM THE KREMLIN

1

A NORMAL COUNTRY

After Midnight

I suffer from insomnia. I get up at 2:00 or 3:00 A.M., pace around the room, drink some tea, and still can't fall asleep. I don't like to take sleeping pills and they don't help anyway. At these times I feel like talking to someone, but everyone's asleep.

I work on my book during these hours; that is, unsystematically, I ponder and recollect and formulate things and sometimes I jot down a thought, sometimes I try to memorize it. At two in the morning, you recall all sorts of things and mull over matters that are not always so pleasant; in a word, you become more open and sincere with yourself than during the day, in your office, when all your buttons are buttoned.

I hope that these notes will elicit the same kind of trust in response.

What do I remember? I ponder my life with Naina Iosifovna, Naina. Or Naya, as I call her. Tender, patient, always understanding. I think of our daughter Lena and her husband, Lyosha, an aerospace engineer now in business for himself; of Tanya and her pilot husband, Valera. I think of my grandchildren—Borka, Katya, and Masha—and wonder what the future Russia will bring them.

I remember how once my wife, Naina, came down seriously ill with pneumonia—she even had to go into the hospital. Meanwhile, our infant daughter, Tanya, who was still being breast-fed, remained at home. Because there was no one to baby-sit her at our house, and it was impossible in those days to put her in day care, I had to take the tiny mite to her grandmother's home in Beryozniki. Going to Grandma's house, however, meant taking a train ride for a day and night—even longer, about thirty hours.

So I wrapped the baby up in a blanket and got on the train. It was a reserved car with open sleeping berths. Everyone stared at me wide-eyed—where was that fellow taking that little baby? Embarrassed, I explained the story to them. The train started to move.

At first, little Tanya slept well. The women on the train helped me change her and everything. But at night, when she grew hungry, the horror began. Tanya cried and screamed and balled her little fists. Everyone in the car woke up. I was shaking as if I had a fever. They all felt sorry for me, of course. People began to look for a young nursing mother who could have spared some of her milk. They ran up and down the entire train, but couldn't find anyone. People advised me to wrap a piece of bread in a cloth and let the baby suck on it. With trembling hands, I took some bread and twisted it into a rag. Sure enough, she began to suckle. But within five minutes she was wailing again, realizing she was being deceived. So I gave her my finger to suck, and a little spoonful of water. What was I to do? I was so tired I was seeing spots before my eyes. What if something happened to the baby? Well, to make a long story short, I opened my shirt and let her touch her lips to my own chest, and she suddenly stopped crying. Everyone chuckled. The women on the train laughed almost until they cried. "See, he fooled her," they said. Perhaps it was the warmth of my skin; whatever, she settled down and finally fell asleep.

That's how I brought my nursling to Grandma's house. It was an emergency, but a funny one. My daughter doesn't remember this story, of course, and when you tell her, she doesn't believe it.

Now I have three grandchildren. There's Borka, my daughter Lena's son, who's thirteen. I think he is like his grandfather in some ways. By nature he's a go-getter. He loves to be a leader among his classmates. He's a real scrapper and, boy, can he fight. I find it interesting to spend time with him. He likes to play tennis. To be sure, he lacks a certain stick-to-it attitude, and I berate him for that. But he knows how much I love him and doesn't take my criticism seriously.

Then there's Katya, my daughter Lena's oldest daughter, who's fourteen. She's a very talented girl involved in all sorts of sports, very agile and strong and very goal-oriented. She radiates a kind of inner calm.

Masha is our youngest. She loves to knit and draw and is very feminine and gentle. She is sometimes teased by her siblings, but she never tattles on them. On the contrary, she always comes to their defense. She is the center of the family even now.

My elder son-in-law is Valera, a pilot. He comes from a family with traditions, with some very fine manners, and these best qualities were passed on to Valera. He is direct, independent, and strong, a real man of the house. Lena and Valera and the children live on their own. Whenever we get together, I always find it interesting to hear his opinions.

Lyosha, my daughter Tanya's husband, worked as an engineer in an aerospace design office but has gone into business for himself. Well, he's a brave lad. I'm worried about this for understandable reasons; his business is just getting off the ground and I'd like to hope he'll be able to stand on his own. I think things will work out for him.

Finally, there are my daughters, Tanya and Lena. They're the most beloved children on earth. Together with their mother, Naina Iosifovna, they make up the "women's great council" in our family, and decide virtually everything in the family.

In general, it's hard to be a wife. Being my wife is even harder. Then, to be the wife of the president—that's sheer horror.

The problems start with trivial things, with the kitchen. The women in my family do the cooking at home. At the dacha, we have a chef because it's a government residence with a lot of visitors there. It's not easy for a woman to get used to having a chef in the house. The housewives exchange skeptical glances. On the one hand, there's less fuss with the meal preparation but on the other hand, there's more trouble. The chef doesn't take into account the children's appetites, their favorite foods and whims. And what's there for Grandma to do?

When it comes to Borka, his grandfather is not objective. I had waited for a little boy for such a long time. There are often three different opinions on what Borka is allowed—mine, his grandmother's, and his mother's. The rest also start to chime in. He looks at us all—which opinion will prevail?—then goes and does what he wants anyway. He gets into the usual scrapes—a fight, a C in school, playing hooky, rudeness to his grandma, an argument with his sisters, or something else.

I imagine the reader has already realized that no one walks around the president on tiptoe in our family. Although they try, they do try. But it does get noisy sometimes and that's to be expected.

I'm very touched by their efforts, of course, both the little ones and the adults, as they try to create an atmosphere of serenity and warmth around me. They must all be in on it together because they look at each other knowingly, even little Masha.

It's Naina and my daughters who are responsible for this. For that I am grateful to them. Even so, they have their temperamental natures and occasionally get worked up about politics and can't stop the discussion, although they try to be silent when I'm around.

Does my wife understand who is my friend, who is my enemy, what is the logic of my decisions, does she try to give advice? It's hard to answer those questions. She advises me without words. She senses everything perfectly, reacts silently with great self-control. But I can tell she's upset.

On the whole, it's just a normal family.

A phrase from a Western newspaper about the "legalized anarchy" reigning in Russia today fairly accurately reflects the reality. Outwardly, Russia has all the necessary attributes of a state: the Justice Ministry, the powerful Security Ministry, and an enormous police force. But internally, there was no law and order.

Given the number of law-enforcement agencies, institutions of government, and state employees, and given such a civilized, cultured people, only one reason could explain the anarchy. The conveyor-belt system of administration was not working and, therefore, the machinery of government would not function. Everything was supposed to be subordinated to a single strictly defined principle, a law, a regulation. To put it bluntly, somebody had to be the boss in the country; that's all there was to it.

Of course, introducing the institution of the presidency to Russia will not immediately resolve all its troubles. A real government must be able to govern and manage. In my view, this is so obvious that I can't understand why many politicians find this matter so intricate and confusing. The main thing is for the government to fulfill its mandate and help its citizens live a good life.

No reform—economic, political, or financial—will solve our problems instantly. They will take a long time to fix, with year after year of painstaking, agonizingly slow work. We have to start somewhere, however. For there to be decent government employees in ten years, they must be trained under two or three presidents or parliaments. But now "they have no czar in their head," as our Russian proverb phrases it. They are almost incapable of doing anything themselves. Regrettably, we have no other staff; where could they have come from except the previous system?

All of us must be patient. And we must all learn.

What is reassuring, however, is that in the larger scheme of things, this situation is not some outright calamity for society. When we were under the Communists—now *that* was a tragedy. When the czar was executed—that was a tragedy. When war broke out with Hitler, it was a question of life or death for an entire nation.

I recall my own life and the lives of my parents. In the last thirty or thirty-five years, Russian society has had a fairly peaceful, calm, and stable life, with the same priorities as the rest of world civilization—the welfare of the family, culture, education, raising children, and duties to oneself and society. This was the age of Khrushchev, Brezhnev and Gorbachev—the fascist Stalinist system gradually turned into "velvet" totalitarianism (like the Franco regime in Spain or the Latin American dictatorships), with traditional, peaceable values still predominant. Society adapted and learned to survive within these restrictions, somehow managing to create a bearable spiritual climate, material wealth, and an atmosphere of moral tolerance.

This is of course a very difficult discussion, but I do want to say one thing: our modern society did not arise in a vacuum. We cannot compare what is happening today with the revolution of 1917, when the whole world was turned upside down. Now society is simply searching for a more convenient, more rational, more modern means of existence. I don't find very acceptable the tragically shrill notes resounding at times in the newspaper columns today. I don't understand them.

We are already living, not getting ready to live. That's probably the premise from which we should start. We live in a normal country—just a country with a slightly complicated heritage and difficult fate.

Journal Entry, May 7, 1993

In the Interior Ministry's Palace of Culture, near the infamous Butyrka Prison, we paid our respects to Vladimir Tolokneyev, a police officer killed on May 1 while helping to quell a violent demonstration. The street had been closed off. It was sunny, empty, and quiet, and as usual in early May, muddy with newly melted snow.

Bidding farewell to a person is an awful thing. Of course we will provide his family with a good compensation and we won't leave his child helpless. But somehow, it just doesn't fit—a May 1 demonstration turning out this way. We Soviets associate May 1 with ice cream, a bottle of beer, an outdoor barbecue, and, of course, bright red banners. But bloodshed?

The television footage of the demonstration was terribly disturbing. Without television, one could perhaps imagine a crush of people, a fight breaking out, and maybe in the pitch of battle a young man was shoved or accidentally struck. But the camera does not lie. The man who jumped behind the wheel of a truck and pushed the gas pedal to the floor knew he wanted to kill a policeman. It was premeditated murder.

Numerous questions arose: why was the line of police with linked arms so defenseless, surrounded on two sides? Where were the water cannons?* Why wasn't tear gas used? When will we get even one weapon with plastic bullets to disperse aggressive crowds if necessary, as should have been done in this case?

I stand at Tolokneyev's coffin and gaze at his young widow.

I, the president, can do nothing.

All of these questions bombard me five months later a thousand times harder. Once again I feel an almost physical pressure, the suffocation of powerlessness.

*Street-cleaning machines used to quell demonstrations.—Trans.

Journal Entry, June 5, 1993

At 9:45 A.M., I telephoned Alexander Korzhakov and asked him to beef up security to maintain order in the hall where the constitutional conference would take place. If there were catcalls, whistles, or disorderly disruptions of the session, the troublemakers should be escorted out immediately. There should be about a dozen people on duty in the foyer. I and Viktor Chernomyrdin, the Russian prime minister, would be presiding on the speaker's platform.

Ten minutes before the opening of the session, Valery Zorkin, chairman of the constitutional court, arrived. I knew that a place at the far left of the first row had been reserved for him. Ruslan Khasbulatov, chairman of the Supreme Soviet, or parliament, was seated at the far right. Zorkin had thought he'd be placed somewhere in the center, stood up, shook his head, then resignedly took his seat. Khasbulatov also stood near his seat for a time thinking, and then sat down after all. No one sat next to him. He squirmed in his seat for a bit, then appeared to bury himself in his papers.

My speech on the Constitution and the new constitutional process ran forty minutes. I had sat up all night rewriting this speech, extensively revising the second draft (I had categorically rejected the first draft after making fifteen major comments). My mood was tense. My heavy foreboding was about to be justified.

No sooner had I begun to speak than Khasbulatov wrote a note and began to gesture to a staff person on duty next to the podium.* The aide took the note and placed it in a box. This did not suit Khasbulatov and he began to make vigorous signs to Chernomyrdin as if to say, "Give me the floor after Yeltsin," despite the conference's approved rules of order. As soon as I took my seat, Khasbulatov jumped up and raced to the podium out of order. Here we go again, I thought.

The people in the hall, who were also agitated and nervous, did not behave very appropriately, either. Some began to clap and whistle.† It was a riotous, jittery atmosphere, ruining the opening of the conference.

*It is common practice in Russian political meetings to send written questions or commentary up to the speaker's platform.—Trans.

†In a Russian audience, claps and whistles are often signs of disapproval and impatience, not of approval.—Trans.

During the break, reporters asked me what I thought about the first day. "The conference is continuing despite the provocative action of the speaker," I replied. Even so, Khasbulatov was not his usual self—he was gaunt, the tone of his voice was imploring, and his eyes had lost their usual sparkle.

Next, Deputy Yuri Slobodkin began to shout and hurled himself at the podium. He had to be forcibly taken out of the hall.

I suddenly had a sharp and clear realization: once again, I was experiencing an overwhelming urge to break up this entire gang.

My irritation had probably begun that morning when the button on my telephone from Rutskoi's direct line had remained annoyingly lit for five minutes. I didn't pick up the receiver, but the light kept glowing. For five whole minutes. Hadn't I told them to shut off Rutskoi's direct line to me? What was the problem? It turned out that over the weekend, a technician who was supposed to turn off the line instead cleaned it, wiping the contacts inside the phone with alcohol, and somehow rejoining the wires permanently. If he was able to rejoin the wires, I asked, couldn't he unjoin them? I was told that no, he couldn't do anything except link the wires.

Still, despite my ruined mood, there had been a beginning.

Journal Entry, October 1, 1993

On the way to the Kremlin, I asked my driver to stop across from the mayor's office on Kalininsky Avenue.* The weather was overcast and very windy. Television camera crews came racing up to me and, as was fitting in this situation, I tried to speak with the utmost firmness and severity: until the rebels surrendered their arms, there would be no talks.

The familiar great hulk of the White House loomed above me. It had become so alien to me in the last year. I felt like throwing off its apparition, breaking off all plans, the whole strategy, and walking right into the nearest doorway, taking the elevator up to the right floor, and sitting down at the negotiation table to compel the rebels to compromise, surrender their arms, and withdraw from confrontation—to do *some*thing.

*Renamed Novy Arbat in 1992. The author uses the names interchangeably.—Trans.

But there was no longer anything to do. The bridges were burned. That explained my oppressive foreboding.

Soldiers had linked arms around the White House and were exchanging glances, calling to one another. They were freezing out here. How much longer would they have to keep standing?

Was Russia really doomed to bloodshed?

Was I right to issue the decree, despite so many objections? Decree number 1400 of September 21 was to have ended the destructive duality of power in the country, the clash between parliament and the executive branch of government. On the one hand, there was the popularly elected president; on the other were the soviets,* local and national governmental bodies drawn from party lists. Not the lists of the various new parties of recent years, but the lists of the one, invincible, omnipotent Communist party of the Soviet Union whose officials packed the current parliament.

The future would tell if I was right to disband this relic of the past. Meanwhile, I would act as I saw fit following the logic of events, relying, in the final analysis, on my own experience and understanding.

Journal Entry, October 4, 1993

At 5:00 A.M., Mikhail Barsukov, chief of the main security directorate, and his first deputy, Alexander Vasiliyevich Korzhakov, head of presidential security, came to see me. They asked if I would meet with the officers of the elite troops for special assignments, Alpha and Vympel.† I immediately understood from their tone of voice that something was wrong. But I did not stop to investigate, saying I had no time to meet them, that they had been given a specific assignment, and they should fulfill it. Barsukov nodded his head and they left. Half an hour later, Barsukov once again asked permission to see me. He was troubled: "Boris Nikolayevich, I really beg you. You must meet with them," he urged. "Not the whole group, but

*Local, regional, and national representative bodies of government in Russia (established during the Soviet era) are known as soviets, the Russian word for "council." The Supreme Soviet was the standing parliament.—Trans.

†*Vympel* is the Russian word for victory pennant. These groups, formerly under the KGB, were moved under the direct command of the president after the August 1991 coup in reward for their loyalty to Yeltsin.—Trans.

at least see the division commanders and the senior officers. The men are anxious about this assignment; after all, it's the second time in their lives that they'll have to seize the White House."*

I thought for a moment, then acquiesced. Soon I was informed that the division commanders, about thirty people in all, were waiting for me on the third floor. As I went to see them, I could not escape a sense of trepidation and a kind of unfathomable grief. I entered the room where they had assembled, and they all rose to greet me. I looked at them one by one, and almost all of them lowered their eyes.

Deciding to take the bull by the horns, I barked, "Are you prepared to fulfill the president's order?" In reply there was only silence, a terrible, inexplicable silence coming from such an elite presidential military unit. I waited for a minute and no one uttered a word. I finally growled, "Then I'll put it another way: are you refusing to obey the president's order?" Again the response was silence. I cast my eyes over all of them—they were strong, strapping, and handsome fellows. Without saying good-bye, I turned on my heels and strode toward the door, telling Barsukov and Zaitsev, Alpha's commander, that the order must be obeyed.

Subsequently, both Alpha and Vympel refused to take part in the operation. With great difficulty, Barsukov managed to convince them to at least go up to the White House. Having them nearby would put psychological pressure on the occupiers; they would surrender faster with fewer casualties. Barsukov put the men from the special units onto buses and had them park near the zoo (about five hundred yards from the White House). Here they dug their heels in, saying they wouldn't budge, without giving any specific reasons. Someone said that the soviet of the Russian Federation† should give the go-ahead for Alpha to take part in a combat mission. Someone else said hesitantly that they hadn't been trained to shoot at unarmed typists in a parliament building.

*The building of the Russian Supreme Soviet, or standing parliament. The first time the troops had been prepared to storm the White House was during the August 1991 coup.

†A special ad hoc body of regional representatives created by Yeltsin in September 1993 as a counterweight to the congress, not to be confused with the soviet of the Russian Federation in the Federal Assembly (parliament) elected in December 1993.—Trans.

Barsukov's tactics were simple—to try to entice the fighters as close as possible to the building, toward the action. Once they had sniffed the gunpowder and cinders and were plunged into the maelstrom of shots and automatic-weapon rounds, they would want to be involved.

Perhaps we could have done better without them. Actually, up to that moment we had not been planning to use Alpha and Vympel, and, instead, were going to use paratrooper divisions and *spetsnaz** army troops for the operation inside the building. But the fact itself was so telling: Alpha was refusing to go! Just like in August 1991! This would evoke definite associations. By tomorrow, the newspapers would be blaring, "Those bloodthirsty leaders sent in special troops against their political opponents, but the soldiers are so rational, so unwilling to mix into politics that they refused to budge." That would be just the external side of the unpleasantness, and no particular attention need be paid to it. But the underlying layer would be more serious. Information that Alpha had refused to fulfill its commander's orders could reach the parliament leadership and really boost their morale. That would give them an excuse to go on shooting and resisting and would lead to further casualties.

Barsukov persuaded several Alpha volunteers to climb on some armored assault vehicles and ride them right up to the building. They weren't going to try to penetrate it, but just take a look around so that if they had to ultimately take action they would know what to do. Four vehicles then drove up to the White House, and it was here that a tragedy occurred. One of the armored vehicles halted near a wounded man who was still conscious and needed immediate attention. A junior lieutenant† climbed out of the vehicle and ran to the fellow on the ground. Just then a sniper's shot rang out. The bullet hit the soldier in the back, right under his bullet-proof jacket. That's how thirty-year-old Gennady Sergeyev was killed, becoming yet another casualty of that bloody Monday. The injured man whom he had tried to help died several minutes later.

Upon learning that one of their comrades had fallen, most of the Alpha men needed no further persuasion to act. Almost the entire

*An abbreviation of the Russian term *spetsial'nogo naznacheniye,* special assignment.—Trans.

†The Russian Army has three ranks of lieutenants: *mladshiy leytenant* (junior lieutenant), *leytenant,* and *starshiy leytenant* (senior lieutenant).—Trans.

team set off to liberate the White House. Barsukov contacted Viktor Yerin, the interior minister, and several more tanks were delivered. The troops entered the building under cover of machine-gun fire. Barsukov and Korzhakov went at the head of Alpha. They figured (probably correctly) that the best form of security for me would be to arrest the leaders of the coup—Ruslan Khasbulatov, Alexander Rutskoi, Albert Makashov, and Vladislav Achalov.

Alpha's appearance in the White House had a shattering effect. Everyone immediately began to surrender. Alpha hardly had to shoot at all.

Such was the inglorious end of the October coup.

2

RUSSIA WINS INDEPENDENCE

Editor's Note: In this chapter Boris Yeltsin describes his increasingly stormy relationship with Mikhail Gorbachev, including the Soviet leader's fatal indecision and his failure at the end of his reign to embrace genuine economic and political reform. The author describes the last-ditch efforts to preserve the Soviet Union in the months leading up to the August 1991 coup, and suggests that the KGB recorded his and Gorbachev's confidential conversations about the fate of the USSR, thus triggering the coup. He also writes of his last-minute selection, almost by accident, of Alexander Rutskoi to be his vice president, which would later lead to bloody confrontation.

After Midnight

Often during my bouts of insomnia I recall some difficult days. Perhaps the hardest period of my whole life was after my expulsion from the politburo.* Gorbachev didn't send me into Siberian exile or to some far-flung foreign country (as was customary with his predecessors); he put me in charge of construction projects.

Sometimes I felt like pulling my telephone right out of the wall. It seemed to be an intruder from the world that had chucked me out so harshly. There was almost a physical sensation that this little

*Yeltsin was a candidate member of the politburo, expelled in October 1987 after a critical speech during the party's central committee plenum.—Trans.

white phone on my desk concealed some threat, that it would explode any minute, bringing new troubles.

I was sitting in the minister's office at Gosstroi, the state construction ministry, and this telephone, white with a red-and-gold Soviet state seal, was sitting on my desk. A feeling of dead silence and emptiness surrounded me. I will never forget those moments of anticipation. It was 1988, the heyday of perestroika. My aide, Lev Sukhanov, would say it was hard to look at me during those moments. I am always grateful to him for learning how to drag me, at least temporarily, out of my depression. For example, he would make a special effort to find a petitioner from a remote province, someone who hadn't been able to get an appointment with me, and would invite him in, carefully telling me, "Boris Nikolayevich, there wasn't a thing I could do. There's a fellow trying to get in to see you . . ." And I would get involved in a discussion and would come out of that emptiness for a time.

Gorbachev appeared to be gracious, sparing and pitying me. But few people know what torture it is to sit in the dread silence of an office, in a complete vacuum, subconsciously waiting for something. For this telephone with the state seal to ring. Or not.

As I whiled away the long hours in the Gosstroi office, I finally figured out my relations with Gorbachev. I saw both his strengths and weaknesses and felt the vibrations of trouble and peril emanating from him. I had never intended to fight with him personally; moreover, in many ways I had followed in his footsteps as he dismantled communism. But why hide it—the motivations for many of my actions were embedded in our conflict, which had arisen in earnest just prior to the central committee plenum in 1987 that led to my being ousted from the politburo.

By late winter and early spring 1991, Gorbachev was sick of perestroika. He clearly saw the dead end into which the country had run. There should have been more preparation for a crisis. The evolution of the situation was obvious: failed reforms and the latest "thaw" had gradually shifted to a freezing of the political climate with stabilization of the situation by forceful methods, with harsh control over political and economic processes.

His first step was creating the institution of the presidency. By the time of the plenum, he had finished the process of formulating his new status. This would be his protection from the Communists: it would be a lot harder to threaten the president of the USSR, as distinct from the general secretary of the Communist party, Gorbachev's other title.

Gorbachev began ridding himself of people who were becoming independent figures—Alexander Yakovlev, Eduard Shevardnadze, and Vadim Bakatin.* He was weary of the troublesome republics, weary of the complete muddle of the economy, and, finally, weary of our passive policy of endless concessions and peace initiatives in international affairs. Gorbachev was sick and tired of being the same old Gorbachev after so many years.

Perestroika's global strategy had run smack up against its inability to make practical reforms; that is, to break things down and build them up anew. Gorbachev's reliance on moral leadership and liberal ideologists had not panned out. Despite his expectations, the magic wand didn't work. The system didn't want to change, just like that, for the sake of its health. It would pretend to do anything you told it.

What kind of reforms did Gorbachev wish to make? Was he organically capable of playing the role of a severe uncompromising master?

Everyone knows that Gorbachev had always been an advocate of socialism with a human face. That looks nice in theory. But in practice, the former general secretary was so afraid of making the painful break with the past, was so steeped in our Soviet system that at first he was horrified by the very concepts of "the market" and "private property." This horror dragged behind him like a long train every time our "party and government"† acted. Even after the August coup, Gorbachev was extremely pained by the decision to suppress the party!

So in 1991, what reforms could we talk about under the new Gorbachev "tough line" team? Hard-liners like Boris Pugo, the interior minister; Alexander Bessmertnykh, the new foreign minister after Eduard Shevardnadze resigned; Valentin Pavlov, the prime minister; Gennady Yanayev, the vice president; and the others?

*Alexander Yakovlev, in charge of the media, and Eduard Shevardnadze, foreign minister, were liberal members of the politburo; Vadim Bakatin was interior minister under Gorbachev.—Trans.

†The stock Soviet phrase to describe the rulers. The party was an intricate part of the state.—Trans.

With this crew, was Gorbachev capable of playing the role of "strong executive"? Let the reader forgive my subjectivity, but I doubt it. By his very nature, Gorbachev was created for diplomacy, compromises, the delicate and intricate bureaucratic game, the cunning "Oriental" type of rule. But he dug himself into his own hole, surrounding himself with "typical representatives," as our school books used to say, of our Soviet state machinery. People like Pavlov and Pugo. In granting them enormous powers, Gorbachev helped push them in the direction of a right-wing policy shift at the same time as his own political background led him to a dialogue with leftist forces, to a political compromise with the democrats.

The fall into the abyss was inevitable.

I recall how after I was elected speaker of parliament in June 1990, Lev Sukhanov and I went for the first time to the office of Vitaly Vorotnikov, my predecessor in the position of chairman of the praesidium of the Supreme Soviet of Russia, as the title was officially known.

Vorotnikov's office was enormous. Sukhanov said in amazement, "Look, Boris Nikolayevich, what an office we've seized!" I have seen many an office in my life but I got a pleasant tingle from the soft modern sheen, all the shininess and comfort. "Well, what next?" I thought. "After all, we haven't just seized an office. We've seized an entire Russia." Even *I* was frightened by that subversive thought.

There was something to that thought, some distinct feeling of a borderline crisis state. And at last I understood what it was. Before, the officials who used to sit in this gorgeous office, in this new spic-and-span building known as the White House, were people upon whom nothing really depended. Vorotnikov, Mikhail Solomentsev, and others were all high officials of the Russian federation. But in the larger scheme of things, everything was decided in other corridors of power. To be more precise, on those upper floors even the biggest bosses were only pretending that they were ruling Russia's fate. Some urgent tactical decisions were made in the politburo, of course, which had its "progressives" and "hawks." But the country no longer sensed any real need for their commands and decisions.

Government officials came to these fancy offices, to this unlimited power, as cogs to a wheel, with the same measure of independence. Russia's main paradox was that its government system had for a considerable time been shuffling along by itself, largely unmanaged. There had not been any real powerful leader in the Republic of Russia. Even the reformer Gorbachev was more afraid of breaking and destroying this system than anything on earth; he feared it would get its revenge. "Perestroika," in his conception, was not supposed to touch the actual mechanisms of the Soviet order.

Starting in 1989, with the first popularly elected Soviet parliament, known as the Congress of People's Deputies, we began our protracted battle with the system. For the first time in Soviet history, we fought legally and we won. We won so that some day we could come into this office, which was to become known as the White House.

My joy was rapidly replaced by a bad case of the shakes, as the athletes say. It was true that under Gorbachev the system had shifted to another modus operandi. It could no longer crush us openly but it was quite capable of quietly eating us, bit by bit. It could sabotage any of our actions, and eventually fly out of our control. It could affectionately and tenderly stifle us in its embrace. There were numerous options. But we had only one—to win.

I felt strange in Vorotnikov's office, realizing how absurd it was. Here the leader of the opposition would be taking charge of the enormous Soviet Russian bureaucracy.

Hearing that a new boss was coming, the employees of the old Russian Supreme Soviet, the nominal legislature, had first frozen in panic, then scurried into hiding. During my first days in the White House, nothing happened whatsoever; nobody did any work. Everyone was expecting a complete clean sweep with scandals and abrupt dismissals. Persistent rumors circulated that Yeltsin was a ruthless and petty tyrant. All he knew how to do was shake his fists at rallies, people said. When he was party boss of Moscow, he drove everyone wild, as anyone could imagine.

I was forced to begin with an elementary political orientation. I called all the employees together and said that I did not intend to fire anyone, that we should work together. If that suited them, fine. If anyone had a hard time or was bored, we'd say good-bye.

Many stayed; a few left.

When I was a deputy in the Supreme Soviet, I had turned down the perks of a chauffeured car and a dacha. I also rejected the special hospitals and registered at my neighborhood clinic.

Now I suddenly encountered a different problem. Instead of rejecting such things, I had to lobby for them! This was not because the leader of Russia needed "privileges," but because normal conditions for work were required, and they were simply absent at that moment.

This revelation so amazed me that I pondered it—would people understand me correctly? For so many years I had criticized privileges, and now I seemed to be asking for them. I decided that people weren't stupid. They had realized even earlier that we had to fight not party privileges, but the unchecked, all-encompassing power of the party, with its ideology and politics.

First, I needed some kind of residence outside of town, so that people could live and work with me—secretaries, guards, aides, analysts—the whole crew. There had to be at least several rooms. Initially I was offered a room in a vacation home in the village of Lipki, but it was noisy and crowded there, filled mainly with clerks from the Russian Supreme Soviet. It was impossible to get any work done.

We worked for several months at the Desna Sanatorium, not far from Moscow. My assistants complained that it was uncomfortable and cramped with bad telephone lines. Finally, we found Arkhangelskoye, the vacation home of the Russian Council of Ministers. I shared half of a two-floor cottage with the deputy minister for agriculture, then the whole house was given to me and my co-workers. This is where we lived until the coup.

I paid for all the expenses at the house myself, right up until I was elected president of Russia in June 1991. After the August coup, I moved into the government residence in Barvikh in the suburbs of Moscow, a specially protected compound, as it is officially termed, with special telecommunications and so on.

For the Russian Supreme Soviet chairman's security detail, for the first year we hired only civilians. A retired instructor taught them all the tricks of their trade. The problem was that the entire government security service in the country was under the control of one institution, the KGB's ninth directorate. Their attitude toward me can be imagined—General Plekhanov, chief of the ninth directorate, had been the one to disarm Gorbachev's security men on August 18 on the eve of the coup. It was he who had run the security for all the meetings of the coup plotters, and to this day, he has not been prosecuted along with them, although surely his case was elementary—a deliberate neglect of his professional duty! Obviously, we feared hiring government security guards after the coup.

Nevertheless, General Plekhanov was still in charge of all the government *spets,* as we say in Russian—the special cars, the special telecommunications, the special buildings—and, of course, the provision of weapons for the security service.

Undiscouraged, my staff employed all their wiles to obtain weapons through legal channels. People helped out at the Soviet Defense and Interior ministries. By the time of the August coup, the Russian Supreme Soviet security directorate had the following arsenal in hand: sixty assault rifles, about a hundred pistols, two bulletproof jackets, and five Austrian walkie-talkies. And that was it.

Let me interrupt my train of thought to put in an enormous question mark.

Khasbulatov also had his home-grown security service at the parliament, answerable to nobody. His people tried to stockpile as many arms as possible at the White House. Does history repeat itself so exactly?

How will our Russian democracy appear to historians if the first time, the Communist putsch was afraid to shoot at democracy, but the second time, democracy itself was not afraid to shoot its enemies? Is there not a malicious irony of fate in this?

Let each person solve this riddle for himself. My answer is as follows: in both the first and second cases, the moral advantage, the force of right, was on the side of Russian democracy because it was forced to defend itself, to protect itself with the help of unarmed people in the first instance and with the help of threatening tanks in the second.

Even so, the fate of the White House of Russia leaves me no peace.

Future generations will also have to grapple with this historical conundrum.

Often I have made unexpectedly sharp statements on television that had the effect of exploding bombs. It doesn't mean I love to strike a pose and appear on camera—just the opposite. I find it hard work to let myself be filmed, as with any regulated, restricted behavior. When I have to go on TV, I sweat bullets and I hate terribly to see myself on the screen. I'll look only when I can't escape it.

But there was a time when I had to fight to get on the air, to get my own broadcast. That was in February 1991, when I publicly proposed that Gorbachev should resign. The March 1991 referendum on the public's attitude to the Soviet Union was at hand, and events were heating up terribly in the Baltic republics. Society was reaching the boiling point.

Everyone understood why the referendum was needed: to give legitimacy to a Soviet Union-wide state of emergency,* and to obtain the "legal right" to fight against the Russian republic's independence.

Each day, the television broadcasters were scaring the public with the specter of the Soviet Union's collapse and civil war. The position of the Russian republic leadership was portrayed as purely destructive and negative. It's easy to frighten people with civil war. In fact, I think many were already seriously expecting something of the kind.

That was why I was feeling an enormous need to explain myself, to tell people that reform of the USSR did not yet mean its collapse. But it quickly developed that no one was going to give me live air time and Leonid Kravchenko, chief of television, was playing games. He wouldn't come to the phone to speak to me, then he set some conditions, then he postponed the date of the taping. This cat-and-mouse game continued for quite some time, and, understandably, I began to get angry. Practically every day, in various newspaper columns or in personal conversations, the democrats were trying to persuade me to make a compromise with Gorbachev, to take the country out of its suspense. And now I was finding out what sort of compromise was really being offered to me—one with a gag in my mouth.

Soon the press was raising a ruckus, demanding that I be given airtime. Kravchenko pretended nothing was happening; it was the usual kind of incident in his line of work. As a result, the opposite of what the guardians of state interests had wanted occurred: curiosity burgeoned.

The problem was to explain my position as clearly and briefly as possible, so that everyone could understand. It was crucial in this current situation not to apologize or be on the defensive.

That was when I got an idea. You're afraid of Yeltsin? Well, then, you'll get that very Yeltsin you fear! I once again decided to go against the grain of established stereotypes in society.

*States of emergency had been declared in some republics prior to that time, but not throughout the USSR.—Trans.

"It has become utterly obvious," I said to the television viewers, "that while preserving the word *perestroika,* Gorbachev does not want to undergo perestroika in reality, but merely wants to preserve the system, preserve the harshly centralized government, and not give independence to the republics, Russia above all. . . . I disassociate myself from the position and policy of the president and call for his immediate resignation . . ."

Getting ahead of myself, I can say that the consequences of my speech were favorable—like some of my other sharp statements, this one did not complicate but ultimately defused the situation. It did, however, offend Gorbachev terribly, although that was not only a matter of psychology.

Why did I speak so harshly then? Why did I demand Gorbachev's resignation? After all, he was still considered the leader of perestroika, he remained the idol of the intelligentsia, and his authority in the world was immeasurably higher than any other politician of those years.

The newspapers of the world were not at all happy with my speech: "Gorbachev's resignation will hardly open the way to democracy" (*Berliner Zeitung*); "Yeltsin's decision to launch an open attack reflects his weakness rather than strength" (*The Christian Science Monitor*); "foreign diplomats believe that Gorbachev remains the most suitable candidate, if not from the point of view of progress, then at any rate to prevent chaos there. Yeltsin remains an unknown quantity and could lead to anarchy . . ." (the *Times*).*

Nursultan Nazarbayev, my good friend and the leader of Kazakhstan, had this to say: "At this crucial moment, when we are suffering an economic crisis, Yeltsin is virtually staging another crisis—a political one, this time."

Why, then, did I come down so hard on Gorbachev?

For one, there was a purely moral reason. I found intolerable Gorbachev's double dealings during the tragedy in Vilnius† and I

*Newspaper excerpts here and elsewhere throughout the book are back translations into English from the Russian translation of foreign news clippings made by Yeltsin's staff.—Trans.

†Gorbachev claimed to have no knowledge that the military would use violence to suppress demonstrations in Vilnius in January 1991, but many believed that he had sanctioned the actions of special assault teams.—Trans.

couldn't forgive him for burying the 500-Day Program* so quickly. It had been our only economic hope at the time.

There were deeper reasons for my attack on Gorbachev, however, and I only began to become aware of them during this period.

A completely new political force had become visible by then that lumped together Gorbachev and me, the leftist opposition and the powers-that-be. All of us were "agents of imperialism," the "American spy" Yakovlev, and the "chief German" Gorbachev! This force was essentially the embryonic National Salvation Front, consisting of the disenchanted Russians in the Baltic states, the new official hard-line Russian Communist party run by Ivan Polozkov, the unofficial "neo-Communists," the reactionary trade unions, the blackshirts, and so on.

Unlike most democrats, I surmised that the threat of dictatorship came not only from "Gorby's" entourage but also from Gorbachev himself. And that was truly terrible. The moment would come when he would have to save himself, and his exit through the back door would have damaging consequences for all of us.

For now the conservatives in the Supreme Soviet, led by the cunning Anatoly Lukyanov, and those in the government, the party, and the security ministries, had a clearly formulated radical ideology—"national salvation." Taking advantage of the economic crisis and the ethnic conflicts in the Caucasus, they designed a step-by-step model for a Union-wide state of emergency, essentially a blueprint for a future coup d'état.

It was impossible to maneuver between right and left in this situation. Gorbachev was now faced with the terrible necessity of having to choose sides. With this harsh choice, he was stripped of his chief weapon—the political game, the maneuver, the balancing act. Without that freedom to make endless promises, blocs with various forces, and unexpected moves, Gorbachev was no longer Gorbachev. Backed into a corner by various political forces, he proposed the idea of a new Union Treaty to be signed by all the Soviet republics. And managed to buy himself more time.

*A program for a staged move to a market economy drafted by reform economists Grigory Yavlinsky and Stanislav Shatalin in 1990. After being rejected by Gorbachev and the Soviet parliament, it was passed in an altered form by the Russian parliament, which, in effect, had no power to implement it at the time.—Trans.

As relations with Gorbachev worsened and the coal miners went on political strikes demanding his resignation, I made a trip to Strasbourg to attend a session of the European parliament. Since the fate of Russian reforms and the Russian Supreme Soviet was still very much up in the air, I decided to bolster myself with support from the democratic parliamentarians of Europe.

No groundwork had been laid for this trip. We figured they were democrats and we were democrats. But I was blasted in Strasbourg with a cold—I would say even icy—shower. The Western newspapers covered the chilly reception:

Le Monde: "Having come to Strasbourg—the gateway to Europe—Yeltsin must note that only one Russian is recognized—Gorbachev. Particularly unpleasant for Yeltsin was the Monday when he was subjected to a severe trial by a group of Socialists in the Europarliament. Yeltsin had not expected that he would be called a 'demagogue' and an 'irresponsible person'; that Jean-Pierre Cot, chairman of the group of socialists, would reproach him for 'presenting himself as an opposition to Gorbachev,' with whom, as he phrased it, 'we feel more reassured.' "

Berliner Zeitung: "The deputies of the Europarliament have taken a definite position. In very undiplomatic expressions they gave to M. Gorbachev's 'chief rival' to understand that his one-on-one fight with Gorbachev did not find sympathy. His effort to establish direct relations between Strasbourg and the Russian parliament were rejected. A Soviet Union disintegrating into pieces would completely destabilize the situation."

New York Daily News: "We have to remember that lacking the experience of democratic institutions, the Soviet Union will plunge headlong into bloodshed, hunger, cold, and anarchy if Gorbachev and the current government, no matter how weak, are undermined. Gorbachev's efforts to prevent the collapse of the USSR are possible only if political reforms are maintained and the economy is definitely improved. To the extent possible, the U.S. and other Western countries must help Gorbachev to achieve these goals."

The Western reaction was a terrible blow for me. When I returned home and cooled down somewhat, however, I realized there had been some sense in my trip. Russia was taking her first steps. If nothing else, the trip was a good lesson. What was important was not merely what I thought I was when I set out for talks; no less important was what my partner believed me to be.

For the Europeans, Russia was only the promise of something to come. From where we sat, we thought everything was fine. But from over there, from Europe, many things looked puzzling and were hardly guaranteed to turn out as we were assuring them they would.

I had already decided that I had promises to my own people that had to be kept.

The party's April 1991 central committee plenum was approaching. This next plenum boded only ill for Gorbachev as the party's general secretary. On one flank, the worsening battle with the democrats was not likely to slacken, quite the opposite. On the other flank, the attacks of hard-line party leaders were becoming more severe. Sensing that Gorbachev's position was weakening, his opponents were preparing a powerful offensive to remove Gorbachev from the post of general secretary and ultimately deprive him of support at the USSR Congress of People's Deputies, many of whom were Communists, thereby making short work of his policies.

Realizing the danger, Gorbachev made an unexpected move. He convened the heads of the Union republics at a government dacha in the suburb of Novo-Ogaryovo and asked me to attend the meeting.

I had just returned from Strasbourg, and the conference at Novo-Ogaryovo came as a surprise. What Gorbachev then said at the meeting exceeded my expectations. The president of the USSR announced that he would consent to signing a new Union Treaty that would significantly weaken the influence of Moscow Center on the Soviet Union's republics. He also very much advocated a new Constitution, after which the existing legislative bodies—the Congress of People's Deputies and the USSR Supreme Soviet—would be dissolved and direct elections for a new president would be held. I agreed to set my signature to a joint statement of the republic leaders that had been prepared in advance. The West approved. *The Washington Post* wrote: "Soviet President Mikhail Gorbachev changed his political orientation today in favor of a compromise with intractable Union republics and obtained support from his chief rival, Boris Yeltsin. At a meeting behind closed doors with deputies, Yeltsin said that Gorbachev 'had made some important concessions,' in decentralizing political and economic power, thanks to which, as Yeltsin noted, the republics 'may become sovereign states.' Yeltsin reminded those attending the meeting that in the fall of the previous year Gorbachev had deceived Russia over the draft of the 500-Day Program. 'This time Gorbachev has sworn to keep his promises. That was the most important thing,' said Yeltsin, remarking that Gorbachev 'for the first time has spoken like a human being.' "

With the agreements reached at Novo-Ogaryovo, Gorbachev was well armed for the central committee plenum. When the torrent of criticism came, he abruptly raised the question of confidence in him. With the republics' support of the Union Treaty, Gorbachev knew the representatives from the republics at the plenum would not back a decision to ask for his resignation. He seized the initiative, and the plenum had no other choice but to approve Gorbachev's line. In his concluding speech, Gorbachev stated that he did not go along with those who intended to declare states of emergency to stop the process of democratization and limit the sovereignty of the republics.

I signed an agreement in Novo-Ogaryovo to declare a moratorium on political strikes. After that, I flew to Kuzbas and asked the coal miners to stop their strikes. The miners went back down into the pits.

Despite these compromises, there was no way that my relationship with Gorbachev could have been called easy at that point. Having met Russia halfway in the Novo-Ogaryovo process, Gorbachev was still making every effort to prevent me from being elected president of Russia.

The question of my presidency troubled him terribly. As Oleg Shenin, former central committee secretary, later told investigators of the Russian procurator's office,* "Gorbachev focused a great deal of attention on Yeltsin's speeches and incidents at rallies and the congresses of People's Deputies. He dogged Yeltsin's every step and repeatedly gave me the assignment to locate some documentation about Yeltsin's health. The health issue was reviewed at the politburo in 1987 or 1988." (Apparently, my first critical speech at the October central committee plenum was believed to be the result of a mental breakdown.)

*The Russian procurator, is roughly equivalent to the U.S. attorney general or the British Lord Chancellor, but with more powers of investigation and prosecution. Shenin was under investigation for the August coup.—Trans.

In a secret memo, the Russian Communist party central committee recommended "diluting the strength of the opponent's propaganda machine" by putting up ten to twelve candidates for the presidential elections of Russia, "none of whom can or should expect to win," thereby taking away votes from me. They urged that a powerful and well-coordinated offensive be launched against my position.

The Communists were hunkering down for a campaign fight, and were doing this with the full knowledge and direction of the general secretary.

After Midnight

In politics you sometimes find yourself in difficult situations, as in life.

I purchased a membership in a tennis club and discovered a new form of sport for myself. The administrator of the athletic complex, a nice, sympathetic woman, tried very hard to help me train. The club was very cozy; the sauna and courts and everything were excellent and convenient. I could never get to the courts at the reserved time and would play only during off hours. I don't know how she did it, but she always managed to find one court free for me.

After a game, she would invite Alexander Korzhakov and me into her office to sit and rest for a little while. She always had some tasty refreshments on hand. After a few months, however, I began to feel a certain discomfort. The gym was invariably packed with all sorts of people playing—scientists, bureaucrats, students—and I began to feel that I was attracting excessive attention. I knew I had become extremely sensitive to the eagerness of outsiders to try to get near me or into my circle—I was really keenly aware of it. Even the slightest indication of such activity would raise my hackles and I would retreat into myself. How could I explain this to the administrator?

It was awkward for me, but there was nothing I could do about it. Like many politicians of my age and status, I had a certain degree of insularity. I also realized that if you sense danger or alarm, if you experience an internal uneasiness, you should act decisively on it.

It turned out later that all our heart-to-heart conversations with that nice lady administrator were being thoroughly bugged by the KGB.

How many accidents I have had! When I was chairman of the Russian Supreme Soviet I got into a very stupid accident in the center of town. The incident attracted a lot of attention and publicity but perhaps left some people with questions.

This was how it happened. One day, Naina asked my security people to drive my doctor, Anatoly Grigoriev, who had treated me that morning, to work. Grigoriev was offered the car that usually accompanies my automobile, forcing me to travel without an escort.

Our usual route was to exit onto Tverskaya Street, with the escort car clearing the traffic ahead of mine. (We had an agreement with GAI, the state traffic police, to halt traffic whenever we approached.) We would then cross Tverskaya, and from there it was a stone's throw to the White House.

I had sat in the front seat so I could stretch my legs out—an old habit of volleyball players who had broken their kneecaps. I settled in and took a little nap.

That particular morning traffic was very heavy—eight lanes—so there wasn't even a lane or a slot for us. A GAI officer halted traffic but since we were without our escort car, not all the drivers ahead of us noticed immediately that the officer had raised his stick, a sign for them to stop. We should have braked and waited for everyone else to stop. But the driver looked at me, and I automatically gave him a hand signal to go forward. He stepped on the gas and we passed a large van heading toward where there seemed to be a clearing ahead. Suddenly there was a terrible crash! And then a ferocious pain in my head. (Frankly, I have only a vague recollection of what happened.)

My driver (whom I had brought with me from Gosstroi) had made three mistakes simultaneously. First, he did not obey the chief of the security service, who had insisted that morning that he take a detour through the city. Second, he was traveling too fast, but without GAI's cover. And third, he forgot to brake. We crashed into a wooden fence, which absorbed the blow—but it could have been a cement wall. Then much of our lives would have turned out differently.

A woman passenger who was in a Zhiguli that rear-ended us was immediately taken to the hospital with scratches on her head. Korzhakov, in a state of shock, managed to rip off the jammed door with his bare hands, something he would never have had the strength to do ordinarily. Then he took me home.

Naina took one look at me and silently sank to the floor at the sight of all the blood, and my face whiter than chalk. She then took herself in hand and helped me climb into bed. An ambulance was called, and the doctors determined that there was no serious damage, just a light concussion. I had struck my temple and hip. But since I was quite weak and could not pull myself together, the doctors forced me to go to the hospital just in case.

There I was given a small private room. I felt fine, but all the nurses, doctors, patients, and visitors began to scurry around me. Everyone wanted to take a look at Yeltsin—alive and in person. I felt like the elephant at the zoo, and I really sympathize with that elephant now. I could only stand one night there.

In the summer of 1993, a rumor circulated that I was ill, suffering from some mythical attack. Once again people telephoned me and everyone was worried. This type of situation—a real or imagined threat to my life—keeps cropping up again and again and continues to hound me. It's as if they want to frighten me. Test my character. Keep me cocked. Well, what of it? It's probably a good thing. And I am very grateful to those who worry about me.

I didn't know whom to choose. Only a few hours remained before the deadline for submitting an application to the Russian presidential electoral commission ran out. A great many people were waiting with sinking hearts to see who my partner would be, who I would name as candidate for vice president. I simply could not decide.

It was the spring of 1991, the peak of the Russian presidential election campaign. Gorbachev was conducting a fairly skillful campaign, spreading votes over a wide range of preferences, proposing a whole spectrum of candidates (he was making these offers behind the scenes, of course, as only he knows how to do).

I believed picking the right candidate for vice president was extremely important. Later, polls showed that the people who would have voted for me would have voted for me even if Ivan Ivanovich Ivanov was running for vice president—in other words, John Doe, a completely unknown person! But at the time, my team and I were very apprehensive, waiting for the "last battle," the voters' day of judgment.

The situation was becoming increasingly ambiguous with each passing day. It was already uncomfortable coming to work and looking people in the eye. I was acutely aware that two people were tensely awaiting my decision: Gennady Burbulis, one of the people closest to me, and Ruslan Khasbulatov, then vice chairman of the Russian Supreme Soviet.

But neither of them suited me. I won't beat around the bush: I feared the purely irrational public antipathy to these figures. I didn't like the loser's image that both of them projected. More important at the time, I sensed that if I chose either one of them, I would be drastically upsetting some kind of balance of power in my team, a certain parity of forces. With one stroke, I would decide the outcome of their hidden rivalry, and just at a time when I didn't need it, I would earn myself a new enemy!

Alexander Rutskoi was selected candidate for vice president several hours before the official deadline.

Ludmilla Pikhoya and the late Gennady Kharin, directors of my speechwriters' group, were sociologists from Sverdlovsk. They were known in that city for their free thinking during the early years of Gorbachev's perestroika, and they had been with me for a long time. Unexpectedly, they had come up with this idea, and hurried into my office in the morning, happy and excited.

There was something to this. I liked the idea instantly because of its novelty. I had never had any close dealings with Rutskoi. Without any involvement on my part, Rutskoi, using his reformist "Communist for Democracy" group, had managed to split the monolithic "Communists of Russia" faction in the Soviet parliament run by hard-liner Ivan Polozkov. Rutskoi had thereby immediately positioned himself among the informal leaders of parliament. How these "democratic Communists" would behave in the future was not entirely clear, but their leader had unquestionably stuck in my mind with his striking appearance and his military man's determination.

He had the look of an accomplished actor, he was a combat pilot, a recipient of the Hero of the Soviet Union Award, and he spoke firmly and eloquently. A real tiger! Middle-aged matrons would swoon with delight at the sight of such a vice president! And then there was the military vote! Rutskoi was simply made for the election campaign. It was if he had been born especially to have his face printed on the glossy, colorful campaign posters, to appear on television and speak before large gatherings of people.

I often return to the memory of that episode and admit to myself the bitter lesson: you should not be drawn to a beautiful form, to a logic of externals. Nothing in life is simple. For every decision that comes too easily, you have to pay dearly later.

To get ahead of myself, our early relationship was cloudless and pleasant. During the coup, Rutskoi behaved staunchly in military fashion, which also merited my trust. There was only one little-noticed detail that almost spoiled the impression of those first "honeymoon" months with the vice president. For some reason, Rutskoi took a deep interest in my outward appearance.

He would come into my office, give me a horrified look, and say, "B.N., where did you get those shoes? You shouldn't be wearing shoes like that; you're the president! That's it. Tomorrow we're going shopping for shoes for you." The next day, Rutskoi would come in and offer me not one, but six pairs of new Italian footwear. It was the same with my jacket. "That color doesn't suit you. Let's go shopping." For me, this love of glitz on the part of an Afghan war vet and a combat officer was somewhat surprising. To tell the truth, I was a bit flustered by such pushiness.

I can't stand it when people try to invade those corners of my private life to which I never intended any outsider to be admitted. Of course we're grateful for your kind suggestions, but we'll get along very nicely without them.

Aside from this irritating feature, Rutskoi's main error—or, rather, not mistake but an inherent feature in him—was his stubborn refusal to understand and accept his own status. From the very first day he believed that the vice president was, to put it simply, the president's first deputy. As even a high school student knows, however, a vice president is a ceremonial figure. He performs one-time tasks and special assignments handed him by the president. By definition, he does not take any independent political positions or actions.

Deep down, Rutskoi did not want to accept a situation where from the outset several key figures in the Russian leadership, including the deputy prime ministers, played a far more serious role in politics than he. He looked for a way out of this impasse, as he realized that things were not working out. He found for himself a role that was truly paradoxical and unprecedented in the customary institutions of power—the role of a moralizer, a guardian of ethics, a sanctimonious figure out of Molière, who, with a humble and inspired expression, claws his way toward the president's seat.

After many months I understood that Rutskoi had never been close to me and in the purely psychological sense had never been a soul mate. The burden of dealing with him only became evident later on, when it was already too late to correct the mistakes.

Our psychological incompatibility was felt in many things, also trivial—for example, I could not stand his habit of letting coarse swear words slip into his speech. But most important, his intrinsic aggressiveness, his obsession with finding an "enemy within" was alien to me. Later I realized that this was common in a person who deeply represses his anger and thus suffers frequent outbursts.

I don't want to exaggerate anything. Rutskoi, like all of us, knew how to be kind, attentive, cheerful, and courteous. Perhaps he was warped by the military life in some way, or perhaps there were some personal problems; it is not for me to know. Rutskoi and I simply did not get along.

Let's remember what candidates ran in the first Russian presidential elections in June 1991 besides me.

There was Nikolai Ryzhkov, prime minister under Gorbachev. The people who were likely vote for Ryzhkov were those who did not wish anything new, who were for the USSR in its previous form, for the planned economy and the quiet life on state subsidies with a stable subsistence wage. Ryzhkov vigorously defended these social priorities. With the fiscal reforms of Prime Minister Valentin Pavlov, the conflicts in Nagorno-Karabakh and South Ossetia,* and with the start of the era of private enterprise, these priorities had come to the forefront for a large part of the population.

There was also—a creature of Gorbachev—Vadim Bakatin. He was yet another person who had resigned from the administration, a nice progressive fellow surrounded by the press. Few people voted for him, actually, but he did have a role to play: he caused a certain confusion and hesitation in people's minds, some of whom began to mix up the candidates and didn't go to the polls at all.

*Nagorno-Karabakh is an Armenian enclave within Azerbaijan seeking independence. And South Ossetia is a region in Georgia that sought to join the republic of Russia at the time.—Trans.

Finally, there was still one more "present"—three odious and very active figures who fiercely opposed the democratic idea entirely, who were against Gorbachev's perestroika, against both Gorbachev and me personally, and who advocated imposing order with an iron fist. They were Albert Makashov, Amangeldy Tuleyev, and Vladimir Zhirinovsky—a general, a deputy, and an independent politician. They were three fairly modern figures (that is, tough, determined, and aggressive), angry but, most important, dangerous. Dangerous because when such black obscurantism poured forth daily from the television, society was paralyzed, or so I understood during those weeks before the election.

Their slogans were both quite awful and attractive in their simplicity. Their recipe was to forbid, imprison, disperse, kick out, freeze, halt, confiscate, distribute, and so forth in the same vein. The slogans had a bewitching effect on public attitudes.

I make this conclusion because according to the results of the election, Zhirinovsky came in third, after me and Ryzhkov. Millions of people voted for this man, who feverishly concocted one absurd idea after another and spouted it over the television. Obviously what attracted people was his slogan that it was time to remove the old party apparatchiks from power, the politburo members, and "make way for the lawyers."* I don't think that was the main point, however. In a complicated society as harried by politics as ours has been, a "mad" leader with a simplistic fascist or semifascist line will always gain a toehold. If other politicians are failing, such a person has the green light. With the disintegrating economy, savagery and darkness were spreading with unusual speed.

The hawks blamed Gorbachev for everything (even Ryzhkov would occasionally take a potshot at him), but Gorbachev did not run for election! Objectively speaking, however, all the candidates were working for him; that is, against me. Through his people he lobbied for all my opponents, with the possible exception of Zhirinovsky. Gorbachev's people helped Ryzhkov and Bakatin organize their election campaigns; deputies' factions in the Russian parliament worked for Tuleyev; and Polozkov and his Communist party supported Makashov.

There were other circumstances working against me, too. For two years (since my election as a people's deputy of the USSR), I had

*Zhirinovsky is a lawyer by profession.—Trans.

remained in the position of the "eternal opposition leader." The 500-Day Program I had backed had been a mere promise. Then I had supported the new and strange idea of sovereignty for Russia.* But now the era of mass enthusiasm for democratic catchphrases had passed. People now associated democracy with Gorbachev's blather and the fall in their own standard of living. This disenchantment with Gorbachev seemed to work in my favor, but also against it: the public was growing rather tired of the same old political stories. Even so, those spoiler votes worked against Gorbachev in the end. Suddenly everyone cottoned to the fact that there were so many different candidates—and all rivals of mine.

It's hard for me to speak objectively of what mainly accounted for my success in the first free elections. Still, I believe that the myth of the "hurt" Yeltsin, the image of an enemy of the regime, was not the main factor here. I believe the most important political motive for my success was the division of roles: Gorbachev represented the Union, the empire, the old power, and I represented Russia, an independent republic, a new and as yet nonexistent country. Everyone was waiting impatiently for this country to appear.

Many Russians came to June 1991 with a sense of the end of Soviet history. Even the very word *Soviet* was no longer possible to pronounce; it had exhausted its resources. The image of the USSR was inseparably linked with the image of a military power. "Soviet man" and "Soviet tank" were both concepts that were inextricably and mysteriously joined. As Gorbachev changed our image in the world community within the framework of our global strategy by silencing our tanks, so he continued to babble on and on about socialism, the friendship of the Soviet peoples, the achievements of the Soviet way of life, which must be developed and enriched—never realizing that he was up the creek.

The Soviet Union could not exist without the image of the empire. The image of the empire could not exist without the image of force. The USSR ended the moment the first hammer pounded the Berlin Wall. Everything that was Soviet in people's heads—not all of them, but the most active and thinking parts of society—had by then receded. It was from this fresh perspective that the country approached the election of a new leader.

*That is, as all the other Soviet republics were seeking at the time.—Trans.

I came to the presidency with the idea of making a clean break with our Soviet heritage, not merely through various reforms but geopolitically, through an alteration of Russia's role as a powerful, enduring, long-suffering nation.

Ordinarily, meetings at Novo-Ogaryovo, one of the Soviet president's residences in a Moscow suburb, went according to approximately the same scenario. First Gorbachev would speak in his dilatory, circumspect, manner; then he would invite us to begin a discussion. In the end, I usually had to seize the initiative myself if a fundamental issue was involved, and do all the arguing. That suited everyone fine. To understand, you would have to visualize the scene in the small ceremonial conference room, where everything glittered with state splendor, as a heavy pause would hang over the long table and those in attendance would try to hide their eyes.

With the existence of two centers, two poles, the Soviet Union and Russia, everyone else found it convenient to choose his own position and maneuver between the two centers. As a result, Gorbachev and I bore the entire moral burden for hashing out controversial issues. Oddly enough, our debates never came to unpleasant scenes or fights, which was surprising since we were essentially negotiating the limitation of the Soviet Union's central powers. Something seemingly intolerable for such a man as Gorbachev was happening—the restriction of power. A number of circumstances must be taken into account here, however.

First, outwardly, Gorbachev seemed to be at the head of this process, preserving his "paternal" image, initiative, and leadership—at least in the eyes of public opinion. Further, no one was infringing on the strategic role of the president of the Soviet Union; all global matters of foreign policy, defense, and a large part of the financial system would remain under Soviet control.

Second, in one stroke, Gorbachev was relieved of responsibility for the nationalities' conflicts. Or rather, his role in reconciling these insane bloody quarrels was changed; from the "man with a musket,"*

*Reference to Nikolai Pogodin's story of Lenin's life as an underground revolutionary. It is also useful to recall that Gorbachev was supreme commander in chief of the Soviet armed forces, which had intervened in local ethnic conflicts in the Soviet republics.—Trans.

Gorbachev was immediately transformed into a peacemaker, an arbitration judge.

Third, Gorbachev liked the role, unprecedented in world practice, of leader of not one but many democratic states. This was a very good staging ground from which to launch his entrance into the role of world leader.

Finally, there was the psychological dimension: the new arrangement dictated that Gorbachev and I remain normal human beings during the negotiations; we could cast aside our personal differences. The cost of each word at these negotiations was high; but when you are psychologically prepared for a difficult conversation, when all the controversial points had been previously worked out then it's no longer like a politburo session, when every step out of line is treated as an attempt to escape.*

After the talks we would usually go into another hall where a congenial dinner awaited us with Gorbachev's favorite cognac, Jubilee. We would come out afterward, warmed and excited by both the reasons for the meeting and the meal.

While I was defending Russia's interests at the negotiation table, my aides had to defend them in other less enjoyable circumstances. They would usually try to put my car (the limousine of the president of Russia) first in line at the entrance. But one evening my automobile ended up at the end of a line of government limousines. My security people sprang forward in alarm, made an incredible U-turn, digging up the Novo-Ogaryovo lawn in the process, and finally put the car back at the head of the line—Russia first! Of course, boys will be boys. The manager of Novo-Ogaryovo was furious and threatened to fine us for the ruined patch of grass. Later, he backed off for some reason.

Perhaps from the outside, such a collection of "presidents," who in fact had no real power, appeared somewhat ridiculous. Nevertheless, I now look back on these meetings without any embarrassment and even with regret. What an opportunity was lost! It is hard to say what could have been made of this Novo-Ogaryovo concept. Perhaps it would have been independence for the republics only on paper, not in reality, and Russia's clash with the central Soviet gov-

*Guards in labor camps used to shout at convicts as they marched in formation, "Any step out of line will be treated as escape!"—Trans.

ernment would have been inevitable in any event. Our departure from the USSR would have been far more peaceful and less painful. But after August 19, the Union disappeared all by itself; it was gone in a day.

Still, it was not just a "civilized divorce," as the press called the Novo-Ogaryovo Treaty. Gorbachev and I felt unmistakably that our interests, finally, coincided, that these roles suited us completely. Gorbachev preserved his seniority and I preserved my independence. It was an ideal settlement for both of us.

We began to meet at length unofficially. Sometimes Nursultan Nazarbayev also took part in these confidential meetings. One such meeting took place in Novo-Ogaryovo on July 29, 1991, and it was crucial. Gorbachev was to leave for vacation in the Crimean resort town of Foros on the Black Sea. The signing of the new Union Treaty was scheduled for August 20, immediately after his return from the Crimea. At this informal July get-together, we had the opportunity to once again go over the most urgent issues that each of us felt were still unresolved.

The conversation began in one of the rooms of the Novo-Ogaryovo house. As soon as we began to address topics that were extremely confidential, I suddenly stopped talking.

"What's wrong, Boris?" Gorbachev asked in surprise. It's hard for me now to recall what feeling I experienced at that moment. But it was an inexplicable sensation, the kind you feel when someone is constantly spying on you behind your back. I then suggested that we go out on the balcony because I thought we were being bugged. Gorbachev protested somewhat unconvincingly, but followed me outside.

I tried to persuade the president that if he was counting on a new renewed federation, the republics would join it only if it would replace at least some of its odious entourage. Who would believe in a new Union Treaty if KGB chairman Gennady Kryuchkov, who had the attempted coup in Lithuania on his conscience, was to remain chairman? Not a single republic would wish to join such a union. Or take Defense Minister Yazov. Could such a hawk from the old obsolete days be in the new commonwealth?

It was obvious that Gorbachev was finding this conversation difficult for he looked tense. Nazarbayev backed me up, saying that Pugo, the interior minister, and Kravchenko, chairman of Gosteleradio, both notorious hard-liners, definitely had to go. Then he added, "And what kind of vice president would Yanayev make?" Gorbachev said, "We'll remove Kryuchkov and Pugo."

Next I tried to convince Gorbachev to abandon the idea of combining the post of general secretary of the Communist party with president of the Soviet Union. Amazingly, this time Gorbachev did not reject my proposal out of hand. He even sought my advice: "Perhaps I ought to run for president in Soviet Union-wide elections?"

All three of us then unanimously decided that after the signing of the treaty, Valentin Pavlov, the current prime minister, had to be replaced. Gorbachev asked us whom we envisioned for this post. I immediately proposed an unexpected and interesting candidate who would have strongly reinforced the position of the treaty itself and the republics that had signed it. I said, "I propose Nursultan Abishevich Nazarbayev for the post of prime minister of the new Union." At first Gorbachev was taken aback, then quickly realized the value of this idea and said he was in agreement. "We'll discuss other candidates together after August twentieth," he said in conclusion of this conversation.

That was our last meeting before the coup, and I think much would have been different if what we had agreed upon as a threesome could have been put into effect. History would have taken a different course altogether.

Only a little time would pass and I would see with my own eyes how a transcript of this conversation could be used against me: After the August coup, investigators from the procurator's office discovered mountains of files with transcripts of tapes of Yeltsin in two safes in the office of Valery Boldin, Gorbachev's chief of staff. For several years everything I did had been taped—and those files were kept in the Kremlin. Among these tapes was the conversation the three of us had in Novo-Ogaryovo. Perhaps it is what triggered the August 1991 coup.

3

THE FALL OF THE EMPIRE: THE AUGUST 1991 COUP

Editor's Note: Yeltsin leads the reader through an hour-by-hour account of the fateful August coup, describing everything from his decision to climb atop a tank in front of the Russian "White House" to his wooing of key Russian generals. Yeltsin describes the bumbling of the coup plotters and reveals that, had his enemies stormed the "White House," Yeltsin and American officials had worked out a plan for the Russian president to take sanctuary in the U.S. Embassy. He also provides a poignant account of how a disoriented Gorbachev returned to Moscow after the coup and only slowly came to grasp that the consequences of the failed coup would mean not only the end of the Soviet Union, but of Gorbachev's career as well.

I believe that history will record the twentieth century essentially ended August 19 through 21, 1991. The election of the first freely chosen president of Russia was a national event, but the failure of the August coup and the disappearance of the Soviet Union that resulted was a global event of the greatest importance.

The twentieth century was largely a century of fear. Humankind had never before known such nightmares as totalitarianism, fascism, communism, concentration camps, genocide, or the atomic plague. Yet during these three days, this century ended and another began. Perhaps people will find this claim too optimistic, but I am convinced it's true because during those days in August, the last empire collapsed. The imperial way of thinking and the policies of empire in the early part of the century were what played such an evil trick on humankind and eventually served themselves as a catalyst of all modern revolutions.

However, soon after the "August revolution," as it is called (although it was no revolution at all, but the opposite, the establishment of a legitimate lawful order in the country), difficult days began for our people. They expected paradise on earth, but instead they got inflation, unemployment, economic shock, and political crisis.

More than enough has been said about the coup—there are documentary films, books, and articles. As a result, the dramatic subject of the August coup and its collapse has turned into a kind of ideological cliché. People have already begun to get irritated with it. Before, people bragged to their friends about the nights they spent on the barricades set up around the parliament building. Now it has become more fashionable to flaunt the fact that they never went anywhere during the coup; they decided to stay on vacation and didn't take any part in the resistance at all. It is still necessary to talk about these events, but difficult.

After Midnight

Naina, Tanya, and Lena. My wife and my children. My kind helpers. When the coup was over, I asked them to dictate their feelings and some fragments of recollections of the three August days into a tape recorder. I knew that some details would escape their memories forever. Now I turn on the cassette player and I hear Tanya's worried voice.

Tanya: Frankly, I didn't yet have a sense of the real danger [the reference is to the events of August 19—Author]. Against the backdrop of that marvelous summer morning . . . Although there were a lot of guys with assault rifles around the dacha.

Papa decided to go into town. He put on a bullet-proof vest and a brown suit. The corners of the bullet-proof vest peeked out from under his jacket. I went up and straightened his jacket so the vest wasn't noticeable. I had the horrible impossible thought that perhaps I was seeing Papa for the last time.

Naina: I said, "What are you protecting here with that bullet-proof vest? Your head is still unprotected. And your head is the main thing." But what was the point of trying to tell him? He was leaving, and the children said to him, "Papa, you're our only hope. Only you can save everyone now." And I said, "Listen, there are tanks out there. What's the point of your going? The tanks won't let you through." He said, "No, they won't stop me." That's when I began to be afraid. I had the feeling that anything could happen. When he left, we were on pins and needles. We kept telephoning the office. Did he get there yet? Hadn't he gotten there yet? Finally they called us and said he'd arrived. The waiting seemed like an eternity.

We decided that we, too, had to do something more. The appeal to the peoples of Russia written in Arkhangelskoye needed to be sent around to those who hadn't received it yet. Someone said that the telephones were no longer answering. Had they been cut off? We only managed to transmit the text of the appeal to Zelenograd.*

Lena: Lyosha and I decided to try to find a fax machine at the dachas. We did find a fax at one dacha and began to send out the appeal.

Lyosha: I called my office—there was a fax there, too—and asked them to start sending things out to everyone from there.

Lena: The first fax went through, but the second was cut off after the first sentence. It just wouldn't budge. We went crazy for quite a while trying to get through to all the numbers, but we couldn't. We started home, and there the security people were, coming to pick us up—a van and some guys with assault rifles. We decided to send Mama and the children away.

Naina: We went in the van and took some circuitous routes.

Tanya: But first we packed some things and I ran into the greenhouse, which we had been tending all summer, where we had planted for the first time some cucumbers and tomatoes, and I picked as many as I could. The children fell silent when they saw the people with assault weapons.

Lena: We put the kids in the car and gave them instructions: if security said so, they had to lie down on the floor and not ask questions. Borka asked, "Mama, will they shoot us in the head?" That phrase just devastated us. I thought to myself, I don't know how all this will end, but it's terrible when children ask such questions.

*An outlying Moscow district of special housing for scientists and engineers who are fervent Yeltsin supporters—Trans.

Naina: When I read today about Georgia, Abkhazia, Ossetia, and Ingushetia, I always see our children in my mind's eye. They were not shot, although what happened was terrible. But to think of the Caucasus, Nagorno-Karabakh, everywhere, where children's blood is shed! And when you see a grandmother, or grandfather, or mother holding a child by the hand, running, in order to save themselves, and those politicians are still arguing somewhere—you just get so angry!*

During those days in August, I was shocked most of all at how the children understood everything, absolutely everything, and were silent.

Lena: Lyosha, Tanya, and I went home in the Volga. While we were driving along Kaluzhskoye Highway, nothing was happening. But when we turned onto the Ring Road, we kept passing tanks. They took the far-right lane and were going along one after another. It was unpleasant feeling that these were our guys sitting in the tanks, so happy and smiling. We wondered if they would really shoot. After all, they were our people!

Lyosha: There was a gigantic column traveling along. Many of their vehicles had broken down, and they were busily pushing them over to the shoulder of the road.

We went along Minskoye Highway to the Hotel Ukraine—it was closed off. Armored personnel carriers were parked there. We made a turn and went toward the Shelepikhinsky Bridge. But it was also closed. We had to go through Mnevniki. Finally we got to the Belorussian Station, right near our home.

Lena: When we were driving through the Fili district, it seemed as if we were in a dream. We were speeding along very fast, with a pretty good idea of what was happening. But people in the street were quietly going to the store. In these districts on the outskirts of town, life was going on as usual.

*Abkhazia and South Ossetia are regions within the former Soviet republic of Georgia seeking autonomy. Ingushetia is a region within the Russian Federation seeking autonomy. Nagorno-Karabakh, the Armenian enclave within the Muslim former republic of Azerbaijan, seeks independence. All of these regions are located in the Caucasus Mountains.—Trans.

Lyosha: What do you mean, on the outskirts, if in the center of town women were calmly buying vegetables and watermelon from the stands outside the metro? It seemed as if nothing was happening.

Lena: It was later we realized that they still hadn't seen the tanks, and had not realized that they were moving on Moscow. We got home and went into the apartment. Zhenya Lantsov [a security employee—Author] was already there. And he told us, "Guys, don't go near the windows." That made the tension worse. We couldn't go near the windows or go out on the balcony.

Tanya: On Monday, Lyosha was raring to go to work. Valera was away on a flight. I said, "Lyosha, you are the only man in the family. We don't know how this is going to turn out, it's such a tense situation. I beg you, please stay; don't go anywhere. Imagine if one of the women should get sick, or anything could happen." So he didn't go to work on Monday. Although all the guys got together at his office.

Lyosha: Monday night and early Tuesday morning were the worst, when we didn't understand anything and downstairs in the guards' room, I remember, the guys from security spent the night on the floor. There were about five of them. I went downstairs to have a cigarette and they told me things could get quite interesting if they decided to take us—we had two assault rifles among five men.

Tanya: We didn't sleep all that night. We had the television turned on, the radio tuned to the station of "Echo of Moscow," and the BBC.

That night I telephoned the White House and was told: everything's normal, Papa has practically not slept at all, he is working constantly, and he is in a fighting mood. But most of all we feared for the people outside the White House.

Lena: A military vehicle that looked like a bread van was parked outside in our courtyard the whole time. All those days. The most difficult moment for all of us was the evening of August twentieth when Sergei Stankevich* announced over the radio, "All women must leave the White House." Suddenly, Zhenya Lantsov came up and said, "Guys, you'd better go. Get the children together."

*A Yeltsin supporter in Soviet parliament.—Trans.

Tanya: I was about to telephone and find out where we could go. But Alexander Korzhakov told us to stay home. So we did.

It was then, by the way, that the children began to get worried for the first time. Borka and Masha had behaved perfectly for the whole time; we didn't see or hear them, they didn't ask for anything to eat or drink. But now Masha came up and asked, "Tanya, they aren't going to arrest us, are they?" It was completely serious.

We couldn't leave. There were roadblocks all along the Garden Ring Road. A curfew was declared. We put the children to bed in their clothes. Just in case.

On August 18, the eve of the coup, I was in Alma-Ata.* It was an important official visit: a bilateral agreement between Russia and Kazakhstan was being signed. Now that the meeting over, it was time to fly home. But Nazarbayev wouldn't let us go, and persuaded us to stay another hour. After a large ceremonial dinner, there was a concert of Kazakh folk music, then another performance, and another . . . Choirs, dance collectives, the clanging of national instruments, colorfully dressed girls whirling around. Frankly, my eyes were already starting to glaze over from it all.

Our flight was postponed for an hour. Then another hour. Nazarbayev was playing the Oriental host—not imposingly, but gently, delicately. Still the grip was just as strong. It was then I felt something was wrong. There was a certain sense of things going too far, too much pressure. I had managed to fit in some swimming in a mountain river that day, so I was sleepy. All I could see were dancers twirling before my eyes. But internally I had a sense of vague unfocused anxiety.

I don't think that our three-hour delay in departure from Alma-Ata was accidental. Perhaps something will come out during the trial of the coup plotters, but one interesting detail is already known. Alexander Tizyakov, one of the conspirators now in Sailors' Haven Prison,† who had a prepared directive for his co-conspirators, said: "It is necessary to recall in the course of the investigation and the judicial proceedings . . . that in the conversation with Gorbachev an option was even envisioned whereby on the eve of the final deci-

*The capital of Kazakhstan, now known as Almaty.—Trans.

†The coup plotters were given amnesty without trial in 1994 and all of them, including Tizyakov, were released from prison.—Trans.

sion to impose a state of emergency, on August 18, the plane on which the Russian government delegation, headed by Yeltsin, was traveling to Moscow from Kazakhstan should be destroyed in the air at night . . ."

Reading this statement I had a vivid recollection of the strange chill in my chest that time in Kazakhstan. We will probably never learn whether there was such a plan in reality or whether the plotters were just trying to mislead the investigation. But as I review those days, I am persuaded once again that we were walking on the edge of a precipice.

By 8:00 A.M. Marshal Dimitry Yazov was holding a meeting with the top military leadership. Designated units were supposed to enter Moscow on the morning of the 19th. A fair number of generals had learned of the impending coup overnight, although they did not know all the details, nor about Gorbachev's arrest.

At 11:00 A.M., KGB Chairman Kryuchkov informed his deputies and the chiefs of the KGB directorates that a state of emergency was being declared in the country. The KGB's third chief directorate (military counterintelligence) and the directorate to protect the constitutional order (former fifth directorate, which dealt with ideology) began to put together special groups to dispatch to the Baltic republics.

The seventh directorate (surveillance) was assigned to monitor the situation near my dacha in Arkhangelskoye and to maintain surveillance, with a team of arresting officers stationed nearby.

KGB Chairman Kryuchkov gave his deputy, Lebedev, a list of people who were to be kept under surveillance and arrested if necessary.

At the same time, Gorbachev's chief of staff, Boldin, and other officials flew to Foros in order to "talk Gorbachev into" signing a decree declaring a state of emergency and transferring power to the GKChP* "for health reasons."

At 3:30 P.M., the three law-enforcement and security ministers—Yazov, Kryuchkov, and Interior Minister Pugo—gathered in Yazov's office at the Defense Ministry (Pugo had just returned from vacation in the Crimea that day).

**Gosudarstvenniy komitet chrezvychaynogo polozheniya,* state committee for the state of emergency. The initials "GKChP" are a mouthful even for Russians. "ChP" has long been used in Russia as an idiomatic expression to mean a crisis of any kind, serious or humorous. From the outset, the name selected by the coup plotters suggested that they were in a state of emergency themselves rather than declaring one.—Trans.

At 5:00 P.M., two military helicopters flew to the government vacation home in Valdai in northern Russia to pick up Anatoly Lukyanov, speaker of the USSR parliament.

At 6:00 P.M., they were all assembled at the Kremlin, with the exception of Soviet Vice President Gennady Yanayev, who arrived intoxicated thirty to forty minutes later, and Lukyanov, who had already called to say he was on his way from the airport.

The machinery of the coup was now working at top speed.

We flew into Vnukovo Airport from Kazakhstan before daybreak. A car drove us to the dacha at Arkhangelskoye.

All my thoughts were filled with the forthcoming signing of the Union Treaty. Would the republics—above all, Russia—have the right to vote in decisions involving the Soviet Union's strategic agenda? Or was Gorbachev hoping to dilute Russia's radical position using the votes of other, more compliant republics? One way or another, an event of enormous import was about to happen. The first stage of the signing was scheduled—I looked at my watch—yes, nearly for tomorrow.

I relaxed and looked out the window. Farms, villages, and telephone poles whizzed by me in the dark. I was in a calm and peaceful mood.

The coup plotters gathered in the Kremlin.

The chief protagonists of the plot—KGB Chairman Kryuchkov; Defense Minister Dimitry Yazov; Oleg Shenin, in charge of party personnel and organizational affairs; Oleg Baklanov, politburo member in charge of the military-industrial complex and space program; and Valentin Pavlov, prime minister, had met the previous day, August 17, at a secret KGB location in the southwest part of the capital. Prior to that meeting, on August 6, Kryuchkov had brought in KGB analysts to forecast the consequences of imposing a state of emergency in the country. They did not merely generate some abstract model of a strategic situation, the kind that KGB analysts, keeping in mind, of course, their bosses' tastes and needs, put together from time to time when assigned by higher-ups. This was a specific order: outline the issues, prepare the main documents, and identify the chief directions of a future coup.

The risk was great that confidential information would leak, especially because Kryuchkov had brought in an expert from another bureaucracy, the Defense Ministry. (That expert was Pavel Grachev, future defense minister of Russia, who, during the coup, played one of the key roles in refusing to support the members of the GKChP.) But Kryuchkov had to take that risk. He had actively negotiated with party representatives—central committee secretaries Baklanov and Shenin. Furthermore, on the eve of the coup, Kryuchkov made direct contact with Boldin, Gorbachev's chief of staff, and one of the people closest to and most trusted by Gorbachev.

Then for a fairly large group of top officials, Kryuchkov laid out his thesis that Gorbachev, president of the USSR, was a hostage in the hands of extremists, in particular, the chief extremist, me. This was grounds for imposing a state of emergency. Kryuchkov not only outlined this idea, but he also argued and persuaded and brought people into the process of the conspiracy. Proof of this was meetings held just before the coup—with representatives of various other power structures in the government. The KGB ordinarily was not so cooperative with the other bureaucracies.

Thus was born the conspiracy, planned quite brazenly and calmly. The plotters seemed unafraid of a backlash, believing they were on solid ground. By this time Kryuchkov had evolved a theory under the influence of various factors that Gorbachev was completely isolated. In the struggle against the KGB, Gorbachev had absolutely no one to rely on, or so Kryuchkov believed. General secretary and now president of the Soviet Union (although it was true he had been elected in a rather strange manner),* Gorbachev was now in suspended animation.

The way to understand the general dimensions of Kryuchkov's theory is as follows: Gorbachev had long since ceased to be leader of the reform process. His concessions to democrats in the course of the Novo-Ogaryovo talks about the new Union Treaty had been forced and in some sense were a bluff. As I have noted, he started the talks in order to buy himself time after being backed into a corner in the struggle between conservatives and liberals.

All the large street rallies of the winter and spring of 1991 that had rocked Moscow (and in some sense had stimulated the president of the USSR toward new ideas and actions) were largely "anti-Gorbachev."

*Gorbachev was not elected by popular vote but by the Soviet parliament, which contained many old-style Communist officials.—Trans.

Neither could Gorbachev rely on the parliament that had once been obedient to him. The Supreme Soviet was entirely controlled by Lukyanov. Its deputies were obviously opposed to economic reform, the new Union Treaty, and Gorbachev's perestroika as a whole. The majority of this parliament was made up of the former Soviet *nomenklatura** elite, who were feeling cramped and unhappy with the reforms.

Enormous displeasure was growing in the army as well. There were numerous reasons: the winding down of the defense industry, the alteration of the country's strategic mission, concessions to the West on disarmament, the completely unprepared withdrawal of forces from East Germany, and the necessitated participation in ethnic conflicts in the Soviet republics, which threatened the life and limb of Soviet military personnel and their families.

Finally, the main bulwark of Gorbachev's power—the executive branch of the government—began to crack. From April to June 1991, Valentin Pavlov very sharply delineated his position, insisting on his own independent opinion on many economic and political matters, in antagonism to the Gorbachev administration's general line. This had a dramatic impact, and suddenly it seemed that Gorbachev had no means of reining in the wayward Pavlov. There was no ruling body that could obediently make hard decisions under the president's guidance because by that time the politburo had been lawfully removed from power, nominally remaining in place but virtually superseded in importance by the new Presidential Council of advisers. Then, after Shevardnadze and two other liberals, Bakatin and Yakovlev, left the Presidential Council, it, too, ceased to be an entity that could provide Gorbachev with support. The Communist party had split into left, right, and center factions and was very unhappy with Gorbachev, its official leader.

No matter how you looked at it, Gorbachev seemed to be alone.

Kryuchkov carefully studied this vacuum around the chief "foreman of perestroika."† Gorbachev's vacillations among the various political forces cost the first and last president of the USSR dearly.

According to KGB reports, Gorbachev had lost the trust of broad sections of the Soviet populace and had begun to lose authority

*The *nomenklatura* was the list of party-approved positions in the party itself, the state, the economy, and other government-controlled bodies. The term came to mean the Soviet power elite, and the usage has been preserved in Russian politics.—Trans.

†A slogan from the early years of perestroika used (often ironically) to describe the leaders of reform.—Trans.

among the major Western politicians as well. A KGB memo submitted to Kryuchkov stated that "those close to G. Bush believe that M. S. Gorbachev has practically exhausted all his possibilities as leader of such a country as the USSR. . . . The Bush administration and governments of other Western countries are trying to identify a possible candidate to replace Gorbachev."

It's not important whether this KGB memo was based on reality or not; what matters is that Kryuchkov clearly made use of such reports in planning the tactic for the coup. It was not strictly a military coup, but was virtually a lawful administrative replacement in the upper echelons of power—a replacement of the Gorbachev "everyone was fed up with."

On the evening of August 18 in Prime Minister Pavlov's office in the Kremlin all the coup plotters gathered officially for the first time without Gorbachev present. It was the entire "presidential team," sent in to replace the original players, who were now conspiring to replace the trainer himself.

This does not only happen in soccer.

Nevertheless, despite the momentum, it was psychologically very difficult to take the step of plotting a coup. Kryuchkov divided all the key players into three groups: the first group were those who made decisions with him. They were chiefly the central committee representatives Baklanov and Shenin and also Pavlov and Yazov, although the latter played a passive role the whole time. The second group consisted of people who had been brought into the plot's orbit through cautious conversations and hints. The third group contained those who would go along once they saw the forces in favor of a state of emergency, and who in fact could not step aside. They didn't have the courage or the foresight. Even Lukyanov did not back out, although he had said from the outset that as a representative of the legislative branch he could not join the GKChP and asked that his name be crossed off the list. Then he fell silent and with the rest began to await the return of the group of comrades who had visited Gorbachev in the Crimea.* They waited for several hours.

*The delegation sent by the GKChP to negotiate with Gorbachev consisted of Yuri Plekhanov, head of the KGB directorate in charge of security for government leaders; Oleg Shenin and Oleg Baklanov of the central committee; and Gen. Valentin Varennikov, commander of the ground forces.—Trans.

Kryuchkov had already informed them of the main facts, but everyone wanted to know the details. They wanted to see the expression on the faces of the people who had spoken with Gorbachev.

Yanayev did not quit, either. When he and others met their fellow comrades flying in from Foros, Yanayev learned that Gorbachev had been abrupt and categorical, cutting off all ties linking him to his old team in one stroke. Yanayev then apparently began to worry and could not force himself to sign the GKChP documents for quite a while. In the end, however, he did sign; they broke each other down, one after another. The last to crack was Bessmertnykh, the foreign minister, who had flown in from a vacation home in Belarus, just as he was, in jeans and a jacket. He was also frightened, saying that he should not sign such serious documents, that he should first communicate with the ministers of foreign countries and needed room to maneuver. But he, too, was forced to support the decisions of the GKChP through the Foreign Ministry.

In fact, there was no resistance among these officials. These three—the vice president, the speaker of parliament, and the foreign minister—at first held themselves back from the coup, but later danced obediently to the tune of its chief instigators.

This third group, dragged into the plot at the last stage, was precisely the group that had some chances to stop it. At the moment when Lukyanov asked to be crossed off the list of the GKChP, or when Yanayev delayed in signing the GKChP's documents, or even when Bessmertnykh entered the picture, there was still time to change everything. But they played by the rules of a criminal gang: each initiate is forced to wear the gang's colors to make sure he won't quit. The main motive of the plotters who had flown in from the Crimea was the infantile desire not to become scapegoats. They were driven by pure fear, and insisted on collective responsibility, on blood brotherhood. And they got it.

They were affected by their lack of experience in making independent decisions, products of their Soviet upbringing with its custom of voting unanimously. And they were also affected by simple human frailty and the grinding of the individual by the millstone of power. But also operating was the wish of this power to prevail, only without Gorbachev, who was irritating and exasperating everyone.

These were the people who were to decide our fate for many years to come. They are the ones to "thank" for the collapse of the Soviet Union, and the terrible tragedy for society that has accompanied it.

At 4:00 A.M. on August 19, a small division of the Alpha group headed by Commander Karpukhin arrived in Arkhangelskoye. Still not briefed as to the purpose of the operation, people in camouflage fatigues cut a path from the highway through the forest, and then heard insane orders over their walkie-talkies: upon a certain signal, they were to arrest me, "for the purpose of guaranteeing the security of negotiations with the Soviet leadership." Nobody understood what was being said, and no explanation followed. The order to attack the dacha was then rescinded at 5:00 A.M. by Kryuchkov personally. He had decided not to rush developments. First, I should be trapped into breaking the law.* Then they could decide what to do with me.

During the wee hours of the morning of August 19, Gorbachev feverishly tried to grasp all the changes that had taken place. Under house arrest, virtually locked behind four walls, ignorant of what would happen literally from one moment to the next—Gorbachev must have found that night very psychologically difficult. These were hours of complete mystery and utter unpredictability.

A little later Gorbachev decided to tape a short statement using an amateur videocamera to express his position regarding the coup. (The guards had let Gorbachev use a videocamera as well as a shortwave radio.)

Most likely at the moment I was driving up to Arkhangelskoye, Gorbachev was desperately twirling the radio dial, jumping from one frequency to another, trying to catch any scrap of news possible. There wasn't any news of the coup—yet. But Gorbachev needed to check what the coup plotters had told him against official bulletins. Would there be any? Perhaps it was all some kind of provocation?

Worse was the complete consolidation of the army, KGB, and police. For a long time these forces had been the most threatening and the most influential in the USSR; the Communist party had always been the sole form of control over them. But the party was no longer in control of anything; it was just going along with the coup for the ride.

Early in the morning, about 7:00 A.M., workers came to our dacha in Arkhangelskoye to put down some pavement. An impres-

*That is, defying the "law" of the coup plotters' declared state of emergency.—Trans.

sive steamroller drove through the lanes of the garden. Workers in orange vests slowly and carefully poured out fresh hot asphalt. This was the result of an old story that had been dragging on ever since we had moved here. The director of the vacation home had been lobbying with his bosses for this pavement for several months. And of all days, the asphalt and the workers were finally allocated on the morning of the coup.

The road workers looked around in fright. People with real assault rifles were rushing all around with worried expressions on their faces. Black Volgas were pulling into the driveway one after another. There were obviously more people outside the gates of the home than usual.

Impulsively, I went up and introduced myself to the guys working on the road. The hell with the coup, this historic event! Our asphalt's getting cold! As often happens on such terrible days, the weather was just perfect. The hot asphalt smelled strangely reassuring. It meant the convenience of a road.

Tanya had woken me that morning, flying into the room, crying, "Papa, get up! There's a coup!" Still half asleep, the first thing I said was, "That's illegal!" She began to tell me about the GKChP, Yanayev, and Kryuchkov. It was all so stupid. I said to Tanya, "Are you kidding me?"

People all over the country were asking themselves the same question. In just those words. None of us could believe that such a thing was possible. It turned out it was.

Continuous columns of APCs and tanks were driving through the streets of Moscow. An unbelievably absurd operation was unfolding—units of several motorized rifle and tank divisions were being sent in at once to a perfectly peaceful city; other units were waiting outside Moscow, assembling on the roads leading toward the capital.

Kryuchkov, Yazov, Pugo, and the other coup leaders decided to shock the city with an enormous display of military hardware and personnel, to give it the look of a war front and drive everyone into hiding. There was a constant heavy drone over Moscow for several hours. "Is it war?" the old ladies of Moscow cried, clutching at their hearts. "No, it's a military coup," the young people explained, although they, too, had trouble realizing what was happening.

The paradox was that the GKChP members were in fact professionals, even first-class specialists and enforcers in their fields. Nevertheless, each one of them had a personality defect not so noticeable from the outside, some deviant behavior, thinking, or psychology.

Gennady Yanayev had stunned all the deputies at the congress when he smirked and publicly replied to questions about the condition of his health that he was "performing his marital duties quite well." Yanayev suffered from a so-called repressed inferiority complex, when a person who has suffered some abuse since childhood suddenly begins to feel superior. This superiority complex helped the bland Yanayev to occupy a high position in the leadership far beyond his capabilities. He would talk forever, arguing and imposing his opinion on you with an extremely confident expression. It was as if he had been born for party and government work. Even so, before the big meeting of the GKChP members, he had to find some courage in a bottle; he was very insecure. After all, the role prepared for him in the coup was quite visible.

Vladimir Kryuchkov was a disciple of the late Soviet leader Yuri Andropov, who had passed through a rigorous schooling in our security services. By both his nature and type of work, he should have been more realistic and sane. But Kryuchkov suffered from an occupational hazard, the most banal of spy manias. He constantly made his reports "classified" and placed secret memos on Gorbachev's desk, all of which boiled down to one thing: the democrats were planning a coup and were agents of the CIA. America was drafting a strategic plan to seize the USSR in order to divvy up its national resources among the NATO countries, reduce its population, strip its land of all its ores, and occupy the country. And so forth and so on. I am not a psychoanalyst, but it seemed as if Kryuchkov had a hypervigilance syndrome practically from his childhood. He was no longer capable of comprehending the ways of the modern world.

Valentin Pavlov was a very strong financial manager. But whenever he got in front of a television camera, he would be overcome by an inexplicable brazenness. He would tell dirty jokes; he would grow savage and put on war paint. On the second day of GKChP's existence, his unbalanced nature was revealed—he had a nervous breakdown.

Dmitry Yazov had served at the front during World War II and was a typical bluff soldier. Life had been brutal to this marshal. He had

had a very difficult hungry childhood, fought in the war, suffered the early death of his daughter, then his wife, and his second wife had been in a serious accident just before the coup. Yazov could no longer look at life with any fresh perspective. He perceived everything with the soldierly bluntness and through the morose bureaucratic prism of duty, obedience, and orders.

You cannot read the testimony of Boris Pugo's family about the last minutes before his suicide without being disturbed. It was a real tragedy. "You have a very intelligent daddy, but they bought him out for five kopecks," he said in a fit of despair. He broke under the weight of all the responsibility heaped upon him.

I suppose the only person among the plotters who kept a cool and clear head, and calculated everything, was Lukyanov. He tried to leave himself a way out no matter what happened. If the GKChP was to win, he would be one of the main ideological leaders of the putschists; if we won, he would have nothing to do with the GKChP. Really, he could say he had always been for legality; he was Gorbachev's best friend.

All in all, I look at the tragedy of the coup plotters as the tragedy of a whole platoon of government bureaucrats whom the system had turned into cogs and stripped of any human traits. Faced with the new reality where a politician, if he wanted to stay in office, had to have his own views and expression, his own individual speech and behavior, his own internal rules, they broke down.

It was a tragedy, but it would have been far worse if that platoon of cold and robotlike Soviet bureaucrats had returned to the leadership of the country, and if the victims of the situation had been us, not them.

Of course, when my daughter Tanya ran into my room I had no time for such lengthy ruminations. I was sitting glued to the television (I hadn't put on a shirt yet) and kept glancing at the faces of my wife and daughters, comparing their reaction to mine. Everyone was shaken. Everyone understood perfectly what had happened. Korzhakov hurried in to see me ten minutes after the first television news report. He had already placed guards around the property and had taken the cars out of the garages.

Naina was the first to get a grip on herself. "Borya, who should we call?" she asked me almost through clenched teeth.

I phoned everyone who was available and told them they would now be needed to work. Naina helped me make the calls. She and my daughters were my very first helpers that morning. My women never cried, never sat around at a loss, but immediately began to act with me and the others who soon appeared at the house. I am grateful to all of them.

We decided to write an appeal to the citizens of Russia. Khasbulatov copied down the text by hand, and all the colleagues from the liberal opposition in the Soviet parliament and the Russian government who were there—Sergei Shakhrai, Gennady Burbulis, Ivan Silayev, Mikhail Poltoranin, and Viktor Yaroshenko—began to dictate the text, with all of us drafting it together. Then the appeal was printed out, with my daughters helping to do the typing. We began to telephone acquaintances, friends, and relatives in order to find out where to send the text first. We sent the text to Zelenograd.

Anatoly Sobchak, mayor of St. Petersburg (Leningrad at the time), appeared at our dacha. He stayed for only a short time because he was hurrying home to St. Pete, fearful that he would be detained en route. He gave his opinion as a legal scholar and left after fifteen minutes, calling to Naina in farewell, "May God help us!" Evidently, these words helped her realize the full horror of what was happening. She watched him leave with tears in her eyes.

Incidentally, while all this was going on, the phones and the fax at Arkhangelskoye, strange as it may sound, were working intermittently. There was actually nothing surprising in this, though. In the two or three years of burgeoning business in our country, an incredible number of new communication lines had been installed. Literally an hour after my daughters typed our appeal to the people, it was being read in Moscow and other cities. The Western wire services sent it out, professional and amateur computer networks transmitted it, and independent radio stations like Echo of Moscow, stock market lines, and the correspondents' network of many national publications also passed it on. And many Xerox machines, previously banned, suddenly appeared out of nowhere!

I think that the middle-aged coup plotters simply could not imagine the extent and volume of the information age, which was so new to them. They were faced with a country completely different from the one they had imagined. Instead of a quiet and inconspicuous coup executed party-style, they suddenly had a totally public fight on their hands. The coup plotters were not prepared—especially psychologically—for an atmosphere of complete publicity.

Our appeal declared the coup unlawful. A precise evaluation of the events was provided, commenting on the president of the USSR, whose status the coup plotters were refusing to reveal; on Russia's sovereignty; and on the civic courage we would all need in order to withstand these hours and days.

But it was all so inadequate.

My intuition told me that the fate of the country would be decided not only on the square, not only by open public demonstrations, but also by the drama behind the scenes.

Shortly before the coup, I paid a visit to the military's Tula Division, a model regiment. Pavel Grachev, commander of the paratroopers, reviewed the combat troops for me. I liked Grachev. He was a young general who had seen action, a quite bold, independent, and frank individual.

I hesitated for a moment, but then made up my mind to ask him a hard question.

"Pavel Sergeyevich," I asked him, "if our lawfully elected government in Russia were ever to be threatened—a terrorist act, a coup, efforts to arrest the leaders—could the military be relied upon, could you be relied upon?"

"Yes, we could," he replied.

The next time I spoke to him was on the 19th. It was one of my first calls from Arkhangelskoye. Upon receiving news of the coup, I reminded him of our last conversation.

Grachev was disturbed, there was a long pause, and I could hear his labored breathing on the other end of the line. Finally, he said that for him, for an officer, it was impossible to disobey an order. I said something to the effect that I didn't want to expose him to attack. He said something like, "Wait a minute, Boris Nikolayevich. I'll send you a reconnaissance squad (or security detachment, I don't recall)." I thanked him and on that we said good-bye. Naina recalls that at that time, which was already early morning, I put down the receiver and said: "Grachev's on our side."

Grachev's first response had not discouraged me. In fact, it wasn't everyone who could give a direct answer in such a situation. Still, an order is an order, and there would be some kind of protection for us; Grachev had not reneged on his promise. That was the main thing.

There are few moments in life when perhaps the main question of a person's fate is decided. While Grachev was sighing into the receiver, he was deciding not only his own fate but also mine. And the fates of millions of people. That's the way it goes.

Of course, for such a high-ranking military commander, things were not so simple. He was too closely involved with the coup plotters' operations. He himself was giving orders to move troops into Moscow, and was actually running the military side of the coup. But at the same time, he was on our side.

That a person of such caliber as Grachev—determined, self-motivated, and independent—was in this post at this time was a real stroke of luck for Russia. It was not just a matter of his personal qualities. The fact was that at that moment there were really two armies. One army was made up of the highly professional combat units that had served in Afghanistan, an army at the highest world standard. The other was the gigantic "kitchen garden" army, many millions strong, used for harvesting crops, repairing roads, and performing other services, although mainly it served itself and didn't do much else, not even defend the country. An internal conflict was brewing between these two camps, the "lean" generals who had seen action and the "fat" armchair generals.

When I had called Grachev he had been forced to think through all sides of the issue simultaneously: political, moral, and, finally, purely professional. As a lean general, Grachev was getting a chance (a historic opportunity, really) to turn the "kitchen-garden" army into a real army. It would take deprivation, suffering, and the most arduous reforms. But it would mean turning the political and ideological machinery of intimidation into the kind of army in which Russia had once taken pride.

The scene outside Arkhangelskoye that morning was bizarre. There were a lot of cars and observation posts, with some of the personnel in disguise and some plainclothed, deliberately demonstrating their affiliation—many were officers of the KGB and other special divisions. Korzhakov remarked that he had the feeling that all of the security people sent out here had trouble telling their own people apart from ours.

Their clumsiness became obvious quite quickly. We did not yet know about the arrest team from the Alpha Division dispatched the previous night and left to freeze in the woods without any specific assignment. We didn't know that deputies Telman Gdlyan* and Vitaly Urazhtsev† had been arrested. Meanwhile, the Russian government's top officials quietly woke up at their dachas, realized what had happened, wrote an appeal to the people, went to the White House, and launched an open resistance to the coup.

For the time being, my attention was solely on the telephones. If they were still working, it meant we could survive.

The jerking puppetlike motions of the coup were just beginning to show through, but I had already realized that something was wrong with this picture. A real military junta would not behave in this way. There was another agenda here. Were they perhaps expecting mass intimidation? That nature would merely take its course?

Whatever the case, their ineptitude had to be exploited. My call to Grachev, as it turned out later, was exactly on target. It was he who had been entrusted with running the whole military operational side of the coup in Moscow. The coup plotters had waged their bets on this display of military hardware, on its overwhelming numbers, and on the belief that Moscow would be completely paralyzed not by special tactical troops but by ordinary soldiers. The putschists did not want bloodshed; they wanted to save face with Western governments. And it was this ambiguity in their motives that undid them. They were grossly mistaken in their choice of tactic, and we owe them enormous gratitude for that error.

Later, I kept recalling that morning, trying to understand what saved us. I turned over various possibilities in my mind. As an athlete, I know very well how sometimes all of a sudden you get a push and feel as if the game were going well, and you can seize the initiative. I felt that kind of uplift on the morning of August 19 in Arkhangelskoye. It was almost 9:00 A.M., the telephone was working, and there were no visible troop movements near the dacha. It was time. I set off for the White House.

We could have been ambushed as we pulled out of the driveway; they could have taken us on the highway; they could have thrown

*A famous prosecutor and member of the opposition in the Soviet parliament who investigated a number of government scandals and became an object of investigation himself.—Trans.

†A member of the radical opposition and founder of Shield, a group lobbying in parliament for civil rights for soldiers and officers and better conditions in the armed forces.—Trans.

grenades or run us over with a tank at any point along our route. But if we just sat at the dacha we would go crazy. By the abstract logic of security precautions, it was foolish to leave the compound. Of course we had an escort car to cover us, although that really had nothing to do with real security.

My security people had a safer route in mind: they wanted to put me in a boat and have me float up the Moscow River to a highway crossing, where a car would be waiting to pick me up. They wanted to disguise me as a fisherman. In fact, we could have dreamed up an even more devious route to—or out of—Moscow for that matter, in order to slip out of sight and escape persecution.

I learned then that the arrest team was watching our movements from the woods. The team leader drank a full glass of vodka to steady his nerves; he was expecting an order to arrest or destroy us at any minute. For four hours, these soldiers who were just regular guys followed our every move. When they saw that we were heading to the center of Moscow, they relaxed. Obviously, we weren't going into hiding; on the contrary, we were hurling ourselves into the very thick of the action.

Silayev's car was the first to leave. He called me after he reached the White House safely. I will never forget those agonizing minutes. Those endless columns of military vehicles. Korzhakov sat with an assault rifle on his lap. The bright sun got in our eyes.

Right before we left Arkhangelskoye, my wife stopped me. "Where are you going?" she asked. "There are tanks out there. They won't let you through." I had to say something, so I gave her my best shot: "We have a little Russian flag on our car. They won't stop us when they see that." She waved her arm in resignation. We left.

I remember so well the feeling when I stood in my heavy bulletproof vest, enormous and clumsy, trying to figure out what to tell Naina to reassure her, and suddenly I came up with the idea of that little Russian flag. It was so tiny.

Frankly, there wasn't much to reassure any of us at that moment. Everything seemed fragile and hopeless. We were hurrying toward the White House, but there might be an ambush along the way. Even if we got through, a trap could be laying in wait. The familiar ground was crumbling under our feet, but this little flag was something real and meaningful.

I think the people around us had the same feeling. We had something to fight for. We had that symbol of hope. This wasn't a political game, which later the Congress and the opposition press would viciously accuse us of playing, but just the opposite. It was a wish once and for all to shake off this filth, this chain of betrayal and slippery schemes, to leave it all and defend this little Russian flag, symbolizing our faith in the future of our great country, a decent and benevolent future.

At 10:00 A.M. on the morning of August 19, Valentin Varennikov, commander of the USSR ground forces, was sitting in the office of Leonid Kravchuk, leader of Ukraine, trying to explain the need for imposing a state of emergency in Ukraine.

Group B, a special division of the KGB's Moscow directorate, was armed and on battle alert, deployed in the center of town, at the Dzerzhinsky House of Culture.*

Kremlin physicians were given a somewhat veiled order to issue a pronouncement on Gorbachev's state of health, one that would be convenient for the GKChP.

The military began jamming the local radio stations.

Troops stationed in the Baltic republics and Georgia began to be transferred.

After we left for the White House, a group of about eight people in jumpsuits approached Arkhangelskoye's gates. Their leader showed our guard a paratrooper's ID card with the name Lieutenant Colonel Zaitsev. He explained that the group had come at General Grachev's command to protect President Yeltsin. As luck would have it, the senior security man guarding our family that day was Sasha Kulyosh, who knew perfectly well that Lieutenant Colonel Zaitsev was no paratrooper, but an officer of the KGB.

Not long before, Sasha had been studying at a KGB school where this Zaitsev had happened to give lectures. Kulyosh definitely remembered his teacher, but Zaitsev didn't recall his student. Another tip-off was that Zaitsev's ID card was brand new —the ink wasn't even dry on his signature. Nevertheless, our security people decided to let them inside the gates and fed them until

*Felix Dzerzhinsky was the founder and first chief of the Soviet secret police. "Houses of culture" were Soviet-era recreational facilities for the masses.—Trans.

they were ready to burst. A soldier with a full stomach is a different soldier altogether. They were given one meal, then another, and finally they relaxed.

The paratroopers' plan had been to take advantage of my phone call to Grachev that morning and his promise to send over some troops (they'd obviously bugged my phone) to worm their way into Arkhangelskoye, to take charge of me as if they were "guarding" me for my own protection, and then turn around and arrest me. Fortunately, their plan went awry from the moment Zaitsev's phony ID was signed. They were too late to boot. My car had already left Arkhangelskoye without a hitch.

This ridiculous delayed appearance of the "paratroopers" at Arkhangelskoye was yet another sign that the tide had turned in our favor and would now be hard to hold back.

I want to say a few words about one of my humble security officers, Viktor Grigorievich Kuznetsov. It was his apartment where my family and I spent the first night of the coup. He had a two-bedroom place in the suburb of Kuntsevo, and according to our sources, the KGB had not yet discovered it as a safe house.

We put the family into a van with shades on the windows and had another car tail us for cover. When the guards glanced into the van on the way out and saw a woman and children, they didn't stop them. The next day the whole family moved to our apartment near Belorussian Station. Naina called me the first night from a phone booth. Thank God no one yet recognized her.

My whole family held up wonderfully during this ordeal.

Shortly after 10:00 A.M., the members of the GKChP once again assembled in the Kremlin, this time without Pavlov. It was their first attempt to analyze what was happening. The reports were still optimistic. The factories were running normally, and people didn't seem to want to go on strike or protest. The need for any kind of immediate punitive measures subsided, and now the GKChP could focus on their short-term tactics. They decided the best idea was to put on television as much *kompromat* (compromising material) as possible on the democratic leaders. They also decided to slash the cost of certain goods in the stores and increase the variety—"to reassure the people." Most important was to gain the Supreme Soviet's cooperation in providing a cover of political expedience and legality to the coup.

Tank units from the Taman Division and armored vehicles from the Tula Division took up their positions by the House of Soviets of Russia,* now commonly called the Russian White House.

The 37th Airborne from Kaliningrad region had been transferred to the air-force base in Riga, the capital of Latvia. The 234th Regiment landed in Tallinn. The 21st Airborne was sent in to reinforce the transcaucasian military district's troops.

That night, two more people joined the GKChP. They were Alexander Tizyakov of Sverdlovsk, a defense plant director who was chairman of the USSR Industrial Union, and Vasily Starodubtsev, chairman of a model collective farm in the Tula region and head of the Peasants' Union. Both had signed all the statements of the GKChP. The new arrivals had not been briefed earlier on the details of the conspiracy, but were enormously enthusiastic about the turn of events. They were immediately assigned security men and large offices in the Kremlin. After all, they were now part of the country's "top leadership." The "peasants and the workers"—in the person of these *nomenklatura* leaders—were now supporting the overthrow of the government.

An order with Yazov's signature had been issued to deputies of the Defense Ministry, commanders of military groups, districts and ships, chiefs of directorates, and other top Soviet army commanders. The troops were put on battle alert.

At the large national factories run by the central Soviet ministries, party secretaries began to hold meetings in an effort to explain the rationale for the state of emergency to their fellow Communists and nonparty workers.

Only one channel was now working on nationwide government television, broadcasting the statements of the GKChP on the hour.

Major General Vorotnikov, chief of the KGB's directorate to defend the constitutional order, later testified during an interrogation that he was given a list of persons to be detained. Besides the leadership of the Russian republic, the list included the chief former Gorbachevites forced out by Gorbachev himself—Alexander Yakovlev and Eduard Shevardnadze. In all there were seventy names on the list. KGB Deputy Chairman Lebedev explained that these Russian republic figures were to be detained upon receipt of

*The building of the Russian Federation government.—Trans.

an additional command. Arresting officers from the KGB's Moscow directorate were standing by on alert in the center of Moscow, awaiting orders. But the orders never came down.

Later that morning, Anatoly Lukyanov, chairman of the USSR Supreme Soviet, broadcast his own statement concerning the new Union Treaty. According to Lukyanov, many of the treaty's articles violated the Soviet Constitution. It needed serious revision. The country's "working citizens" had many questions about it. ("Working citizens" was one of those wonderful Communist phrases that despite their seeming simplicity evoke a tremendous psychological resonance in a public subjected to decades of propaganda about the "dictatorship of the proletariat.") Lukyanov was seriously concerned that the treaty had been signed too hastily.

The official propaganda office had included Lukyanov's statement in the same package as the GKChP's "Appeal to the Soviet People," their decree number one, and other emergency announcements.

The scale of the conspiracy was such that almost everyone who had directly worked with Gorbachev was involved. The coup was uncommonly similar to the removal of Nikita Khrushchev in 1964, which was also bloodless and quasi-legal. Like Khrushchev, Gorbachev was on vacation (although in the Crimea rather than the Caucasus); it was the "velvet season," when the weather was cloudless and not so sweltering. Then *bang!*—and Khrushchev was forced to surrender before the absolute unanimous opinion of his entourage. He had not been prepared for such a turn of events and had no one upon whom he could rely. Ultimately, he was forced to concede political defeat.

The August coup plotters had the same intent vis-à-vis Gorbachev.

As I read Lukyanov's statement about the Union Treaty, I tried to understand what was behind it. The first possibility was that Lukyanov had betrayed his friend and boss, Gorbachev. The second possibility was more complicated but had to be taken into account: Gorbachev knew about the whole situation, and the coup was being executed according to a scenario he had prepared. The idea was to have other people do the dirty work to clear Gorbachev's path, then he could return from vacation to a new country under a state of emergency. That would enable him to put the democrats, the Russian Federation leadership, in their place as well as those upstart Baltic countries, and the rest of the Union republics that had lately been rearing their heads. With this plan, Gorbachev could take care of everything. Meanwhile, we—the Russian leaders—would be shown as calling for civil disobedience and protest actions. Barricades would be put up around the White House any moment and clashes were inevitable. Gorbachev would then appear on the scene, having used Yanayev and Lukyanov to torpedo the Union Treaty.

With these doubts about Lukyanov's and Gorbachev's role uppermost in my mind, I called the leaders of the major republics who had helped draft the new Union Treaty. (The special government telephone lines at the White House had been shut off. But one telephone, that of my aide Viktor Ilyushin, just installed and turned on the day before the coup, was still working! They hadn't yet managed to put it into the Red Book, [the list of government telephone numbers] so it became a kind of secure secret line.)

When I got the leaders of the republics on the phone, I was shocked to find them responding extremely cautiously. They, too, had been disturbed by Lukyanov's statement. They, too, wanted to find out what Gorbachev's real role had been in the events before saying anything. The main thing driving them was a wish to distance themselves from events in Moscow, to preserve at least the appearance and formality of sovereignty, to maintain—to put it bluntly—power, and then enter into a dialogue with the GKChP as equal partners. The heads of the republics had to remain neutral. That would, perhaps, leave them some authority. At least they could keep their offices and their privileges. This was a purely bureaucratic machination, and had nothing to do with political logic. Although it did have a hint of clever but transparent diplomacy.

The republics' leaders did not seem to grasp that Anatoly Lukyanov had already publicly denounced the Union Treaty, and that if the Supreme Soviet was to grant the actions of the GKChP the credibility of lawful force (the coup plotters apparently had no doubt of that), then within a week or so, the coup would turn into an irreversible event that would shake the world, and, of course, the Union republics first and foremost. Out there in the provinces, in Kiev, Alma-Ata, Tashkent, and other capitals of the republics, troops would be mobilized, little local "mini-coups," with tanks and APCs, and local versions of the GKChP would appear, who would be obedient to the center but nonetheless take power into their own hands. Surely the republic leaders could see the impending crisis?

In the meantime, Kryuchkov was attempting to harness events so that the coup would indeed be bloodless. He canceled the planned arrests, although the machinery had been in place for them. As I mentioned, the hit list contained the Russian government leaders, the Gorbachev liberals, as well as some Moscow city authorities.* The people on the list had been put under surveillance so they could all be arrested within an hour, but the machinery of persecution itself abruptly ground to a halt.

I think at first Kryuchkov believed he could get away with arresting everyone. But he quickly saw that such a roundup would provoke a sharp backlash of resistance leading to the possibility of excessive force and bloodshed. Second, such arrests would be too harsh a transition from the Gorbachev thaw. The new leadership would not only be subject to numerous international sanctions but relations could also likely break off altogether. For a country like ours, with its numerous interests in various corners of the globe, this would be extremely painful. Kryuchkov, clever intelligence apparatchik that he was, was thinking pragmatically.

In Kryuchkov's notion of the coup, the army rather than the KGB would serve the function of intimidating the public. The huge display of military hardware on the streets of a peaceful city was bound to paralyze the democrats' will. Resistance in the face of such force was unthinkable. He was banking on an apparatchik's coup, reasoning that Lukyanov's role in giving the coup the fig leaf of legality would tip the balance in his favor. This back-room politicking was what made the coup appear so strange from the outset.

On the morning of August 19, the job of constructing the cover of legality for the coup was top priority for the GKChP.

By about 10:00 A.M., I was convinced that the White House would be the chief staging ground for subsequent developments.

What sort of building is the Russian White House? Built by commission, it is perhaps the first post-Stalinist government building of such size in Moscow, a building for a new generation. The architect Chechulin worked hard on the blueprint of the gigantic structure, achieving wonderful results. People can spend days roaming its corridors. The numerous wings and offices as well as the underground

*E.g., Mayor Gavriil Popov, democrat and member of the Soviet parliamentary opposition.—Trans.

bunker and tunnels exiting the building make for a good security system.

Circumstances dictated that we had to stay in the White House. Our job was just to wait and sit it out. The longer I could sit here, the worse for the coup plotters. The longer the sit-in could continue, the louder the political uproar would be, and that would be terribly damaging for them. The longer the situation, the more ambiguity and the more chances their plot would self-destruct.

I looked around me now with a fresher, keener eye. I had never even had a chance to get used to these cold imposing offices in the White House. Would I really have to stay in one place for many hours? No one knew when the nightmare would end.

By this time, all of us were together—Rutskoi, Burbulis, Silayev, Khasbulatov, Shakhrai, and the other leaders of Russia. We discussed Lukyanov's statement. Our own statements were before us on the table: the appeal of the Russian leadership to the peoples of Russia that had already been sent out all over the country and the draft decree stating that all organizations and persons who would violate the Russian Federation Constitution would be subject to prosecution. At the time of the coup, the Russian Federation was still Soviet and Socialist, and, therefore, its Constitution was a product of the old order. Even so, under that Constitution, the highest official in the government was the president. A sovereign Russia could not be driven into a state of emergency without the consent of its highest bodies!

As we sat there with our papers, a tank was parked outside. It was absurd, and yet real at the same time. I looked out the window. As I watched, the armored vehicle was surrounded by a crowd of people. The driver stuck his head out of the hatch. People were not afraid to approach the tanks; in fact, they were even throwing themselves under them. They weren't afraid—although they were Soviet people, raised in the Soviet system. People were even lining up; they weren't afraid of the tank treads. They weren't afraid of being arrested, although they were being threatened with a crackdown every hour over the radio and television.

Suddenly, I felt a jolt inside. I had to be out there right away, standing with those people.

This was easier said than done. The security precautions for such a simple operation took quite awhile. Finally, my guards raced into the street, and then I determinedly went downstairs to the people. I clambered onto a tank, and straightened myself up tall. Perhaps I felt clearly at that moment that we were winning, that we couldn't lose. I had a sense of utter clarity, complete unity with the people standing around me. The crowd was large and some people were whistling and shouting. Reporters, television crews, and photographers were everywhere. I took out the piece of paper with the text of my appeal and held it in my hands. The shouts died down and I read the text loudly, my voice almost breaking. Next I greeted the commander of the tank upon which I was standing and talked with the soldiers. From their faces, from the expression in their eyes, I could see they would not shoot us. I jumped down from the tank and was back in my office within a few minutes. By that time, however, I was already a completely different person.

This improvised rally on the tank was not a propaganda gimmick. After coming out to the people, I felt a surge of energy and an enormous sense of relief inside.

At midday on the 19th, Gorbachev sent a note to the guards keeping him under house arrest containing his demands: a plane to fly to Moscow and a communication line through to the government in Moscow. He knew that these demands were hardly likely to be fulfilled. Still, he had to do something, to find some outlet for his energy.

Like me, the president of the USSR could not sit cooped up for long without any glimpse of light.

Gorbachev's note was sent to the officer in charge of the Dawn Compound (that was the KGB's code name for Gorbachev's government dacha). The officer called his immediate superior in Moscow, and then nothing seemed to happen. There was a long wait. A delicious lunch and dinner, a look at television, and a stroll around the guarded beach awaited Gorbachev and his family. As someone wrote at the time, Gorbachev was living in a "golden cage."

What was the actual size of the strategic territory guarded around Gorbachev? Three platoons of forces were involved in blocking the Dawn compound: the navy, the air force ground service, and the border guards.

A curious detail: after speaking with Gorbachev, Varennikov held a briefing for military district commanders who were brought especially to the Crimea for that purpose. He informed the high-ranking generals who flew into the Crimea that a state of emergency was being declared in the country.

All of this was very reminiscent of an undeclared start of war. It wasn't real yet; it was still a "cold war," but it was on the brink. The grandiose parade of tanks in Moscow plus the house arrest of Gorbachev reinforced with radar, missiles, and ships, plus the very delayed transfer of the nuclear button to Yazov made it seem like martial law. In its scale and possible consequences, this operation was the kind of global event we had seen in the 1960s, like the Cuban missile crisis or the invasion of Czechoslovakia.

It seemed to me that the radical wing of the conspiracy—Baklanov, Tizyakov, and Varennikov—had envisioned a heavy backlash. I and the rest of the Russian leadership would of course resist. In order to avoid unrest, their rebellion would have to be put down with force. And then . . .

Putting the Soviet armed forces on combat alert, and having the world community reacting sharply, still didn't mean war. The world has lived through such situations many times before. But, as the conspirators reasoned, now the problems related to Gorbachev's "incorrect" foreign policy would be removed. In virtually a day, the USSR was returning to its previous international stance, say, pre-SALT. On the one hand, there were bound to be some difficulties. On the other, in the opinion of the coup plotters, the chief strategic problem—foreign policy—would be resolved. Once again, the empire would prevail and diplomacy would be conducted from a position of strength.

The trial of the putschists will prove whether I am right in my analysis. Obviously, from beginning to end, the coup was extremely inconsistent.

The military-industrial complex was raring to flex its powerful biceps. Varennikov was its personification. By August 19, he was already phoning, telegraphing, and dictating dispatches from Kiev, demanding that this "playing democracy" and "the opportunist Yeltsin" be put to a stop. And Baklanov was another indication, for his part pressuring Kryuchkov and Pugo. But the KGB and interior ministers realized that while it would be easy to get into this bloody mess, getting out would be a lot harder. Clearly, whoever could strike a moral, political balance—whoever could win public opinion over to their side—would prevail in this situation.

The coup revealed how the interests of two large bureaucracies, two approaches, two types of thinking honed in the Soviet system for years were now clashing. These were the interests of the military-industrial complex (the MIC as we have come to call it) and the KGB. What the MIC needed was a real full-fledged full-throated putsch that would force the world to believe in the might of the Soviet tank once again. The KGB, however, needed as clean and as sophisticated a transfer of power as possible. In fact, neither agenda was feasible. The coup collapsed the moment they sent such an inherently weak delegation to Gorbachev in the Crimea. By definition, Gorbachev could not be afraid of officials at the level of Baklanov, Shenin, and Varennikov. Even *they* didn't believe he'd be frightened of them; they had merely decided to take him out of the game for a while. That was a stupid idea. The brazen lie that the president of the country was allegedly ill merely aggravated the situation instead of quelling it.

As the driving force behind the putsch, the KGB did not want to bloody its hands. It had hoped to extract victory with merely the rumble of tanks and perhaps a warning cannon shot or two.

The presence of these two incompatible approaches to the coup was easily explained: the GKChP had no leader. There was no authoritative person whose opinion would become the clarion call to action. Yanayev was no good for this role. He was too spineless a character. Who, then, remained for the role of official leader?

The balance of forces among the eight coup plotters on the morning of August 19 was as follows: Baklanov, the MIC, and the armed forces chiefs of staff were a counterbalance to the wait-and-see position of the KGB, particular its intelligence directorate. Pugo and Yazov, demoralized by what was going on, were awaiting instructions from someone else, and therefore could not actually influence the situation. Tizyakov and Starodubtsev filled a purely representational function. And Yanayev, as I've mentioned, was not capable of making his own decisions.

That left Pavlov and the "shadow" member of the GKChP, Lukyanov, the speaker of parliament. These two were ambitious, intelligent apparatchiks who were quite capable of assuming responsibility. Pavlov, however, was undone by that well-known politicians' disease—a heart attack. This was not just a trick. He really could not tolerate the sleepless nights and the excessive alcohol, but mainly it was the incredible nervous anxiety. Pavlov crumpled under the pressure and took to his bed. Ironically, he had probably been the only one of the coup plotters who had not been afraid of clashing with Gorbachev's line and engaging in open confrontation with him. He had been the one to vigorously support the idea of using the military to impose a state of emergency, seeing great economic sense in it.

Kryuchkov's attitude toward Lukyanov was ambiguous. On the one hand, Lukyanov's legal and political support of the coup, expressed in his televised statement had come in extremely handy and was worth a great deal. On the other, Kryuchkov was cautious with Lukyanov since he didn't know how much he could trust him. But this turned out to be another mistake for Kryuchkov. With his experience and understanding of Gorbachev's nature, Lukyanov was just the man needed and was a great asset for the GKChP. Now, however, Lukyanov was distancing himself from the putschists and largely watching the events from the sidelines.

None of this came as any surprise. Both the coup plotters' supporters and rivals were gradually peeling off. Now the red button of the coup was in Kryuchkov's hands alone, but what was he himself thinking?

It was very important for me to understand the mindset and the train of thought of the KGB's chairman. A quiet old man with a steely gaze, Kryuchkov was the most dangerous of the conspirators. Every minute we remained in the White House shortened the life of their state of emergency. Did Kryuchkov understand that? Could any kind, tender notes be detected in his voice? Or would I hear the gloating of an executioner who had already pushed the button?

I reached the KGB chairman on the special government line. I don't recall our conversation word for word, but its overall tenor was interesting. Kryuchkov tried to justify himself.

Do you really not understand what you are doing? I asked him. People are throwing themselves under tanks; there may be countless casualties. No, said Kryuchkov, there won't be any casualties. First, this is a strictly nonviolent operation: no ammunition will be used in order to impose order, and no military objectives have been set. All the agitation is coming from you, the Russian leadership. According to our reports, people are calm and life is normal.

When I later analyzed Kryuchkov's logic as the central figure of the coup, I understood that he was almost telling the truth. He reasoned that the coup would proceed the way the crackdowns had in Hungary, Czechoslovakia, and Poland. In 1956, there had been a lot of bloodshed in Hungary, but it was the first armed aggression in

Europe after the war, people reacted very strongly to the sight of foreign tanks, and even the Hungarian Communists were not really in earnest. In Prague in 1968, there were relatively few casualties. True, people demonstrated and there were various incidents but on the whole, it went quickly and "rather well." Still, it was a foreign army once again! In Poland in 1981, martial law was imposed in one day. A column of tanks ran down the central streets of the city, and that was it—resistance was cut off. Later, the Poles were afraid martial law would continue and chose a bad peace rather than a good war.

In dealing with his own country, Kryuchkov was taking his cue from the Polish example and the other precedents established in the Socialist countries. It was as if Kryuchkov had once gone up to the mirror and said, yes, I'd make a good Wojciech Jaruzelski (the Communist leader of Poland during martial law in the early 1980s). I could be like him, a middle-aged military man in dark glasses with a soft voice, who would quietly but firmly lead the country out of the impasse.

The coup plotters expected no outside aggression when the coup was declared—after all, the tanks were all our very own—they had not expected any resistance either. And that was Kryuchkov's mistake. People reacted to the cartoonish high jinks of the coup as they did because they were not afraid of our tanks—precisely because they *were* ours!

Finally, it became obvious the putschists would have to use force, but by then it was too late. No one was able or willing to shoot, because it would mean firing on a live swarming crowd.

The first reaction Muscovites had had to the announcement of the coup was to quickly dart into the grocery stores and snatch up all the bread, butter, and cereal. Lines formed for vodka. Fearing drastic changes, ordinary people—housewives, mothers, and grandmothers—grabbed everything they might run out of soon.

There were long columns of tanks on all the main streets leading to the center—Tverskaya, Kutuzovsky and Manezh Square. Many curious people who had been paralyzed with fear during the first few hours of the coup gradually crept closer and closer to the tanks, drawing the soldiers into conversations, offering them food and drink, asking and finally demanding an answer to the main question of the day: *why?* The soldiers, who had awakened in the middle of the night by alarm bells, were tired, hungry, and wound up, but not aggressive. They didn't have a clue, either. No briefing had been provided them in their units, and they didn't have even the remotest notion of the battle objective. The commanders' explanation—that the operation "was to preserve calm in Moscow"—contradicted what they could see with their own eyes. It was the appearance of the tanks themselves that was disturbing Moscow's calm.

People were walking around with transistor radios. The first independent radio station, known as Echo of Moscow, was broadcasting every bit of news that journalists could glean as well as snippets of contradictory rumors swirling around the government, and news briefs from the White House. The mood of those listening to the radio was already different from those of mere curiosity seekers. Alarmed and worried, the citizens of Moscow were assembling. Crowds were circulating back and forth between the center and the outskirts of town, looking at the tanks, and then returning directly to the White House. Traffic was halted in many areas of Moscow.

International and intercity communication lines were down at the central telegraph station, and the building was occupied by a platoon from the Taman Division.

The business community in Moscow had issued statements condemning the coup, and all the stock markets were closed.

The GKChP's decree number 2 was entitled "On the Publication of Central, Moscow, City, and Regional Newspapers." Almost all the press was shut down except for a few central newspapers ostensibly supplying official soothing information to their readers. Representatives of the GKChP went to the editorial offices of these newspapers—*Pravda, Izvestia, Trud,* and *Sovetskaya Rossiya*—and indicated their desire to "have a glance" at the contents of the next day's headlines.

On the bridge opposite the White House, people had stopped the flow of tanks. Kalininsky Avenue was blocked off by buses, as was the Garden Ring Road. People were lying down in front of tanks. They were sticking broken-off pieces of metal into the wheels of the halted military vehicles. The frightened combat squads were not receiving any orders over their radios except to remain calm.

There was another focus of tension on Manezh Square, immediately in front of Red Square and the Kremlin. Tanks, APCs, and soldiers with assault rifles were lined up along the Manezh, pushing the crowds back. Two APCs crashed into one another as they entered the square from Herzen Street. There were APCs even in front of the Bolshoi Theater.

Yanayev issued a decree declaring a state of emergency in Moscow, which meant there was a curfew. Everyone was waiting for the GKChP's press conference scheduled for 6:00 P.M.

Evidently, Russians have a love-hate relationship with Moscow. They may curse it and knock it, but they still love it. The threat to Moscow's security was perceived by everyone as a threat to the security of the Russian nation as a whole, as an attempt to violate sacred national ground. Every person who could think and feel normally had his or her own personal national liberation that day. The Soviet empire was finally divested from the image of the motherland; Russia was separated from the USSR. This was particularly true of the officers and soldiers who suffered the most severe psychological ordeal that day.

People understood perfectly well that the coup plotters—the Communist leadership—had "dumped Gorbachev." And they had different reactions to this news. People were sick of Gorbachev's failed reforms and his long rambling speeches. Quite a few people, unhappy with the instability and uncertainty brought by democratization, advocated an iron hand. KGB analysts had counted on precisely such sentiment, and it was the centerpiece of the game plan for the coup, drafted deep within the secret police.

I have found that during such grave, uncertain situations, details that seem secondary can play an important role. It's the psychological factor. As I have mentioned, the GKChP did not have any internal leader, and it didn't even have any external leader, a figure "for show," either. The figure of Kryuchkov evoked gloomy associations with Stalin's purges. Marshal Yazov was not appropriate for a civilian role. The obnoxious Pavlov had already infuriated the public with his unpopular monetary reform, forcing people to trade in their large banknotes, and with price increases that had drastically depleted their savings. The cunning and hypocritical Lukyanov did not evoke any positive emotions, either; he was too cold and calculating an individual.

Perhaps a figure like Baklanov, new to the public, could have played the number-one role in the government. But the coup plotters were afraid of violating the Constitution, so they propelled Vice President Yanayev out in front, hoping he would show confidence and determination. They were wrong.

Despite the public's mixed attitudes toward Gorbachev, the uncertainty of his fate managed to raise his ratings more in one hour than all his years of reform. In the eyes of the public, the president of the USSR became an innocent victim—possibly soon to become a martyr.

Finally, everyone was outraged by the pointless lumbering of tanks and armored vehicles around Moscow. The military hardware put on the street for show provoked angry protest. The popular base of support for the state of emergency and "restoring order" was dwindling with each passing minute.

Unquestionably, yet another reason for the coup plotters' fiasco was their collective responsibility—or irresponsibility—for the events occurring. The nocturnal huddle in the Kremlin that preceded the launching of the coup would have made sense if Gorbachev could have been forced to "abdicate the throne" and officially hand over his presidential powers. But since the coup plotters' delegation had returned empty-handed from the Crimea, which could have been predicted, the meeting of all the country's top leaders (many of whom had been urgently hauled out of the resorts and sanatoria where they had been vacationing) had a completely different flavor. The point of the gathering was to have a bonding ritual, to look around the circle at one's neighbors and carefully coordinate all actions. As a result, there was no driving force, no forward tackle on the conspirators' team. The GKChP was operating according to the old tried-and-true method of the Brezhnev (but not Gorbachev) politburo: a nominal leader placed out front with the truly powerful shadow figures and struggling mysteriously behind the scenes.

The lack of an auteur, the facelessness of the GKChP's decrees, was supposed to make the public quiver in awe, as in the days of stagnation,* and consign themselves to the iron will of fate, but much had changed in people's psychology during Gorbachev's perestroika. The public had grown accustomed to the fact that all of us, including the leaders, were individuals. Whether good or bad, there was still individuality, not a nondescript collective. No two leaders were alike, and there were quite a few colorful figures around Gorbachev.

The collective-style decisions made in the Brezhnev manner (a small group of top bosses leisurely passing resolutions to be carried out by zealous functionaries) only hampered Kryuchkov and the other comrades. The consequence of this style was delay and indecision.

*The popular perestroika term for the Brezhnev and post-Brezhnev era.—Trans.

The scores of journalists at the White House with tape recorders, videocameras, and photo equipment were very courageous. They were constantly in the background during all the events, breaking through the most inaccessible doors, patiently waiting for an interview, and simply joining our "people's irregulars." The sight of these people obsessively going about their work—and as far as I could tell, not so much for the sake of money but simply from the unchecked enthusiasm common to all members of their profession—always had a calming effect on me. Of course a KGB agent or provocateur could have entered the White House posing as a reporter. Nevertheless, all sorts of people were walking and running up and down stairs throughout the building, and it was virtually impossible to stem the flow. People kept coming and coming, breaking through the cordons. There were deputies, representatives of various parties and movements, military people, well-wishers offering help—arrangement of security, funds, food, office equipment, and so on.

This flood of people had to be directed and regulated somehow, so we divided up our roles. The "sociopolitical" headquarters was in Burbulis's office, where lots of famous people came and reporters brought in news and rumors. I assigned a retired general, Konstantin Kobets, chairman of a parliamentary committee, to coordinate the work of the armed forces. He gathered the military people in his office, they cogitated over the floor plan of the building, and used their internal channels to try to discern which units had been mobilized in this enormous military-political parade. Together they drafted a plan of action in the event the White House was stormed.

Rutskoi was in charge of security and public liaison; that is, he worked with the masses of people who began to crowd around the building early every morning. He also directed our "combat troops"—the presidential security detail, a small police division, and the former officers, professional security people, and other fighting men who had volunteered. Basically, Rutskoi's top job was to organize rallies, human chains, inspect guard posts, and make up security instructions like, "In the event the White House is attacked with tear gas and nerve gas, wet a handkerchief and hold it over your face."

I knew that this flurry of activity was somewhat illusory or at least amateurish. It was the typical struggle of dilettantes at the barricades, an odd contingent of guerrillas in an urban setting. But with each passing hour, the GKChP's state of confusion became more and more evident and that worked in our favor. The powerful popular support for the White House was preventing the conspirators from staging the coup with the lightning speed they had originally planned in the Kremlin.

Our next political action was a memorandum addressed to Lukyanov containing our demands to him as head of the Soviet parliament: to provide accurate information about Gorbachev's state of health and location; to convene a session of the USSR Supreme Soviet immediately and have a legal appraisal of the state of emergency; and to rescind the orders of the unlawful GKChP.

Silayev, Khasbulatov, and Rutskoi took the memorandum to Lukyanov, which was a fairly risky business in that nervous and unpredictable atmosphere. They were able to deliver the text safely, however.

At midday we decided to create a government in exile if the White House fell. According to international custom, a foreign minister may declare a government in exile without special authorization. Foreign Minister Kozyrev thus flew to Paris for that purpose the next morning. We next dispatched a group headed by Oleg Lobov to Sverdlovsk to lead the democratic resistance in Russia in case the Russian leaders were arrested and the coup ultimately succeeded in Moscow. We held a press conference at the White House and reiterated our basic principles: we need the truth about Gorbachev; the GKChP was illegal; and all the coup plotters were outlaws.

I sensed the situation gradually shifting. The putschists had underestimated the changes that had occurred in the country. Under Gorbachev's rule, aside from the official government, there had emerged leaders of public opinion, political forces, independent authorities in culture, the democratic press, and others. Their mouths could be stopped only with the most brutal, bloody persecution, with a wave of arrests and executions. If the conspirators did not have the will for that, they could make some clever moves, some inventive exploitation of information under the news blackout in the state of emergency, manipulating public opinion—but they were not even capable of that. They had failed on all counts. The coup plotters would also have to contend with people outside Moscow. In the provinces, there was a completely different scene. In one of our statements we had called for a political strike and acts of civil disobedience. By afternoon we learned that three mines in Kuzbas, where there were strong trade-union leaders, and possibly several plants in Moscow were prepared to declare a strike. But most of the population was still waiting to see what would happen.

The coup plotters' strong suit was the harsh vertical system of subordination preserved from the old regime whose iron rule was deeply embedded in the country. The central structures of the Soviet Union worked mightily in favor of the GKChP: government telephones rang, coded telegrams went out, instructions were handed down, a wave of meetings were held by the Soviet "public" in support of the GKChP in institutes, offices, and factories. Not everything went as smoothly as they would have liked; protests resounded in some quarters. On the whole, however, these Union structures did not let them down even now. With one phone call from Moscow, emergency bodies made up of party leaders, military people, and state economic managers were created in every city and town in the country. Miniversions of the GKChP were formed in the provinces at the district and city levels. Everything was done by rote and in the usual leisurely provincial manner.

At 6:00 P.M., the cabinet opened session at the Council of Ministers, chaired by Grachev, who was on the verge of nervous collapse. Almost all the ministers had supported the imposition of the state of emergency—some tacitly by lowering their heads, some fervently and zealously. This meant that on the following day, the enormous bulk of Soviet industry would work overtime because of the emergency, which was really terrible. Another three days and we would awake in a different country. There was no way Russia could revert to such a government regime of curfews, administrative restrictions, censorship, and "special measures" restricting rights and liberties.

I was particularly concerned by the position of the USSR Foreign Ministry at this Cabinet meeting in contrast with the position of the Foreign Ministry of Russia.* We were receiving reports from our embassies, which were openly supporting the GKChP. Although almost all the Western leaders had expressed complete and unconditional support to me personally over the telephone, the trend among our ambassadors definitely gave us pause.

*The Soviet Foreign Ministry tacitly supported the coup. The Russian Foreign Ministry openly denounced it.—Trans.

But the greatest of all the question marks was the position the army would take in this civil conflict sparked by the coup.

Military people were clearly the driving force of the coup and certainly had their reasons to dislike—if not hate—Gorbachev. However, there was much we could not understand. If the army was disposed toward resolute action, virtually put on battle alert, if OPERATION PUTSCH had mobilized such enormous forces, then who was the enemy? A handful of democratic figures? The people outside the White House? But then . . . but then why were all the tank commanders unanimously claiming they had no ammunition? Why did the soldiers not even know why they had been sent here? What was causing such incomprehensible chaos, the restationing of the troops?

Several times I tried to reach Marshal Yazov at the Defense Ministry to find out what was happening there, and finally I got through. Yazov sounded gloomy and I sensed a certain depression in his voice. When I pushed him, he answered almost as if coached: there was no communication with Gorbachev, the Russian leadership should cease the criminal resistance to the lawful authorities, the troops are fulfilling their constitutional duty, and so forth. I learned later what a state of shock he had been in. His wife, who had recently been in a car accident, had come to see him at work. She had known nothing of her husband's plans and was really frightened. Calling him by his nickname, her voice shaking, she said, "Dima, who are these people you've gotten mixed up with here? Didn't you used to laugh at them? Call Gorbachev!" Then this woman broke down in tears, in the office of the defense minister of a mighty country. Yazov could reply only that there was no communication with Gorbachev.

There was a GKChP press conference scheduled for that evening. They were supposed to prove their sincerity and the lawfulness of their actions. No one knew what sensations or surprises might lie in their briefcases. Although it was already clear they had lost the first day of the coup, much could still work to our detriment at this press conference.

As evening approached on August 19th, as president of Russia, I appealed to Muscovites not to obey the decrees of the self-styled emergency committee and to take possession of the Russian White House.

The Soviet presidential plane flew from Foros to Vnukovo Airport. On board were Gorbachev's own security guards, personal secretaries, and stenographers. The plane was also carrying away the presidential communications system, thus depriving Gorbachev of contact.

Vremya (*Time*), the news program on Channel 1, unexpectedly ran a totally accurate and truthful report from the barricades of the White House. A tank platoon from the Taman Division under the command of Major Yevdokimov came over to the side of the White House defenders. There were tanks at the Defense Ministry on the Arbat, on Zubovskaya Square at the Foreign Ministry press center, where the GKChP press conference was under way, on Gorky Street in front of the *Izvestia* building, and on Pravda Street, where the editorial offices of all the major central newspapers were located.

"I would like to announce today that the state committee for the state of emergency in the USSR is completely aware of the depth of the crisis that has beset the country. It is accepting responsibility for the fate of the motherland and is filled with determination to take the most serious measures to bring the state and society out of the crisis as quickly as possible. . . . At the pace, ladies and gentlemen, at which President Gorbachev has been working these last six years . . . he has naturally become rundown a bit. I hope that my friend, President Gorbachev, will soon be back on the job and we'll be working together again."

The long-awaited press conference was a total flop. Both our own journalists and the foreign reporters openly asked direct questions: was this a military coup? Yanayev's and the others' hands were distinctly shaking and their faces were flushed and mottled. When asked about Gorbachev's health, Yanayev mumbled some nonsense, completely evading the question.

Once again it was obvious that the GKChP did not have a leader. Pavlov had taken to his bed, apparently aggravating his health crisis with fresh doses of alcohol. Kryuchkov didn't show up at the press conference. As for Yanayev, the expectations that he would be self-confident were mostly misplaced. The vice president simply looked silly. Indeed, how could anyone not look stupid in a situation where he had nothing to say? None of them presented a single fact about Gorbachev's medical condition. There were no clear explanations of what the country could expect in the near future. While superficially legal for public consumption, the bloodless and bureaucratic nature of the coup exposed its chief flaw—the coup plotters were not capable of appearing openly in public. They were apparatchiks who frankly were ill suited to the role of political leaders, ill prepared for speeches or any kind of definite understandable behavior.

The camera lights illuminated their disgustingly pathetic faces, which all seemed to swim together. Every Russian who saw this press conference was gripped with an ineradicable sense of shame before the entire world on behalf of these men. The "determination" that Yanayev strained his hardest to convey didn't change a thing. With such determination, it would be easy to bring the country and the world to the brink of disaster; it was the determination of a man walking off the gangplank blindfolded.

The coup people left the press conference angry and depressed, and went to their offices to try to come to some kind of conclusion. Finally, in the best of the old Russian traditions, they put off their main decisions until the next morning.

Late in the evening of August 19, Ivan Silayev, chairman of the Council of Ministers, came to see me in my office at the White House. "Boris Nikolayevich," he said, "I'm sorry, but I'm going home. I want to be with my family tonight." I could read in his eyes the following: "Defeat is inevitable. I'm an old man. I want to see my wife and children for the last time."

My first reaction was a certain anxiety. Cowardice I could have expected—people leave quietly, simply disappearing, and that's it. And I could have expected a readiness to stand until the end, as the majority of defenders of the White House in fact did. But Silayev's statement was some kind of third option. In the final analysis, politicians are not Samurais; they do not sign an oath in blood. I understood Silayev very well. Still, it was the departure of one of the leaders, and that meant a heavy psychological blow to those who stayed behind. We therefore tried to make this episode look like a necessary security measure, one of the leaders of Russia should remain outside the walls of the White House. (Silayev later returned to the White House, and left once again, and things went back to normal.)

I went to the window and noticed a group of students, I believe from the Bauman Institute. About two hundred people. The kids were warming themselves at a bonfire. In the darkness, lights in the windows of apartments on Kalinin Prospect glowed serenely. The noise in the hallways at the White House also seemed to have died down. Behind me was the most difficult day of my life. And ahead was the most difficult night.

Immediately after Silayev left, I was suddenly impatient to see my own family. We were quite close. I knew that at any moment Naina would be calling me from a phone booth, calling from somewhere this night, which was becoming more and more difficult for me. Looking through a crack in the window blinds, I could see a swarming ring of people and tank after tank everywhere. Then there was a smaller circle of armored vehicles parked flush against each other. These were the airborne troops, the Tula Division, which, like several other divisions, had been dispatched to Moscow even before the coup. It was the same division I had visited before the coup, not so long ago.

Antihelicopter prongs were placed on the roof of the building to prevent the combat group's choppers from landing. Everyone was issued gas masks in case of a tear-gas attack. I also tried one on, but you can stand it for only about a half hour, then it becomes impossible to move around easily—you start to steam. The reception area was barricaded with chairs, tables, and safes; it would hold several minutes in the event of an attack.

My nerves were humming despite my exhaustion, but my body knew that if it did not shut down for at least half an hour, I could make mistakes tomorrow. There was a deadly risk of making a wrong decision. With an effort of will, I took a short nap and then jumped back on my feet.

During the coup, this is how I would take a rest: a soldier with an assault rifle stood guard outside my office. But I would be in a completely different wing of the White House in some little back room about which only two or three people would know.

Despite all our plans and preparations for an attack, our overall situation was quite desperate. The White House could be taken fairly easily. Using two grenade launchers to create a deafening and blinding effect, the first floor would be knocked out completely. In the smoke, the SWAT teams would have no problem climbing to our floor, especially if they were covered by a helicopter above.

Such operations had been planned down to the last detail in theory. There were even special textbooks about them. The only thing textbooks forgot to factor in were the people in front of the White House. Psychologically, this was an enormous problem since this living mass would simply have to be crushed and shot during the course of the operation.

Throughout the coup, I had the feeling that some sort of miraculous force was helping us. As we began to analyze the details, this sensation of mine grew even stronger. There is a simpler explanation for everything, of course. On one hand was an impersonal machine that seemed invincible by virtue of its incredible might and the resources invested in it. On the other hand, in the end everything depends on people. During the coup either people didn't understand anything, like the tank officers, or they acted spontaneously or simply refused to follow orders. On our side there was no machine—just the opposite—but whether by instinct or inspiration, the right people were at the right place at the right time.

Everyone knew that several snipers were supposedly targeting us. It was our own sniper who discovered the other snipers. (Among the various firearms in the Supreme Soviet security service's arsenal there happened to be a sniper's rifle with a telescopic sight.) Our sniper surely knew his business. He went onto the roof, looked around at nearby points of elevation, and spotted the enemy. During World War II, snipers used to have an unwritten law: if they caught each other simultaneously in their respective sights, they would part amicably, so to say, and not shoot. I think such a convention was in effect at that moment.

More to the point, the presence of the sniper perched on the roof of the building next to us, right behind the Pavlik Morozov* Children's Park, was a danger sign. We were being watched. We were also being watched from the roof of the Hotel Mir next to the American Embassy.

After that we didn't go near the windows, and my planned balcony speech to the White House defenders was moved to another part of the building. We discussed the option of seizing the snipers, but our military people said that each sniper was covered by a small KGB division. That would entail a battle in the building entrance, with cross fire and explosions. It would mean an escalation to outright combat; what's more, in an urban setting. We decided not to take the risk.

Then the snipers realized they'd been discovered. As we had expected, they quit working that night and soon afterward left their positions. The coup plotters were now betting on a storming of the White House.

*Soviet propaganda made much of Pavlik Morozov, the boy who informed on his own father during World War II in loyalty to the Communist state.—Trans.

Alexander Korzhakov and the small presidential security detail probably had the most definite objective. By now almost everyone in the White House realized that those damned coup plotters would likely storm the building. The security people decided to first save the president.

I knew that Korzhakov was thinking up one escape plan after another, and going over and over each one to determine which was the most reliable. I knew that if my security people were given their way, they would escort me out of the building, drive me someplace, hide me in underground tunnels, float me away on barges, or lift me into the sky in a balloon. At the time, I did not become involved in these numerous plans; I only learned of them much later. From Korzhakov's combative and intent expression, I knew he had once again devised something new. A disguise had been ordered for me from the makeup room at the Taganka Theater: a beard, wig, and mustache. How handsome I would have looked in that getup!

It so happened that Mstislav Rostropovich, the outstanding Russian musician, had twice visited Russia (although he lives in the United States and travels a great deal all around the world) at most urgent and critical moments. The first time was during the August 1991 coup, and the second was in late September and early October of 1993 during the parliamentary rebellion. Both of these meetings seemed symbolic to me, not just an episode in our lives, but a spiritual landmark.

During the August coup, I learned that outside, down below the White House* *tout le Moscou* had gathered; that is, the most vigorous, prominent people in the capital, including actors, artists, writers, and musicians. Rostropovich was a special person with a special kind of magic. I understood that ancient Russia, Russia the Great, was blessing me by the highest possible art.

Both inside and outside the White House, many people found their nerves were giving out. Some people just couldn't or didn't know how to behave in such a stressful situation. There were hysterics. There were quite a few drunks. When we went into the bunker below the building, one prominent democrat got quite drunk, which was very depressing to see. In general, a seething undirected crowd is a double-edged sword. We tried to govern it but,

*The White House is located on a hill overlooking the Moscow River.—Trans.

obviously, not everyone was under our authority. I realized this, and each moment in anticipation of the coup plotters' next move added to the weight on my shoulders.

Suddenly Rostropovich walked in and everything fell into place. All the trivial concerns and inanities fell away. The repressive atmosphere, making me feel alienated even from myself, evaporated. Of course Rostropovich was a great man who performed a magnanimous, bold deed: he asked for an assault rifle and was loaned one for a time, although every firearm was needed.

Later, in 1993, Rostropovich gave a concert in Red Square. The cold wind tore at the flaps of the musicians' frock coats. They were only wearing tuxedos and hats and their fingers were blue from the cold, but they kept on playing. Playing for all of us. Just as during the coup in August Rostropovich had blessed democracy in Russia with his heartfelt gesture, so during the parliamentary rebellion in 1993, it was as if he were telling us with his beautiful music to be prepared for great ordeals. And may God help you.

Yet another late-night meeting in the darkened White House left a lingering impression. Yuri Luzhkov, at that time not yet mayor of Moscow but premier of the Moscow city government (as the position was called at the time), did not come to the White House alone, but brought his pregnant wife. In the harsh glare of the fluorescent light bulbs, in the dim corridors of the underground bunker, it was awful to see her pale face and the anxious Luzhkov, who would not leave her side. They sat together for a long time and no one bothered them.

This episode reminded me once again that we were playing, as a poet once wrote, "for keeps to the after death." Luzhkov's tough masculine nature brought him to the White House, but he and his wife could not leave each other. They waited together to see how the night would end for them and their future child.

I was informed that Gen. Alexander Lebed had appeared at the White House. Rutskoi, Security Council Secretary Yuri Skokov, and Korzhakov held preliminary talks with him, then I met him for the first time. Lebed is an interesting individual. A general who had served in the Afghan war, Lebed was able to perform the paratrooper's routines better than any soldier. Strikingly tough in manner, he was a blunt man who placed his military officer's sense of honor above everything.

As more and more army units were arriving in Moscow on Marshal Yazov's orders, Grachev needed to determine what was actually going on at the White House and had sent Lebed on a reconnaissance mission. Lebed explained to our people that all it would take would be to release a few antitank guided missiles and the plastic in the building would ignite. The fire would burn so fiercely that people would jump out of the windows. So there was no point in talking seriously about defending the White House.

Next Lebed announced that eight of the APCs parked outside had come over to our side and would help defend the White House. Rutskoi and Kobets argued over how the armored vehicles could be better positioned; their disagreement led nowhere. Lebed was convinced he was dealing with people who were largely dilettantes and weren't capable of resisting even a small professional military division, although there were already dozens of such divisions in and around Moscow.

During our meeting, Lebed dryly and politely explained to me that my appeal to the army not to obey the GKChP was provoking the soldiers and officers into insubordination, and that was a violation of their oath. In order for my call to have some force and backing, said Lebed, I should assume the office of supreme commander in chief of Russia on its territory. After all, the supreme commander in chief of the Soviet Union was not Defense Minister Yazov, but President Gorbachev, and Gorbachev's location was now uncertain. Therefore, as president of the Republic of Russia, I had the right to head the armed forces of Russia.

I thanked Lebed and we said good-bye.

I could not immediately make up my mind to start calling myself supreme commander in chief, so I did not sign the decree about this new title until the following day.

I assigned Yuri Skokov to contact the top leadership of the Soviet Army and the Interior Ministry. We had to maintain informal communications with them, so these contacts did in fact take place during the coup. Skokov met with Pavel Grachev and Boris Gromov, Pugo's deputy. Both had served in Afghanistan and been through the awful school of a colonial war (as it would have been called in the past), but neither of these generals had any desire to fight in Moscow.

The morning of August 20 KGB analysts sent a memo to Kryuchkov outlining the GKChP's grave errors in attempting the coup.

Moscow journalists from newspapers banned by the GKChP pooled their efforts to issue *Obshchaya gazeta* (*Common* newspaper), printing it out from their computers as fliers and distributing thousands of Xerox copies.

A quick survey of fifteen hundred Muscovites found only 10 percent who supported the GKChP. Yevgeny Primakov and Vadim Bakatin, members of the USSR Security Council, now came out publicly against the coup. Alexander Yakovlev, former member of the presidential council and close adviser to Gorbachev, also urged the nation to resist the coup.

Many thousands had been rallying for hours. Occasionally, they would pause to listen to local radio reports. One of the dispatches said that Yanayev had ordered my arrest.

The previous evening, Oleg Baklanov, the coup plotter in charge of the military-industrial complex, had sat down at his desk to address a statement to Yanayev. He had begun, "Dear Gennady Ivanovich: Due to the inability of the GKChP to stabilize the situation in the country, I consider it impossible to participate further in its work. I must admit that . . ." Here he broke off and threw the letter away. Then he went in person to try to persuade Yanayev that the coup was going awry. Ground troops Commander Varennikov sent a coded telegram from Kiev: "We all urge you to take measures immediately to liquidate the group of the opportunist B. N. Yeltsin. The RSFSR* government building must be immediately and securely blockaded, and all water service, electricity, telephone, radio communications, etc., must be terminated." Apparently, Varennikov already had in mind a ready-made "liquidation" plan. He was obviously suffering from having been stuck in Kiev, away from all the action.

An entire night and then an entire morning passed, and still there was no storming of the White House, nor even a blockade. The troops continued to stand outside and there was a lot of tank movement. Was Kryuchkov really so stupid that he didn't understand how dangerous such indecision could be?

Here is what General Lebed wrote in his memoirs of the coup:

*Russian Soviet Federated Socialist Republics.—Trans.

> There was a terrible mess at the Chkalov and Kubinka Air Force bases. The Volgograd Division had been flying around the "hot spots"* for three years, and with their experience and given the right approach, could land anywhere. But now their planes were off schedule, flights were mixed up, and aircraft were suddenly showing up and landing at the wrong air bases. Divisions of regiments were intermingled and the chain of command partially disrupted. . . . A forceful, deliberate intention could be sensed directing all this disorder. Grachev called early the first night. "Get back here!" he said. I returned. The commander was agitated. Karpukhin called and said that Alpha would not take part in either a blockade or a storming. It wasn't clear what the Dzerzhinsky Division would do. Apparently its tanks were leaving but there was no accurate information. He suggested calling the division's command post. When a sleepy junior sergeant was roused and asked how many vehicles had left and when they had begun to move, he asked, "Vehicles? What vehicles? Nobody's gone anywhere." The Tula Division had not budged from its location in Tushino.† The Tyoply Stan Brigade‡ had gotten lost somewhere.

General Lebed hinted that the chaos reigning in the military that day was the work of some terribly cunning conspiracy of dark forces. But chaos—real chaos—cannot be so cleverly organized or managed. It happens for the most elementary reasons. What was the number of the paratroopers' division that Lebed went to meet in Kubinka? What were the numbers of those who were brought into Moscow during those days? The fourth? The fifth? The sixth? With so much traffic, it was easy to see how mixups could happen.

In fact, the White House could have been stormed with just one platoon. The military people made up for their lack of an advance plan with the usual Russian overkill, sending out as many tanks and divisions as could be mustered.

This exaggerated response wasn't the main problem, however. Even before the military had made contact with us, the highest-ranking command had very mixed feelings about the coup. The army realized that the KGB had been late in acting by whole days. Now, as Lebed recounted in his memoirs about his report to Grachev, "any violent actions on the approaches to the building of the Supreme Soviet will lead to massive bloodshed." That would be

*That is, of ethnic conflict in the USSR.—Trans.

†Tushino is a suburb of Moscow. The Tula Division had been transferred there.—Trans.

‡Tyoply Stan is a district in the southwest of Moscow.—Trans.

a severe psychological blow for the military people from which they would not recover. There was no single strong figure behind the army urging it on. That was why they were only imitating the preparation of a storming and imitating acts of war in order to buy time. Nevertheless, the moment of resolution was imminent.

On the morning of August 20, KGB analysts prepared an instant analysis of the situation for Kryuchkov (in response to his query on the GKChP's options in the immediate future):

1. Massive civil disobedience, a revolution from the left. A return to the situation prior to August 20, but now with a regime of terror against Communists and the highest echelons of the government.
2. A sharp turn to the right. Accusation of the existing post-Gorbachev leadership of abetting Gorbachev. Worsening of the struggle for power with a gradual transfer of power to forces of the orthodox right-wing orientation. The principle will be that everyone who was with Gorbachev is to blame. The possible time period for this option is from two weeks to two months.

The leadership of the Komsomol's* central committee issued a statement that the coup jeopardized the policy of extensive reforms associated with Gorbachev's name. The Komsomol appealed to young people, primarily soldiers, urging them not to succumb to provocations—a characteristically lukewarm call from that organization. Academician Tikhonov of the Agricultural Sciences Academy appealed to cooperative owners and entrepreneurs to boycott officials who implemented the GKChP's decrees. The USA and Canada Institute declared a strike on August 20. The USSR Journalists' Union expressed "resolute protest" in their statement of August 20.

The country was awakening. Only yesterday, most people were discussing the news in half whispers. Now they began to declare their protest against the GKChP in public, written statements. The Komsomol, the trade unions, academicians, institutes, artists' unions, labor collectives, and commodities markets all weighed in. All of this information immediately came to the desk of the KGB chairman.

*Young Communist League.—Trans.

The coup plotters had let the day for decisive actions go by. During that day, they had tried to see where they stood, argued among themselves, tried to find the right "image," and attempted to steer matters into a constitutional framework. As Baklanov, Varennikov, and others had warned, all this effort to create a legal cover for the coup did was unleash new, far more severe problems. Now they would not only have to crush the resistance of desperate masses of people, growing by the hour outside the White House, and not only confront the resolute stance of the world community and commit massive bloodshed, but they would also have to impose a far harsher regime than they had previously planned. It was practically a military dictatorship. Anyone protesting today was to suffer harsh punishment tomorrow; at the very least, they should be arrested. But how many hundreds of people would have to be jailed? And then how would the rest react? Ideally, mass arrests should have begun with the Komsomol central committee secretaries, the newspaper editors, the Writers' Union, the members of the Security Council, but the country had not known purges of that scale since Stalin's day.

One of the few leaders of the new political parties who supported the coup was Vladimir Zhirinovsky, who spoke at one of the rallies on August 19. At least he was consistent: the Liberal Democratic party that he led had always advocated a Russian empire, iron-clad borders for the USSR, and the imposition of order by military means. When the coup came, he could only say, Hurrah!

Getting very far ahead of myself, beyond the bounds of this book entirely, I would like to take this opportunity to say that in the elections of 1993, Zhirinovsky revealed social, psychological, and moral wounds in our society whose presence we had not suspected. One of them was the absence of immunity to fascism.

Pushed by the GKChP members, the military people were, finally, forced to determine a time for the storming of the White House and met to draft a plan for the next phase of the operation. At first the attack was scheduled for the evening of August 20 and then postponed until 2:00 A.M. because of "insufficiency of forces" and the need to bring in new, fresh platoons who had still not succumbed to the agitation of Muscovites. The maneuvers were coordinated among the army, KGB, and Interior Ministry. On paper, the plan was as follows: paratroopers under the leadership of General Alexander Lebed, cooperating with the Interior Ministry's Special Assignment Motorized Rifle Division, were to block the Supreme Soviet building from the direction of the U.S. Embassy and Krasnopresnenskaya Embankment, after surrounding the White House and closing off access to it.

The OMON* and paratroopers were to drive a wedge through the mass of defenders, leaving a path behind them for Alpha, then Group B, and then Volna (Moscow and Moscow region KGB divisions) to advance on the White House. These special divisions had the best physically trained officers. Alpha would use grenade launchers to knock out the doors, penetrate to the fifth floor, to my office, and then seize the president of Russia.

Group B would put down centers of resistance. Volna would divide into teams of ten and together with other forces from the KGB Moscow directorate would perform what they termed *filtratsyia,* identification and detention of those subject to arrest, including the entire leadership of Russia. Photographers included in the groups of ten would take snapshots as the defenders fired in self-defense in order to make it look as if they had been the first to shoot. The KGB's *spetsnaz* would block all the exits from the building.

Special vehicles would blaze a trail through the barricades. Three tank regiments would deafen the defenders with cannon fire. A squadron of combat helicopters could provide air support for the attack.

At about 2:30 A.M., August 21, I looked at my watch, closed my eyes, and was out like a light. When the shooting began, my aides shook me awake. They took me downstairs, put a bullet-proof vest on me right in the garage, put me in the backseat of a car, and said "Let's get going!" When the engine turned over, I woke up completely, saying, "Where're we going?" My first reaction while still half-asleep was: that's it. The storming has begun.

The White House is an enormous building with different wings exiting onto various streets. One exit leads to a side street where the Americans had recently built a new residence for their embassy. It would take fifteen seconds to get to the American residence, and that route was chief among the options for my evacuation. We got in

***Otryad militsii osobogo naznacheniya,* special assignment police detachment, or riot troops, under the control of the Interior Ministry.—Trans.

touch with the embassy, the Americans immediately consented to the idea, then ran with it themselves. Later they started calling us on their own, even coming over to see us and offering help.

I was not informed of any of the exact plans for my evacuation. Another secret escape plan was to whisk me out through the underground tunnels below the White House to a spot near the Hotel Ukraine across the river. I was to change clothes and put on a disguise and then my security people were to pick me up somewhere else in the city. There were other variations of that escape. Since the plan to go to the Americans was the simplest and most reliable, that is the one they put into motion when the first shots rang out.

When I realized where we were headed, I categorically refused to leave the White House. From the perspective of security, the plan to go to the U.S. Embassy was 100 percent correct. But from the point of view of politics, it was a 100 percent failure. Thank God, I was immediately able to recognize that while I was still in the car. If people learned I was hiding in the American Embassy, their reaction would be unequivocal: they would see it as virtual emigration, though in miniature. It would mean I had gotten myself to a safe place, but had left them under the gun. That would probably be their logic. There were other nuances involved in seeking haven with the United States. Despite our respect for the Americans, people in our country don't like it when foreigners take too active a hand in our affairs.

Late on August 20, day two of the coup, all sources were reporting that the GKChP had decided to go ahead with the storming of the White House. Fresh troops began to be dispatched to Moscow, so we decided to go into the bunker.

The bunker was a modern bomb shelter, not just a basement, but a facility that had been cleverly designed and built very deeply and securely under the ground. It took a long time for our security people to figure out how to work the special large hermetically sealed doors.

There were several exits from the bunker. One tunnel led to the metro. This route involved climbing a steep metal ladder for about fifty yards, and it was mined just in case. The second exit was a small inconspicuous door near the security desk where passes were issued, which led immediately to the street. There were other exits through underground sewage pipes.

Inside the shelter were several rooms with bunk beds. We brought chairs with us and spent several very exhausting hours of the night there. Although there had been an order for the women to leave, the women did not leave us, not even the typists. For some reason, no one wanted to go home.

The most difficult moment came at about 3:00 A.M., when the shooting started up again. It was obvious that it would be impossible to leave the bunker unnoticed. Worse, upstairs, people were perhaps already being killed.

I couldn't just keep sitting there. I decided to leave the bunker and go upstairs. The deserted floor where my office was located gradually came back to life, lights were turned on in the rooms, telephone calls were made. I was informed that three people had been killed. I called home and barely managed to squeeze out three words: there are casualties.

After Midnight

The onion-skin paper was yellowing and almost crumbling. Before me was an office file folder marked in thick purple ink containing case number 5644, under which a group of former peasants who had worked at a construction site in Kazan were tried in 1934. Among them was my father, Nikolai Ignatievich Yeltsin. At the time, he was twenty-eight years old. His brother, Andrian, even younger at twenty-two, was a codefendant in the same case.

Before the brothers' arrest, the family had fallen under the government's campaign to "de-kulakize" the countryside.* Although we have gradually come to forget what that meant, at that time, everything was "as plain as a boiled turnip," as the Russian saying goes. As the local government officials had written in a background check sent to the Chekists† in Kazan, the Yeltsin family had rented about fourteen acres of land:

*The kulaks were wealthy peasants (*kulak* is the Russian word for "fist") massacred through artificial famines under Stalin in a campaign euphemistically called *raskulachivaniye,* or "de-kulakification."—Trans.

†The Cheka was the first secret police formed under the Bolsheviks (named for the Russian acronym *Chrezvychnaya kommissiya* [Extraordinary Commission]). The secret police continue to be called Chekists even today.—Trans.

> Before the revolution, [Yeltsin's] father's homestead was of the kulak type. He owned a water mill and a windmill. He owned a threshing machine, he owned permanent farmhands, he owned about twelve hectares of cropland, he owned a harvester and a binder, and he owned about five horses and about four cows.

Owned, owned, owned. That was why he was guilty—he had worked a lot and had taken a lot of responsibility upon himself. But the Soviet government liked modest, retiring people who didn't stick out. It didn't like large strong vivid characters and was merciless with them.

He and his family were evicted and my grandfather was stripped of his civil rights. The authorities levied a steep tax on him as an individual farmer. In short, they put a bayonet to his throat as only they knew how to in those days. So my grandfather went into hiding. As they grew up, his sons realized that there was no life for them in the village. They went away to the city to find construction work. Where once there had been a flourishing farm, a large country home, peasant stock rooted in the earth, now there was desolation.

Well, the rest of the story was only too typical. For two years the sons worked construction at Kazmashstroi, the Kazan machine-building plant. They did carpentry, toiling hard for the good of Stalin's industrialization. The elder brother, my father, had already started a family by then. A son was born—that was me.

But in April 1934, even this barely started new life was ruined. On one of the pages in a case file the words *fellow villager* appeared. That's what the secret police called the defendants in a trial of six former peasants, the brothers Yeltsin, the Gavrilovs (father and son), Vakhrushev, and Sokolov. But "trial" wasn't the word for it. A "special troika"* simply issued sentences "extrajudicially," as they phrased it, under Article 58–10 ("counterrevolution"). Some of the men were sentenced to five years; my father and uncle got three years of labor camp.

In fact, the codefendants were not fellow villagers at all. The Gavrilovs and the Yeltsins were from different areas of the Ural Mountains region. Vakhrushev was from Udmurt, an even more remote area. They had not known each other before they met at the construction site. The Chekist reasoning behind the case was that

*Three-man commissions composed of a judge, prosecutor, and party representative, which functioned as kangaroo courts during Stalin's purges.—Trans.

someone had noticed that the remnants of strong peasant families, which had been de-kulakized and abused by the Soviet government, had all happened to meet in one barracks. That could spell trouble; hence the trumped-up charge.

As I leafed through the old case file, I wondered about the identity of the main person who informed on them. How had the case started? I came to the conclusion that the case was part of a quota. About that time in Kazan, there were all sorts of huge "conspiracies," "wreckers," and "saboteurs' groups." That made it possible to arrest dozens of people at once. Six workers was an easy job for the troika. The case was needed so that investigators could report to their superiors that they were doing their job. In perfectly ordinary workers' barracks number 8, among plain, honest working stiffs, suddenly the authorities discovered "enemies of the people." A boss or a party worker or a plainclothes informer working for the secret police pointed the finger—there they are; they're former kulaks.

Neither my father nor his brother admitted to anything and refused to plead guilty. I was struck by the fact that in other times such non-compliance would have cost them dearly. The secret police would have grabbed them by the scruff of the neck and beaten the living daylights out of them until they died. It was only a few years later that widespread torture was sanctioned—in fact, quite officially—during interrogations. But in 1934, the investigators were in a hurry. The main thing was to get the paperwork done, to do everything according to the regulations for "Soviet legality"—the interrogation transcript; the witnesses' testimonies; the forced confrontations between defendants and witnesses; the compromising material sent from hometowns; and so forth. All of this had to be collected, signed, copied out, and bound in a case file. Even so, the work took less than a month.

What were the charges against this "wreckers' group"? Once when rotten soup was poured onto the ground right from the kettle, the twenty-two-year-old Andrian Yeltsin angrily shouted, "What, do they want all the workers to run away from the construction site?" Then, citing some vague state exigency, the bosses organized a "loan" at the site; that is, they took away everyone's wages and gave them promissory notes instead. Page three of the case file states: "During a sign-up for a loan, Ivan Sokolov said, 'I'm not going to sign for a loan that you're grabbing from us. You still haven't returned the old loan to us, and now you're making us give you a new one' (testimony from witness Kudrinsky, May 7, 1934)."

Still another time the workers had a nip on Easter Sunday. Somebody informed on the peasant fellows—drinking was considered a grave offense. Interestingly, the case didn't quote any especially audacious statements from my father. It was mainly his brother and the other codefendants who had shot off their mouths. But my father was the brigade leader in this kulaks brigade, and, evidently, a rather good one. That was all it took.

Investigator Denisov recorded the testimony of one of the witnesses called in to give testimony. The witness, Raskolnikov, signed the transcript and wrote "faithfully recorded from my words" at the end. I have preserved the atrocious spelling and grammar of the document:

> This hole group was pretty tight among themselves which was showed at work and also during nonworking hours. All the kamrads would get together at Yeltsin's apartment. They were kulaks but they all tried to hide it. In order to hide there soshul origins, this hole brigade would fulfil there quotas good at work. But even despite there good work, they systamatikly got together at Yeltsin's apartment to discuss some issues, which I can't say nothing about being as I didn't take part in there private huddles.

Such haphazard incoherent witness testimonies were allegedly all it took to "completely expose" the defendants. Finally, the investigators had an indictment with six names. Nikolai Ignatievich Yeltsin was the third in the list. They were accused as follows:

> . . . after starting work at Kazmashstroi, being hostile-minded toward the Soviet government, under the leadership of the kulak Sokolov they systematically conducted anti-Soviet agitation among workers, having as their goal the demoralization of the working class and the sowing of dissatisfaction with the existing law and order. Exploiting the difficulties in provision of food and supplies, they tried to create ill will, spreading provocative rumors of war and the rapid demise of the Soviet government. They waged agitation against the loan, and spoke out vigorously against helping the Austrian workers; that is, they committed acts proscribed under Article 58–10 of the penal code.

Finally, I found a last little slip of paper at the end of the file, a third of the size of a usual page:

> Excerpt from transcript number 12 of the session of the Judicial Troika of the State Political Directorate of the Tatar Autononomous

> Soviet Republic of May 23, 1934. The following case was heard: Case No. 5644–34, on the accusations against Nikolai Ignatievich Yeltsin, born 1906, of the village of Basmanovo in the Ural region, a de-kulakized kulak who worked as a carpenter at Kazmashstroi. Under Article 58–10 of the penal code. Resolved: To incarcerate Nikolai Ignatievich Yeltsin in a corrective-labor colony for a period of three years.

On the back of the slip was written "Read 5.25.34" and the signature of my father. The file—indeed the whole "case"—gave me a heavy sinking feeling. I kept leafing through the documents, trying to understand. Shouldn't there have been some kind of logic to these stories? Did the Chekists' machinery really so senselessly gobble up people? Perhaps my life would have taken a different turn if I had been able to see my father's file earlier. If I could have been convinced without a doubt of what ordinary, banal horror our industry, our powerful Soviet reality was steeped in.

My father never spoke about any of this with me. He blanked this piece of his life out of his memory as if it had never existed. It was forbidden to speak of this subject in our family.

I was only three years old at the time of my father's arrest, but I remember to this day all the horror and fear. One night people came into our barracks room. I remember my mother shouting and crying. I woke up and also began to cry. I was crying not because my father was going away (I was still too young to understand what was happening to him). I was crying because I saw my mother crying and saw how frightened she was. Her fear and her tears were transferred to me. My father was taken away, and my mother threw herself at me, hugging me until I calmed down and fell asleep. Three years later, my father returned from the camps.

If we curse the past, if we blank it out of our memory as my father did, nothing will get better. Our history is both cursed and magnificent. Just like the history of any state or people. It is fitting that in Russia, the tragedies, these contradictory strands of history are woven so tightly together. To this day, I have chills when I see that yellowing file, case number 5644.

The tension around the White House was increasing with every hour. Women and children were asked to leave the danger zone. Some paratroopers had shut off Echo of Moscow's radio transmitter, and people in the square were left without information.

By evening, through the efforts of deputies who literally ganged up on the minister of communications, Echo was back on the air, broadcasting minute-by-minute news reports of troop movements.

In this situation, the generals' beautiful plan, drafted hastily under Varennikov's pressure, was impractical. In order to work, the operation at least had to be directed in person, the divisions had to be individually persuaded to attack, to go with assault rifles against unarmed demonstrators who had formed human chains three, four, and five layers deep, hanging on for dear life. They would have to pass through old people and women, through a whole mile of live human bodies. They would have to shoot the pride and hope of Russia right in the face—its most famous people and its political symbol, the Russian parliament and government.

Obviously, the army could not do this. They could not go further, always behind a step, always chasing events, always trying to keep up with the inconsistent and hysterical moves of the GKChP. The combat troops now retreated to their bases in agonizing shame, or turned on their transistor radios, or else drove off course, a shapeless black mass frozen on the outlying streets of Moscow in the darkness of the night.

In all their interviews and memoirs about the coup, the military people for some reason stubbornly insist on calling the movement of columns of armored vehicles along the Garden Ring Road, and from Chaikovsky Street to Smolensk Square, the "patrolling" of Moscow's streets. This was not just "patrolling," however, but a last-ditch deployment of hardware in a desperate attempt to intimidate, dislodge, and scatter the crowd at the White House. Whatever the case, as one of the armored vehicles rolled into a tunnel, people threw a tarpaulin over it, a young man jumped onto the vehicle, warning shots rang out from the hatch, and the young man fell off. The armored vehicle then backed up abruptly in reverse, dragging the helpless body underneath it along the pavement. Two other young men who ran to the rescue of the fallen man were shot.

The bloodstains remained on the pavement for a long, long time. Three young people departed from this life: Dmitry Komar, Ilya Krichevsky, and Vladimir Usov. May their memory be eternal.

What happened that night was not something which we or the military had wished. What happened shouldn't have happened. Only one order had been broadcast through the headphones in the tank commanders' helmets—stay put; don't move. What happened could have been expected when people are under horrible stress for many hours at a time and near hysterics.

Nevertheless, the casualties helped sober everyone. By morning, under pressure of his deputies, Marshal Yazov gave the order to withdraw the troops from Moscow. The coup plotters, who just yesterday had felt so confident behind the protection of so many guns, were now face-to-face with their own destiny. They were in shock.

Their last disorganized meeting was accompanied by endless hysterics, most vividly demonstrated by Yuri Prokofiev, first secretary of the Moscow city party committee, who said, "You better give me a pistol so I can shoot myself."

By the way, Prokofiev is now a successful businessman.

On the morning of August 21, everyone in the country woke numbed in fear: would there really be more bloodshed? Was this really not the end? Television and radio continued to broadcast the GKChP's decrees. Although the previous day there had been a breakthrough in the situation, the risk was still great that the coup plotters, now afraid of the consequences of their deeds, would retaliate in desperation.

The Supreme Soviet of Russia opened session.

On the 21st of August, at 2:15 P.M., the Soviet presidential plane set off toward Foros. On board were Kryuchkov, Yazov, Baklanov, and Tizyakov. Lukyanov and Vladimir Ivashko* were on another plane.

At 4:52 P.M., TU-134 bound for Foros left Vnukovo Airport carrying Silayev, Bakatin, Rutskoi, Primakov, and ten members of the Russian parliament.

At 7:25 P.M., the plane carrying the coup plotters touched down at Belbek Air Force Base in the Crimea.

Gorbachev refused to speak substantively to the coup plotters, and restricted himself to giving them a stern moral upbraiding. There really was nothing else to say. Before the general secretary stood a team of suicides—they were all different in their way but

*Vladimir Antonovich Ivashko, Deputy General Secretary of Communist Party (1990–91).—Trans.

still alike in one thing: the word former had just been added to their job titles. The GKChP was the last page in their biography.

When Raisa Gorbacheva, Gorbachev's wife, saw Alexander Rutskoi armed and other people toting assault rifles, she asked in fright, "What, have you come here to arrest us?" "Why?" asked Rutskoi in surprise. "We're liberating you!" She broke down in tears.

Late that night Gorbachev came down the steps of the plane onto the tarmac of Vnukovo Airport, "with his face inside out," as someone wrote. His family was with him. I watched the news coverage of his arrival. Although Gorbachev was and is my political opponent. It was wonderful that such a terrible story had such a happy ending.

But ahead was still an extremely difficult day of demonstrations and funerals; an incredible crowd of people stretching from the White House to Vagankovo (the cemetery); a heavy oppressive atmosphere; and an unbearable sense of shame for all of us. Gorbachev could not take it and left, and I remained with the grieving ashen-faced mothers of the young men.

Who could have guessed that these were not to be the last funerals in our country?

I have been criticized many times for demonstratively signing a decree to suspend the activity of the Communist party at the first Supreme Soviet session after the coup. Yes, I did it demonstratively, but not in anger. No one can deny that the main event that occurred in these three days was the complete and final collapse of Communist rule in our country. The party remained, the idea remained, but as a militant state ideology, communism receded into the past.

I remember another depressing episode from the August coup, my telephone call to Yanayev. I told him that their statement about Gorbachev's health had to be a lie. I demanded a medical report or the president's own confirmation. "There will be a medical report," he replied hoarsely. My heart sank.

Only later did I realize they weren't capable of such brutal cynicism and were bluffing. They didn't have the guts. They were, after all, average, ordinary Soviet people. No, there was no "evil genius" among them. The chief catalyst of the coup was still in Foros. Much depended on Gorbachev's behavior and the subsequent reaction of the plotters.

If they were to break him and resort to violence, the repercussions would reach to Moscow and from there run through the entire Soviet

Union. Even though cynical, the coup plotters of August 1991 appreciated the value of human life and had some reservations before committing a crime—that was already something. Their entire background had trained them to think only in technocratic terms, and they turned out to be incapable of overstepping that barrier.

I think something happened to people in the seventy years since the Great October Revolution, the term with which the 1917 revolution has always been dignified. There cannot be that kind of explosion again. Because we Russians and other peoples of the Russian Federation have become more normal, more cultured—kinder, if you will. And perhaps more enlightened.

Killing other people because they are richer? Shooting a whole family because they are of different blood? Fighting, shooting one another, and dying—for my sake, Khasbulatov, the Constitution, or the Communists? No, I can't believe the people of Russia are capable of that.

The trial of the August 1991 coup plotters has dragged on for several years now. It is an exhaustive, uproarious, and messy trial—the judicial machinery simply cannot digest this enormous case. First it was delayed for political reasons (the hope that my power would collapse), then on procedural grounds, and then for medical reasons as the GKChP members began to fall ill. Now they have all been released, they write poetry, they take part in demonstrations, and they are elected to the state duma, the new parliament. That's the way it goes.

Their cells in Lefortovo Prison have now been occupied by other people, thereby proving that the power of democracy is, alas, unstable.*

In fighting for democracy and freedom, the people who fought in August 1991 were actually fighting for the motherland. It was more important for them than their own lives. The inability of the coup plotters to kill and the sacred desire of ordinary people to die for something higher than themselves was a moral lesson, the legacy bequeathed to us, as strange as it may seem, by Soviet rule, with its education and way of life.

*Both the August 1991 coup plotters and the leaders of the October 1993 parliamentary rebellion were amnestied without trial by parliament in February 1994. The coup plotters had been released in 1993, many for health reasons. The October rebels were also released from prison.—Trans.

I often think of this now. Totalitarianism has vanished into the past. But have those moral inhibitions without which there is no morality, and those ideals without which there is no civil society, have they vanished into the past as well?

Another era has begun. A time of troubles and uncertainty, forcing us to rack our brains to find a way out of desperate stalemates. It is an era continually compelling us to recall that translucent time of well-defined objectives and clarity, the era that ended on August 21, 1991.

Once again, I turn on the cassette player.

Tanya: There was a horrible moment when we were told an explosion had taken place in the White House. Mama's knees collapsed and she sank to the floor. "It can't be!" I said, and ran to call the White House. Lev Sukhanov said, "No, Tanya, everything's okay. We're all working. It's just disinformation."

Lyosha: We were listening to Echo of Moscow and heard the gunfire on Kalinin, and then the announcer reported that a tank was burning there and there'd been a clash . . .

Lena: For about a month afterward, whenever I heard trucks passing by, I would rush to see if they were tanks. I knew that they couldn't be, but I would still jerk my head up.

August twenty-first was my birthday. That evening we decided to celebrate it somehow, but only the women came. Everyone's husbands were there at the White House. And Papa wasn't home since, of course, the danger hadn't passed yet completely. People spent the night on watch at the White House on August twenty-first and twenty-second as well. And they gave me a spent cartridge for my birthday present.

Papa called again at five A.M. to wish me a happy birthday. "I'm sorry, I didn't give you a present this time," he said. And I said to him, "Papa, you've already given me the best present there ever was. You have defended democracy!"

And to be honest, that high-flown phrase didn't seem too bombastic to me at all.

4

AFTER THE COUP

Editor's Note: Yeltsin writes of the awkward months between August and the end of December, when Gorbachev finally yielded power. The shift in authority is peaceful but strained. At their last meeting, Gorbachev seemed more interested in his compensation package and in handing over the top-secret historical files of the general secretary of the Communist party than he was in the significance of a historic transition of power in Russia.

After the August coup, all the republics had instantly reacted with declarations of independence. Presidential elections were scheduled immediately, declarations were made, and press releases were issued, by Georgia and Moldova in particular, saying that now they would not sign any Union treaty. All the governmental bodies of the Soviet Union were in suspension, and it was obvious that the real power was in the republics, above all the Republic of Russia. Neither the Council of Ministers nor Gosplan (the state planning agency) nor any of the other all-powerful bodies were making any real decisions; their function was merely limited to registering the existing situation.

The economy follows politics, after all. And in the political sense the principle of ruling from the center had so compromised itself that the republics had no other alternative but to opt for independent development.

Instead of a gradual transition from the unitarian Soviet Union to a softer, freer confederation, we had a complete vacuum at the political center. The center—in the person of Gorbachev—was totally demoralized. The emerging national states had lost faith in him. Something had to be done.

From August 1991 until the moment of Gorbachev's resignation in December of that year, we had approximately eight to ten meetings. I don't know if Gorbachev realized how changed the nature of our relations were by then. I had told him that the coup had taught us a bitter lesson, and therefore I had to insist that he not make any personnel decisions without first obtaining my consent. He looked at me intently, with the expression of a person backed into a corner, but I had no other alternative. Everything depended on my taking a position of brutal consistency. In time I was proved right.

Despite my urging, Gorbachev made the first personnel appointments on his own: in place of the jailed coup plotters, Mikhail Moiseyev was chosen as defense minister; Leonid Shebarshin was appointed KGB chairman; and Bessmertnykh was retained as foreign minister. I knew very well that all of these people had been either overtly or covertly involved in the coup.

After the news agencies had run the reports of these appointments, I called Gorbachev at night and said: "Mikhail Sergeyevich, what are you doing? Moiseyev was one of the organizers of the coup and Shebarshin is a man close to Kryuchkov, the chief coordinator of the coup." Gorbachev began to hem and haw: "Yes, it's possible I've gone off track, but now it's too late. All the newspapers have published the decree; it's been read over television." Finally, at the end of the telephone conversation, I said to him: "I will be in your office tomorrow."

I was amazed at Gorbachev's argument: it would supposedly be awkward to retract the announcement of the appointments. But were outward formalities more important than this real threat to the country's security? In his office the next morning, I first demanded that he dismiss Moiseyev immediately. He put up a fight, but finally conceded that he had made a mistake. He said: "I'll think of how I can correct it." I said: "No, I won't leave until you do it in my presence. Have Moiseyev come here right away and send him into retirement."

That very day, Moiseyev ordered his staff to destroy documents, particularly the coded messages dealing with the putsch that he himself had signed. Fortunately, one of the officers, a senior lieutenant who had been given a direct instruction to destroy the coded messages, made contact with our security service and informed them of the order. I was given a memo with the name and telephone of this senior lieutenant after Moiseyev arrived in my office. I gave this note to Gorbachev and said: call this telephone number and just ask this officer what he is doing right this moment. Gorbachev called him, and he answered: Captain So-and-so here. Gorbachev introduced himself and asked: what were your instructions? The captain replied: I received a directive from Moiseyev to destroy all the coded messages concerning the August coup. Gorbachev turned to Moiseyev and said: is there anything else you need to know?

Gorbachev and I agreed that the appointment of the new defense minister would be coordinated with the Council of Leaders of the Republics. The council was scheduled to meet within a few hours. I proposed Yevgeny Shaposhnikov, commander of the air force, as a candidate for defense minister. It was well known that he had comported himself courageously during the coup. No matter how much Marshal Yazov and those around him pressured him, Shaposhnikov did not succumb to provocation and did everything to prevent the air force from participating in the coup. There were no problems with his appointment.

No less important was to find a decent person for the role of KGB chairman, especially because such a person would have the job of destroying this terrible system of oppression that had been preserved from Stalin's day. The person who accepted this post would have to have experience managing a government agency. As I saw it then, Vadim Bakatin, who had headed the Interior Ministry before Pugo, could handle this job. Unexpectedly, Gorbachev consented to this proposal.

Next we came to the Foreign Ministry. I said that Alexander Bessmertnykh had followed instructions from the GKChP, that all the Soviet embassies abroad were sent coded messages in support of the GKChP, and that he had oriented the entire foreign service toward helping the coup plotters. We agreed on Eduard Shevardnadze, who had been Gorbachev's celebrated foreign minister, and had resigned predicting, correctly, a coup would happen. At 11:00 A.M., the Council of Leaders of the republics opened session and all of our proposed candidates were approved.

But each of these victories took an incredible amount of effort. How many more of them could there be—one, two, three? It became increasingly clear to me that these were all temporary concessions. Gorbachev had no evil intent in his unfortunate appointments to the three key posts in the government, defense, security, and foreign affairs. In the first two cases he had appointed the first deputies of the dismissed officials; in the third case he simply left the former experienced executive in place. But the evolution of the coup had illustrated that not only the first echelon of Soviet government leaders had been involved but also the second tier of their deputies. This was, after all, not a conspiracy of a few desperate generals, as happened later in October 1993, but a conspiracy of a government system that did not wish to be dismantled.

A paradoxical ambiguous situation seemed to emerge of its own accord. Gorbachev, the head of the country, was appointing as his immediate subordinates people who intended to overthrow him. The mechanism itself, the machinery of the coup, was being preserved untouched—the bureaucracies of the Union, where at all levels there were people prepared to impose a state of emergency.

I did not believe the people in the country wanted that. And I could not, I did not have the right to allow the rise of a new threat to Russia's security.

One night before the forthcoming session of USSR Congress of People's Deputies, the leaders of the Union republics gathered in the Kremlin to plan their tactics before the audience of the Congress. Long ago the majority of republic leaders had formed an unequivocal opinion: the Soviet Congress should be disbanded. This government body had outlived itself and was a relic of the past. But they also realized that the Congress would not agree to part with its former unlimited power without putting up a fight.

After intensive work, a joint statement of the heads of ten republics was drafted in which it was proposed to the Congress that interrepublican governing bodies be formed for a transitional period until a new USSR Constitution could be ratified. As soon as there was a new Constitution, the Congress should quickly wrap up its work and cease its existence. If this proposal was accepted, certain important articles of the current USSR Constitution should be suspended and power should pass from the Congress to a Council of Heads of State, made up of the president of the USSR and the leaders of the Union republics.

lead a nation as vast as
ssia, you need to appeal
all the people – from all
lks of life and of all ages.

Resisting the Reactionaries. Young army conscripts were prepared publicly to declare their faith in those who resisted the coup during the uprising of August 1991 (*left*); while, to the outside world, the pictures of a city littered with barricades must have brought home the realization that a revolution was underway – and in peril (*below*).

Before August, when we were working on this and other documents, Gorbachev kept making compromises, did not dwell on trivialities, and maintained a coordinated position with the heads of the republics. But after the coup he did an abrupt about-face. In declaring sovereignty, republic after republic was drastically changing—as was plainly evident to everyone—the political composition of the already former Soviet Union. In the new reality, Gorbachev was left with only one role: the unifier of republics that were scattering.

We asked Nursultan Nazarbayev to present the statement to the USSR Congress of People's Deputies. The proposal of a Council of Heads of State did not come as a big surprise to the Congress; it'd been prepared for such a scenario. Even so, the most excitable of the deputies threw themselves into defending the continued existence of the Congress. Words like *treachery, conspiracy, plundering of the country,* and so on were hurled from the speaker's platform. Gorbachev always had trouble restraining himself when people said such nasty things around him, and when they finally drove him to the wall, he went to the podium and threatened that if the Congress didn't dissolve itself, it would be disbanded. That cooled the ire of some of the speakers and the proposal for the Council of Heads of State went through without a hitch.

Next came vigorous, intense work at Novo-Ogaryovo. Gorbachev was now playing catch-up as the republics stayed always one step ahead of him. He made concessions that would have seemed unthinkable before August, conceding that the future Union could become a confederative state. Nevertheless, in Gorbachev's conception of the union, a strong center would be preserved that would determine matters of defense and some fiscal issues. A single president would remain to serve as guarantor for compliance with the treaty; he would also represent the Union of Sovereign States (the "USS" was the proposed new abbreviation for the former USSR) in dealings with foreign countries. The post of prime minister was retained in the central government, and a bicameral parliament would be convened in Moscow.

To Gorbachev's immense consternation, one after another of the former Union republics began to drop out of the Novo-Ogaryovo process. The first to go were the Baltic States (Lithuania, Estonia, and Latvia), although Gorbachev had not really counted on them to stay. Then Georgia, Moldova, Armenia, and Azerbaijan withdrew. The atmosphere at the Novo-Ogaryovo sessions in October and

November of 1991 was now quite different from before the coup. Back then, most heads of republics could not bring themselves to argue with the president of the USSR, and even accused me of "extreme radicalism." Now they were pouncing on Gorbachev themselves without letting me get a word in edgewise.

Parallel to these meetings, an active process was underway in the republics, with announcements of their independence and election of new presidents. They all dreamed of elevating their own status; all of them wanted to become full-fledged members of the UN.

It was obvious that Gorbachev, not because of anyone's ill will, was, historically speaking, painting himself into a corner.

The situation grew more dramatic on November 25 when Gorbachev told the press at the opening of the next Novo-Ogaryovo meeting that the chiefs of state had convened to initial the treaty. In fact, the treaty was not ready for initialing since Leonid Kravchuk, president of Ukraine, had not come to the meeting, and the Azerbaijani leader Ayaz Mutalibov, as Gorbachev explained, "had been unable to come to Novo-Ogaryovo because of the difficult situation in his republic."

Gorbachev's announcement of the signing forced the republics' leaders to make fundamental changes in the draft treaty, largely involving a transfer of the center's remaining powers to the republics. The president of the USSR first began gently to persuade the others, then became nervous and irritated. His reassurances were not helpful, the leaders of the republics stubbornly demanded greater independence from the center, and neither gentleness, persistence, nor finally harshness on Gorbachev's part could stop the Union republics now that they'd had a taste of freedom. When Gorbachev ultimately tried to insist on his own formulation and we unanimously rejected it, he lost his patience, jumped up from the table, and ran out of the meeting hall.

We were left alone in the room, and precisely then, as a heavy, oppressive silence hung over the room, we suddenly realized that it was over. We were meeting here for the last time. The Novo-Ogaryovo saga had drawn to a close. There was no more progress in that direction, and never would be. We would have to seek and conceive of something new.

All recovered from their surprise and dismay and gradually began to talk. No one wanted an uproar. Downstairs, reporters were impatiently waiting for news from a meeting that was supposed to be historic. It was already clear that it would not be historic, but a decent face had to be put on it anyway. We had to fetch the runaway president, something nobody wanted to be the one to do. Finally, Belarussian leader Stanislav Shushkevich and I were asked to go and bring him back. We went upstairs to his office and said, "Mikhail Sergeyevich, let's work together. We need to look for a way out together." He had been expecting us and immediately rose and came with us. The meeting continued.

No one signed the compromise draft that had previously been approved. Essentially, it was the death knell of the Novo-Ogaryovo process, not the Union Treaty. The official version of the story was as follows: the treaty was being returned for discussion to the supreme soviets of the republics, and after they approved the draft, it would be signed officially by the heads of the republics and the president of the USSR.

Unlike previous meetings, none of us went to speak to the reporters at the press conference. Gorbachev appeared alone, calling the meeting a success and announcing that on December 20, he hoped, the new Union Treaty would triumphantly be signed.

Nothing could be hidden from the political analysts, however. By the next day, virtually all the newspapers came out with pessimistic assessments of the prospects of the Novo-Ogaryovo Treaty. Everyone was struck by the fact that Gorbachev had appeared all alone at the news conference and that the signatures of the republic leaders were missing from the draft treaty. If the heads of the republics had not initialed the document at this meeting, what was the point of the supreme soviets ratifying the draft?

The following day new developments altered the situation even more drastically. In a December 1 referendum in Ukraine, the people of that republic unanimously voted for their independence. Kravchuk stated unequivocally that his country would not take part in the Novo-Ogaryovo agreements. This was the final blow to Gorbachev's protracted attempt to save the crumbling Soviet Union.

We had to find another way.

It was a wonderful winter evening with a soft snowfall—real crisp weather. Shushkevich, Kravchuk, and I had gathered at the residence of the chairman of the Belarus Supreme Soviet in the Belovezhsky Nature Reserve in Belarus. We were meeting to decide the fate of the Soviet Union.

Looking at the outwardly calm but still very tense, even agitated, faces of Kravchuk and Shushkevich, I could not help but think that we were quite seriously letting go of Ukraine and Belarus perhaps forever, offering them in a new agreement a guaranteed status on a par with Russia.

The Belovezhsky meeting took place in the utmost secrecy; the residence was even guarded by a special security division. (Because of this extreme caution, some unexpected situations occasionally cropped up. We realized there was no Xerox machine in the residence. Each time we wanted to make copies of a document, we had to pass it through two telefaxes standing next to each other. At least we had them, thank God.) It seemed to me that Shushkevich was not prepared for such a psychological atmosphere and had imagined that this meeting would be different, more reflective and calm. He suggested we go hunting or take a walk in the woods, but no one felt like strolling. We were all too overwrought.

The tension at the meeting increased with every minute. Burbulis, Shakhrai, and Ilyushin had labored over the documents from our side. An enormous amount of work went into the conceptualization and formulation of the new Belovezhsky Treaty, and it was clear that all the agreements had to be signed right here without delay.

The idea of a new kind of state system had not been born yesterday, and not just in my head or that of Shushkevich or Kravchuk. If we recall the years 1917–1918, immediately after the democratic February revolution, the republics immediately began the process of sucession, eventually moving toward independence. Several new national governments were declared in the territory of the Russian empire, including in the Caucasus and Central Asia. Ukraine led the process. The Bolsheviks managed to suppress all the nationalist uprisings, forcing peasants and soldiers into a civil war, although the revolution was supposedly spontaneously proletarian. With an iron fist, the Soviets strangled the liberation struggles, executed the national intelligentsia, and dispersed national parties.

As soon as the word *sovereignty* resounded in the air, the clock of history once again began ticking and all attempts to stop it were doomed. The last hour of the Soviet empire was chiming.

I understood that I would be accused of settling scores with Gorbachev and that a separate multilateral agreement with other republics was only a means to remove him from power. I knew that I would be hearing these accusations for the rest of my life. Therefore, the decision was doubly difficult. Besides the political responsibility, I had to accept the moral onus as well.

I well remember how a sensation of freedom and lightness suddenly came to me in the Belovezhsky Nature Reserve. In signing this agreement, Russia was choosing a different path, a path of internal development rather than an imperial one. It was not a question of parts of the body of the former empire breaking off, although they had been conquered and annexed centuries ago. The cultural, social, economic, and political integration would sooner or later do its work, and these parts would still remain in a zone of common cooperation.

Russia had chosen a new global strategy. She was throwing off the traditional image of "potentate of half the world," of armed conflict with Western civilization, and the role of policeman in the resolution of ethnic conflicts.

Perhaps I did not completely fathom the prospects opening up before me, but I felt in my heart that such major decisions had to be taken easily. Did I realize that by not preserving a central government in Moscow we would not be preserving an entire country, the USSR? I did. By that time, however, I had long since ceased to link the fate of Russia with the fate of the Communist party, the Council of Ministers, the Soviet Congress of People's Deputies, the state supply office, and the other "historically" evolved bodies that had in fact always been a hindrance to Russia as a nation. Russia had only interested them as a source of raw materials, labor, and cannon fodder, and as the chief imperial "magnet" to which everyone—even Cuba—was to be attracted. Its order was to be imposed everywhere!

A united empire is a powerful and basic force, evoking both awe and respect; but how long could it have remained an empire? By that time all the other empires of the world had collapsed—British, French, and Portuguese—and it was even not so long ago that the United States as well had tried to take almost direct control over a whole range of countries on its own and neighboring continents, but had failed.

The Belovezhsky agreement was not a "silent coup," but a lawful alteration of the existing order of things. It was a revision of the Union Treaty among three major republics of that Union.

We articulated and preserved the idea of the coexistence (actually quite strictly regulated) of states in one economic, political, and military region. But we departed from the old formula of Union government and control of everyone by Moscow. This seemed to us to flow from the spirit of the Novo-Ogaryovo process that had been interrupted by the coup plotters. The idea was to change the political climate utterly. Instead of dragging the republics by their ears into signing the new documents, we were demonstrating that we Slavic states had already achieved a working association, although not giving the others the opportunity for prolonged hesitation and bargaining. If you want, join us. If you don't, that's your prerogative.

The Belovezhsky agreement, as it seemed to me then, was needed more than anything to reinforce the centripetal tendency in the disintegrating Union and to stimulate the treaty process. Therefore, it is strange today to hear our actions being called a coordinated collapse of the Union or its "sudden destruction." I know that this myth is not easy to overcome, but I want to emphasize once again: at that moment, the Commonwealth of Independent States (as it came to be called) was the only possible preservation of an integrated geographical region.

As I stood among the Belovezhsky pine trees, I recalled the tragedies of Tbilisi and Baku, the seizing of the television tower in Vilnius, and the OMON attack in Riga.* All of this had not been so long ago! The next phase of these armed interventions was already in Moscow, in August 1991! Were we really going to wait calmly for a new tragedy, with our paws folded back like timid rabbits? No, I would not tolerate any more of it.

Starting in 1990, on the enormous territory of the former Soviet Union, Gorbachev's vacillations between liberal and conservative policies began to wreak a mortally dangerous state of havoc. Freedom for the nationalities was lawfully permitted and even encouraged, in words. National parties were formed and elections took place. However, the Union tried to keep everything in its clutches. Then its grasp began to loosen. In Tbilisi, they wanted "merely" to clean the square of demonstrators—and nine people died. In Baku, in order to "stop the pogroms," which had already ceased by that

*Nine people were killed in Tbilisi, Georgia, in April 1989 when Soviet troops attacked with tear gas and shovels peaceful demonstrators. More than one hundred were killed in Baku, Azerbaijan, in January 1990 when Soviet troops imposed a state of emergency after pogroms of Armenians. Thirteen unarmed civilians, including a famous filmmaker, were killed by special Soviet units in Vilnius in January 1991, followed by OMON attacks in Riga in which some citizens were injured.—Trans.

time, they brought in Soviet troops. I am certain that Gorbachev could not have helped knowing about all these actions.

In my view, Gorbachev's swings were an insane policy, a double game, a deceptive compromise that had the country a hair's breadth away from an inevitable bloodbath and war between the center in Moscow and the republics. In order not to provoke a new, violent coup, and to defuse the situation, it was necessary to change the very warp and woof of mutual relations. If we were to take this in its larger political context, it would mean changing the relations between a new sovereign Russia and the USSR.

I was convinced that Russia needed to rid itself of its imperial mission; nevertheless, Russia needed a stronger, harder policy, even forceful at some stage, in order not to lose its significance and authority altogether and in order to institute reforms. I was convinced that Gorbachev had exhausted his mental and decision-making resources, making him vulnerable once again to evil forces. That was how the decision came to me to make the multilateral agreement. That was why I was in the Belovezhsky Nature Reserve.

We decided, when the drafts were more or less ready, to get in touch with Nazarbayev to invite him as president of Kazakhstan to become a founder of the new commonwealth. Nazarbayev was at that very moment in the air en route to Moscow. It was an appealing idea to have his flight turned around so that he could immediately come to Belarus. We tried to communicate with his plane, but discovered there was no system we could use to get through to him. Then we tried to contact him through the dispatcher at Vnukovo Airport. This was a more realistic notion since Nazarbayev could speak to us from the pilot's cockpit and turn the plane back in our direction. But soon we learned that the heads of the Soviet Ministry of Civil Aviation were forbidding the airport dispatchers to let us use this official radio link. We were forced to wait for Nazarbayev's plane to land, whereupon he called us himself from Vnukovo.

Each one of us spoke to him in turn on the telephone. I read him the documents that had been prepared for signing. "I support the idea of creating the CIS," he said. "Wait for me. I'll fly out to see you." But we waited in vain for Nazarbayev that day. A little later, someone from his office called and sent the message that the president of Kazakhstan would not be able to travel to Belarus. When Gorbachev learned from Nazarbayev that he was intending to fly out to see us, he weighed in very heavily, calling in every marker to persuade him to abandon the trip.

It was important for us to have Nazarbayev present, at least in an observer capacity, but he decided otherwise. I don't think he canceled his flight to Belarus just because it was awkward to refuse Gorbachev. In those hours, Nazarbayev must have been thinking of the Eurasian context in which Kazakhstan was situated. To be sure, Kazakhstan shared extensive borders with Russia and common ties and interests. Still, situated as Kazakhstan was in the Central Asian region, Nazarbayev's other neighbors were most important, too. They had ethnic and spiritual ties. Well, what can I say—it was an independent decision. So, Nazarbayev did not come to the meeting, and the three of us capped this historic Belovezhsky Agreement with our signatures.

Some will say that surely there was some alternative, some other way out of the situation. I had not lost sight of the option of attempting to take Gorbachev's place lawfully. To stand at the head of the Union, to begin his reform "from above" once again. To traverse the same path that Gorbachev could not take because of the treachery of those closest to him. To gradually, carefully dismantle the imperial machine, as Gorbachev had tried to do.

There were various ways to achieve this. We could fight for elections for the president of the USSR throughout all the republics. We could declare the Russian parliament the legal heir of the dissolved Soviet legislature. We could persuade Gorbachev to make me acting president, and so on.

That path was barred to me. Psychologically, I could not take Gorbachev's place. Just as he could not take mine.

After Midnight

I really love cold water—I like it to be even icy cold. In late autumn when there isn't a soul on the beach, I plunge into the sea. I love clean forest ponds and creeks with stingingly fresh springs. I don't get leg cramps in even very low-temperature water; I am impervious to the cold. The water stings but draws me to its embrace.

It's the greatest thing after a sauna to jump into the water through a hole chopped in the ice. Saunas are also my weakness; not the dry Finnish sauna but the Russian *banya,* or steam bath, where you pour water on hot rocks. I've loved the *banya* since my childhood. My father brought me up to endure this tempering, the steamy pleasure of the *banya* so hot that your breath leaves your body, your pores open, and you can't wait for the blessed iciness of the cold-water dip afterward.

I am one of those fairly well-known types of Russian who needs to constantly prove his physical strength, his ability to overcome something, to breathe deeply (fresh air, of course), and load himself up to complete exhaustion.

For me, this is connected with my childhood (from which come all examples, which the child assimilates deeply and forever). My childhood is associated with the countryside, with physical burdens, with labor. If you don't develop your strength there, you'll be lost. Fortunately, I was born physically strong. In addition to being strong, however, you must have the desire to win. I must say the will to win was a quality that came in handy in my life. I've had quite a few unpleasant adventures in my life.

My accidents are a separate discussion; here I will cite just one example of a mishap. Once I was operated on for some intestinal ailment. The next morning, the effects of the anesthesia were wearing off, and I wanted to go to the bathroom. I thought I should press the button and summon the nurse, although it was awkward and embarrassing somehow to have to ask. The doctors said that I should lie prone for a minimum of a week. Nevertheless, I got up, took several steps, and then fell. Near the bedside were two buttons, above and below. I crawled toward the lower button, my eyes misting, rapidly losing consciousness. I kept thinking to myself that there was a button here somewhere, it was supposed to be here, and that I had to get to it. Somehow I made that last effort, and I pushed the button before I passed out.

I lay for a while not moving hand or foot. It took me a long time to recover. At first I could not walk or even catch my breath. Eventually, I recovered and even began to play sports again. Sports have always saved me, and created a store of energy in my youth that has lasted my whole life.

Sometimes I take risks with my health because I really rely on my body's resilience and I don't always take care of myself. In Sverdlovsk I had otitis, an inflammation of the inner ear. Any child knows that you have to stay home and keep warm until it goes away. Although the weather was freezing with wind, snow, and blizzards,

I decided to go to Severouralsk on a business trip. Such travel requires looking around, talking to people, getting into things a bit, or you'll forget it all later. I was still making a career for myself. But there was an awful wind in that northern city, enough to knock you off your feet, and I was frozen through to the bone. When I returned home, I immediately had to have an ear operation. My carelessness thus affected my health and sense of equilibrium, and it took more than a month to recover.

I last played volleyball in 1986 in Pitsunda, a government resort on the Black Sea. Afterward, I developed a pinched nerve in my spinal cord. It was a severe condition, Moscow was far away, and the local doctors couldn't do anything. Then a folk healer was found who performed therapeutic massage. She seemed a fragile woman at first glance even though she had very strong hands and knew how to find every little bone in your body. While she massaged me, it was terribly painful, and I even felt like shouting. Somehow, she restored me.

One of the worst of my accidents was an operation in Spain. I had attended a political science seminar where I had been invited to speak in a little village that could be reached from Barcelona in a small six-seater plane. As we prepared for take-off, I clapped the pilot on the shoulder and joked, "Well, are we going to crash today?" The crew smiled—they flew every day, and such an accident hadn't even occurred to them. My aide, Lev Sukhanov, and I sat in the very back seat, in the tail of the plane. We weren't even halfway there when suddenly something went wrong with the plane. The pilot turned us around and headed back. The aircraft rocked back and forth from wing to wing while the pilots worked the manual controls, but to no avail. The plane fell into a tailspin. Some of us turned pale; others were completely nauseated. Oddly enough, I find myself joking during such moments. I said to Sukhanov: see, nobody has any privileges now. We're all in the same boat—no parachutes! We would all fall at the same rate, with no pretensions of leadership. Mountains seemed to rush up from below, but the pilot couldn't find even a small plateau on which to land. The plane traced a large circle, then another, like a glider, plummeting lower and lower, and the pilot looked to see how we were doing. We saw a river below and shouted, let's go in the water, we'll be able to jump out before the plane sinks! We were already quite blithe about escaping.

We finally made it to an air base. The pilot began his descent, but now he had a new problem—the landing gear would not come down; the mechanism was jammed. The moment we touched ground, it seemed as if the plane simply collapsed.

Some of us were injured badly. I suffered a blow to the spinal cord, and the pain was simply unbearable. It later turned out that a disk had slipped between the third and fourth vertebrae. We transferred to another plane and proceeded to Barcelona. Once again there was a lot of turbulence and we encountered a thunderstorm. In Barcelona, I felt worse, as if the entire lower half of my body was paralyzed. I couldn't move. I was taken to the hospital, and as luck would have it, I fell out of the sky right into the hands of one of the best neurosurgeons in the world! Professor Josef Llovet, a wonderful man and the most talented of surgeons, happened to be in this hospital. The hospital itself was quite unique; it was run as a cooperative. Local residents were registered at this hospital, and a certain percentage was taken out of their salaries to cover hospital costs. There was order, cleanliness, well-trained personnel, and a computer at each nurse's station.

At night, the laboratories were still running and there was an on-duty shift taking X rays, doing blood work-ups, and everything else. Within thirty or forty minutes, they completed a full array of tests. The surgeon then said there was only one choice: to operate immediately or there would be paralysis. He told me I would not be able to fly to Moscow; my legs would go completely numb and I would not be able to regain feeling in them. He gave me five minutes for reflection, and I agreed to the operation. I merely asked him how long I would have to lie there. He answered quite confidently that the operation would take three hours. It was a difficult and complex procedure that required using a microscope. After twenty-four hours, when the general anesthesia would wear off, I would be able to get out of bed. All right, I said, go ahead, although I did not completely understand how long I would have to stay in the hospital after such an operation. I knew that in Russia they would have kept me for weeks.

The operation took about three hours. I was put in a private room (all four wings in the hospital had such separate rooms). There were no luxury or semiluxury suites. I stayed for one day, slept through the night, and in the morning, the doctor came to see me. Reporters were already peering over his shoulder. That's it, they're demanding that you get up, he said. I practically broke into a sweat. I thought perhaps they would give me some crutches or something, but no crutches. Just get up and go. I was in a panic—everything had been cut open and wasn't healed yet.

Soaking with sweat, I stood up, took a step, with people standing by, of course, so I wouldn't fall from the unfamiliarity of it. I made it to the wall, and everything was fine. Television crews were there filming me. That's it for today, the doctor then told me. Go back and lie down. They forced me to get up and walk in this way three times, and finally I moved around without fear.

The scar along my spine is a souvenir from Spain. It's hard to say what they did; their technology is different from ours. In our country, patients would stay in a hospital bed for six months after an operation like that, but abroad they just tell you to get up and go.

I will always be grateful to all those people—the orderlies, the doctors, my surgeon, the president of Catalonia, who came to visit me and many others. Strangers came to visit me and brought presents. What was I to do with so many gifts?

My doctor said I would be playing tennis in a month, and he wanted to receive a telegram from me with my winning score. Five days later, I flew back to Moscow. I walked around very gingerly because it still hurt constantly, but gradually it became tolerable. When I was able to play a game of tennis again, I did send the doctor a telegram. I telephoned him a number of times, and we met again.

Both misfortune and luck inevitably find me. Sometimes boiling water, sometimes icy water. It makes for a good tempering.

Before resigning, Gorbachev submitted a list of claims—his "compensation package." It was enormous and ran to several pages. Almost all the items were purely material demands. He wanted a pension equaling a presidential salary indexed to inflation; a presidential apartment and dacha; a car for himself and his wife. But more than anything he wanted a foundation, a big building in the center of Moscow, the former Academy of Social Sciences, and with it car service, office equipment, and security guards.

Psychologically, his reasoning was very simple: if you want to get rid of me so badly, then be so good as to dig deep into your pockets. For my part, I tried to conduct myself firmly, saying that the matter would be put on the agenda of the Council of Chiefs of States. At the council meeting, however, many advocated stripping the ex-president of everything, and leaving him with the same income that any average pensioner would receive in our country. I urged that a precedent be created for a chief of state making a decent departure into retirement without an atmosphere of scandal. Almost everything that Gorbachev asked for, with the exception of something very inordinate, was given to him.

He and I met for the last time in his office in the Kremlin on December 24. For the last time I was going to visit the president of the USSR. Our conversation was protracted and difficult and lasted several hours. Alexander Yakovlev and Gorbachev's aide, Georgy Shakhnazarov, joined us. Gorbachev, of course, saw the handwriting on the wall and none of it came as a surprise to him, so he had spent a long time carefully preparing his compensation package.

The first time the topic of his resignation arose was immediately after my return from Belarus. The Belovezhsky agreement was signed and I went to talk with Gorbachev. At that point, I said to him: there's no more Union, don't you see? And there's no turning back. Therefore, a way out of the dead end had to be found. We've found it. I am sure that the other republics will support it.

Several days later, Nazarbayev and the other leaders of the Central Asian republics announced their support of the Belovezhsky agreement. Everyone was prepared to join CIS except the Baltic republics and Georgia, whose president was Zviad Gamsakhurdia at the time.* A commonwealth was therefore formed of eleven newly independent states. For the first stage we decided that we should not have any coordinating bodies, but the chiefs of state should meet once a month to resolve problems as they arose.

(After Gorbachev stepped down from the post of president, I visited his former government apartment on Kosygin Street. It was a museum, not an apartment; everything seemed very stiff and formal. I refused to move in there.)

*Gamsakhurdia, formerly a prominent dissident and political prisoner, was popularly elected president of Georgia after the coup. He soon turned into a dictator and was eventually overthrown. Ultimately Shevardnadze was elected president. Gamsakhurdia fled to neighboring republics where he continued attacks against the existing government with a renegade army. He eventually committed suicide in 1994 while still in exile.—Trans.

The press devoted enormous attention to our final summary meeting, because we performed the ritual of relaying the nuclear "button." More or less everyone knows that there is no button as such, but a little suitcase guarded by two special officers. In the event of war, they are to help the president punch in the necessary code, which will tell the nuclear forces to be on battle alert for a counterstrike against the enemy. For a time the nuclear forces of the former Soviet Union were not subordinate to Russian command but to the leadership of CIS's joint armed forces; specifically, to Marshal Shaposhnikov. Now that the Joint Armed Forces have ceased to exist, control over Russian nuclear forces is under Russian Defense Minister Grachev. Much has changed; in particular, our missiles have been retargeted in compliance with SALT-II. Nevertheless, the two officers with the little suitcase are still on round-the-clock duty. They are supposed to be with the president twenty-four hours a day, on any business trip, at any location on earth. They are always with me.

I was struck by how Gorbachev turned over his secret archives to me.* He took out a pile of file folders and said: this is the archive of the general secretaries. Take it. Now it's all yours. I said that until all of it was studied by specialists and archivists, I would not touch the papers. I knew that there was nothing at all of strategic value among them; it was material that was mainly interesting and important for historians, such as letters from persecuted writers addressed to Stalin, unknown episodes from the political careers of Khrushchev and Brezhnev, the story of the Chernobyl disaster, the Afghan war, and so on.

In fact, several months later, the originals of all the famous secret protocols to the Molotov–Ribbentropp Pact were found in this archive. There were maps six feet wide with the signatures of Stalin and Ribbentropp—Stalin had a red pencil, and Ribbentropp had a blue pencil, apparently to "correct" the borders. One would fix a border in one place; the other, in another place. . . . Then there were their signatures in large letters. Ten secret agreements were found. In them the entire filthiness of the Hitler and Stalin partnership is indisputably revealed.

At the Soviet Congress of People's Deputies, Alexander Yakovlev had been appointed chairman of the commission to analyze the

*The text of some of those documents can be found in Appendix B.

Molotov–Ribbentropp Pact. That commission was able to find only one copy of the documents, and not even all of them: three were missing altogether. Yakovlev appealed to Gorbachev at the time to help locate the documents. Gorbachev had replied that they had been destroyed in the 1950s. Now it has come out that packets with the original documents were opened by Boldin, Gorbachev's chief of staff. Naturally, Boldin reported to his boss that documents had been found which historians all over the world had been seeking.

When I was informed that these documents had been discovered, I immediately called Yakovlev. "Alexander Nikolayevich, the documents have been found," I told him. At first I heard his joyful exclamation, "*Finally.* I always believed they would be found!" Then he angrily added a few choice words, which I'd rather not repeat.

Many people around me were rather surprised at my decision to move from the White House into the Kremlin. It seemed that the White House we had defended would always remain the state symbol of Russia. Moreover, by moving the residency of the president of Russia to the Kremlin, we were giving the newspapers an excuse to carp about the "great power legacy" of the new government, and leaving the Supreme Soviet (Khasbulatov's bureaucracy, although frankly at the time I wasn't thinking of that at all) a kind of independent territory, a staging ground on which they could flex their muscles. Voices began to be heard that it was time to turn the Kremlin into a museum of history and culture.

After weighing all the pros and cons, I nevertheless decided to make the move. I must say that it was largely a matter of principle and strategy. The Kremlin, after all, is not just an artistic gem but—and I'm not revealing any secrets here—the most important government compound. The country's entire defense system is hooked up to the Kremlin, the surveillance system, all the coded messages from all over the world are sent here, and there is a security system for the buildings developed down to the tiniest detail.

Now I see that it was the right thing to do. It wasn't just a question of the technical, administrative, and other facilities of the Kremlin. In politics, everything is symbolic. Starting with my famous Sochi vacation in September 1991 (everyone complained that instead of consolidating the victory over the coup plotters, I was resting), I try to make sense of what's happening. I felt that a new era had really begun in our history. No one knew yet what kind of era, but I knew that ahead was an incredibly difficult, onerous time, with many ups and downs. Politics and my own life were taking a sharp turn in a new direction that was unprecedented. The Kremlin had become a symbol of this turn. To put it crudely: in order to knock someone out of the Kremlin, you'd need at the very least a new committee of coup plotters. The Kremlin was the symbol of stability, duration, and determination in the political line being conducted. If reforms were to be my government line, that was the statement I was making to my opponents by moving into the Kremlin.

We warned Gorbachev and his staff a week before the move of our intentions. It was a period of time quite sufficient to pack up one's papers. However, as is always the case, friction among the clerks was inevitable. From the outset I proceeded calmly. I did not want Gorbachev and his team (or, rather, its remnants) either to be thrown out of the Kremlin or allowed to linger an extra month packing. Long farewells make for too many tears. It was nothing out of the ordinary.

Ordinary—but not so very. That is why I didn't like either the rumors circulated by the press that we literally threw the former general secretary's possessions out of his Kremlin office. The old tenants did not unscrew the handles from the doors, of course, but they did remove some furniture and even took some official state gold fountain pens from their inkwells. Well, that kind of thing's a habit in our country. . . .

In the difficult months of the Gorbachev transition, I was already giving serious thought to how the Russian government should be reorganized; bringing in some fresh faces. I didn't like the composition of the Council of Ministers. With all due respect to Silayev, I realized that a person of his type could no longer remain prime minister. It was high time to bring in an economist with his own original concept, possibly with his own team of people. Determined action was long overdue in the economy, not just in politics.

Once, at the first sessions of the Russian Supreme Soviet in the spring of 1991, we had tried to find an intellectual prime minister with his own program and had considered Mikhail Bocharov, Chairman of the Supreme Economic Council, and Yury Ryzhov, member of the Presidential Council as possible candidates. We talked about Stanislav Shatalin, Yeugeny Yasin, and Grigory Yavlinsky, the authors of the "500 Days" Plan for economic reform. Our efforts fell through at the time because we were still operating within the context of the Soviet Union. Certainly now it would be a strategic mistake if Russia did not find itself an architect of economic reform. I also saw that it would not be possible to confirm such a person as head of government; he would have to be given the title of deputy prime minister, minister of the economy, or something like that. Once again, I had requested input from my staff and various concepts and programs now lay on my desk.

Why did I choose Yegor Gaidar? My selection of many other key figures had been in haste. I wanted to choose the chief economic helmsman intelligently. However, without looking over my shoulder, there was no question that other people had opinions: Burbulis favored Gaidar; in fact Gaidar was "his man," as we say in such cases. I want to make it clear, though, that such serious nominations cannot be made without recommendations. The president must make his selection from a whole range of proposed candidates.

Gaidar impressed me most of all with his confidence. It was not the confidence of an arrogant person or the confidence of someone who was strong and energetic, like many people in my entourage. Rather, this was a completely unique poise. It was immediately evident that Gaidar was not what we would consider high-handed or out for himself. He was simply an independent man with an enormous but not ostentatious sense of his own worth. That is, he was a member of the intelligentsia who, unlike the dull bureaucrats in the government administration, would not hide his opinions, his reflections, or his weaknesses. He would fight for his own principles and ideas to the end, precisely because they were his own, achieved through suffering and not a case of "If the party says so," or "Ours is not to reason why, ours is but to do or die."

Obviously, Gaidar would not be one to fawn, and for me that was invaluable. The responsibility for "shock therapy" ultimately fell on me and it was very important that people not even think of trying to conceal something from me.

Gaidar had a knack for speaking simply, which figured prominently in my selection. He—not I—would have to talk to opponents of reform sooner or later. He did not water down his ideas, but he knew how to speak plainly about complicated things. All economists try to do this, but Gaidar was able to do it the most persuasively. He was able to infect people with his ideas. Listening to him, you would start to see the route we had to take. Gaidar's theories coincided with my own private determination to go through the painful part of the economic reform route quickly. I couldn't force people to wait once again, to drag out the main events and processes for years. If our minds were made up, we had to get going!

Gaidar also let me know he had a whole team of very young and very diversified specialists. They weren't just a group of experts, but individuals, younger people without any hang-ups, independent thinkers raring to go. I realized that besides the old hardened Soviet operators, the kind of people who would get involved in Russia's business would be these arrogant young upstarts. I was dying to test them out and see how they performed in reality. In short, I very much wanted to choose a different kind of person for this top economic post.

At that time, indisputably the most popular economist in the country was Grigory Yavlinsky. But harried and harassed over his ill-fated 500-Day Program, he had already developed a kind of oversensitivity. Besides, psychologically it was difficult to return a second time to the same "500 Days" Program and its creators, even if it had been reworked.

I believe the most important opportunity missed after the coup was the radical restructuring of the parliamentary system. I have a sneaking suspicion, though, that society might not have been ready to nominate any decent candidates to a new legislature. The idea of dissolving the Congress and scheduling new elections was in the air (as well as a Constitution for the new country), although we did not take advantage of it. But this is not the main thing for which I am blamed by the democratic press. The main criticism is that I preserved the system of state security. I did not issue a decree that would have immediately removed from their government posts all former employees of the Communist Party's central committee and regional committees (and some say even the district committees). I do have some doubts about that. The mood in society after the coup was pretty definite: destroy the party! I myself saw the crowd that gathered in front of the central committee building and other party buildings. They were already starting to break windows.

I began to have visions of the ghost of October—pogroms, disorder, looting, constant rallying, and anarchy with which that Great Revolution of 1917 began. It would have been possible to turn

August 1991 into October 1917 with one sweep of the hand, with one signature. But I didn't do that, and I don't regret it.

In seventy years, we have grown tired of dividing people into "clean" and "unclean."

Furthermore, I saw a continuity between the society of the Khrushchev and Brezhnev period and the new Russia. To break everything, to destroy everything in the Bolshevik manner was not part of my plans at all. While bringing into the government completely new, young, and bold people, I still considered it possible to use in government work-experienced executives, organizers, and leaders like Yuri Skokov, the director of a major Moscow defense plant, a man of intelligence and strength.

Was I mistaken in this approach? Possibly. But time has proved that the main threat came not from the *nomenklatura* dressed up as democrats. Rather, the greatest danger was from my closest comrades, the new leaders carried away by the parliamentary tide, who rapidly fell in love with power and its attributes.

Rereading these comments now, I don't want to rewrite anything. Maybe I was in fact mistaken in choosing an attack on the economic front as the chief direction, leaving government reorganization to perpetual compromises and political games. I did not disperse the Congress and left the soviets intact. Out of inertia, I continued to perceive the Supreme Soviet as a legislative body that was developing the legal basis for reform. I did not notice that the very *Congress* was being co-opted. The deputies suddenly realized their omnipotence, and an endless bargaining process ensued.

This should not have been pursued, but the painful measures proposed by Gaidar, as I saw it, required calm—not new social upheavals. Meanwhile, without political backup, Gaidar's reforms were left hanging in midair. Indeed, this was an era of issues hanging in midair, laws not passed in final draft, incoherent decisions taken. It was the era that finally brought the country to October 1993.

From the outside, it could have seemed that the president was "betraying" some people and "taking others God knows where." In reality, the people around the number-one man in the government cannot help but be replaced. It's different in a stable society where the government staff, the parliament, the press, and the courts clearly know their functions and operate in an already established system of relationships. But what happens in Russia?

Let's take, for example, the story of my aide Gennady Burbulis. From the very beginning, I suspected that with his very public, social persona, things would not work out (that was back when I was considering candidates for the vice president). Let me reiterate that I knew this about him, but I did not expect such a unanimous reaction from the press, the parliament, and the politicians. By his job description, Burbulis was not supposed to be so visible; he was the state secretary, a crucial position that was meant to be a staff job, in the shadows. Suddenly, there was all this hostility toward him. "Where did he come from?" people would ask. "A former teacher of Marxism," "a provincial," an "éminence grise," and all the rest. The film director Nikita Mikhalkov even dug up a few copies of some dissertation Burbulis had written as a young graduate student and waved it in front of a television camera, as if to say, look at what kind of person is ruling us.*

On the one hand, it was a normal situation: people were not afraid to criticize the government, to express their dislike of even the highest officials. That was good. But on the other, why did they have to launch a harassment campaign against a person just because they didn't like his face? In fact, no one appraised Burbulis's work objectively; they made their judgments on his appearance and speech. Perhaps it stands to reason that Burbulis developed a sense of injured pride and ceased to react appropriately to the situation, but there's another aspect to this issue. People are just raring to go into politics these days. That's the case all over the world, but it's especially true in our country now. The problem is that our politicians are totally devoid of any professional ethics. There are no traditions for political behavior. You often have to look not only at someone's professional skills, but at their personal qualities as well. In a new situation, in a situation where a person acquires enormous power

*Burbulis was head of the department of social sciences at the Advanced Training Institute of the Ministry of Non-Ferrous Metals in Sverdlovsk. The unsubstantiated implication is that a professor in that field during those years would have had to teach from a Marxist perspective. Like many people of his generation, Burbulis had written a paper loyal to the party as a graduate student. As Yeltsin explains later, Burbulis did not work for him when Yeltsin was party secretary of Sverdlovsk, but later, after the two men had come to Moscow.—Trans.

and a high position, he may unexpectedly show his true colors, and turn out to be different from what you thought.

There is a third and main reason for the changes in my team. In Western politics a person is brought to a ready-made position (let us take the United States, for example, where a new president comes in and brings new people with him). The priorities of the job are well known, they have been established virtually for centuries, the system is in place, and you can jump right in and work. It is no secret that a significant portion of the staffs of the Democrats remain in place and are inherited by the Republicans, and vice versa. But it's completely different in our country.

I can't say that we had to start from scratch, but almost. We utilized everything we could. It would have been disastrous to destroy the government administration of such an enormous state. Where it was possible to put in experienced "old" staff, we did. And sometimes we made mistakes. A number of times Rutskoi tried to insinuate General Alexander Sterligov* as one of his close deputies. Wasn't this absurd? Where else but Russia could such a person who openly advocated military dictatorship (his own personal dictatorship, to be sure, and not somebody else's) end up as one of the most important officials! There were surely more than one such mistake.

Meanwhile, we had to figure out everything from the start. What was a vice president? How should a Russian constitutional court look? There was nothing but blank space because no such institutions had previously existed in Russia. How was everything supposed to be? We constantly required analysis (what would international practice suggest?) but at the same time we couldn't help understanding that what was abroad was one thing (and actually different everywhere) but what we had in our country was something else. We had to proceed not from how people did things somewhere else, but from our own experience. But we didn't have any.

As a result, there emerged beautiful structures and pretty names with nothing behind them.

*General Alexander Sterligov. Former KGB general who previously worked in the economic directorate of the Council of Ministers. As one of the organizers of the White House defense in August 1991, made the arrest of KGB chairman Kryuchkov. Now leader of the Russian National Assembly, a nationalist movement.—Trans.

There were other fairly serious reasons—developments were happening rapidly and the political context kept changing constantly. Not a single other large country has known so many upheavals as we have in recent years. And that dictated the necessity of changing horses in midstream, although for me personally, this process was truly anguishing.

This was not the most important thing, however. I didn't try to change people. The very nature of power, power under totally new conditions, is what changed them.

5

A NEW RUSSIA AND THE WORLD

Editor's Note: In this chapter Yeltsin offers a mix of impressions and observations about his contacts with world leaders. From his earliest trips abroad as, in effect, Gorbachev's leading political opponent, Yeltsin reflects a blend of boldness and insecurity. In the aftermath of the coup, Russia's relationships with other countries underwent profound changes. Instead of being an imposing superpower, the role and future of the country was undetermined.

Something amazing happened; something I myself wouldn't have believed before August 19, 1991. Overnight, a new Russia—"Boris Yeltsin's Russia,"—took the place of the Soviet Union in international politics. We were the heirs to the entire tragic history of the USSR, to say nothing of the legacy of the Russian empire. Even as this new Russia was struggling to be created it carried the burden of its past.

I had not yet fully realized the significance of the change that had occurred when the first telephone calls came from Western leaders. It was August 19, 1991, the very beginning of the coup. There was no time for analysis then.

John Major, the British prime minister, was the first to call me to express support for a democratic Russia and confidence that everything would turn out well. The British confirmed their moral authority in international politics.

For Americans, the number-one politician in our country continued to be Gorbachev. What if he really were sick? What if he did support the GKChP, which was his own team, anyway? And what if, now, Yeltsin was only king for a day? Morality was one thing, but what if they were forced to deal with the former Gorbachevites, with Yanayev, for example? Surely the president of the United States would have had to think about these things; as the coup unfolded indeed, it was his duty. Yet George Bush not only called but also immediately organized international support for Russia, talked with the leaders of the NATO countries, issued political statements, and so on. Mr. Bush unquestionably displayed himself first and foremost as a moral politician. George Bush is older than me. He is a member of the war generation. And for me, his support was invaluable and meant a great deal personally.

Helmut Kohl happened to be hunting in a remote mountain area the day of the coup. Many people say that he and I have a similar appearance: we are both husky; we have similar habits, perspectives on life, and ways of behaving. I have always felt a particular fondness for him. Despite difficulties, Kohl was able to get a call through to me. I think he would have done that no matter what, even if the tanks were already firing in Moscow. (Concerning the tanks, Bush said that if we could fight our way out of a tank encirclement, it would be a final victory. Russia would have paved the way to the civilized community of nations.)

The Italian prime minister, and the prime ministers of Spain and France, the leaders of Argentina, Japan, and Canada all telephoned. I am enormously grateful to all of them. They demonstrated solidarity, not in some drawn-out long-term political campaign, but instantly, when they had to get their bearings within minutes.

The GKChP was taken aback by the rapid response of the Western countries. That evening the members mumbled and grumbled at a press conference about "premature reactions" and "interference in internal affairs."

Now, in hindsight, I see the reasons for such a rapid and unequivocal response. Western analysts had long since predicted the coup, and it came as no surprise to them. It was more apparent from the outside; in our country, however, no one believed it could happen—the very thought seemed outrageous. Finally, despite all the mystery surrounding Gorbachev's situation (although for Western intelligence agencies, I think it was probably clear from the start), the coup seemed too much a caricature of itself (although frightening), too crude, even stupid, I would say, for anyone to hesitate about whether to go with those self-styled leaders of the USSR. These reactions by foreign leaders to the coup were a prologue to a new international policy toward Russia. Before and after the fall of the Soviet empire, my dealings with leaders abroad provided an education for me about their countries and my own.

Also among those who telephoned me during the coup was Margaret Thatcher. There are few figures like Mrs. Thatcher in international politics. Their opinion will always be heard, regardless of the office they hold. But even among these few individuals, Thatcher stands out in particular.

The summer I had gone to Spain to the ill-fated seminar that ended for me on the operating table, Mrs. Thatcher and I had spoken about my flying to England to visit her. I was in the opposition at the time, and was neither speaker of the parliament nor president. Nevertheless, as a woman who knew her own mind, she invited me to visit, even though few leaders of the world were very enthusiastic about meeting with me, a leader of the opposition in Gorbachev's Soviet Union.

I flew to London and we drove to 10 Downing Street. The meeting lasted forty-five minutes, and I don't recall ever having a more interesting conversation with anyone. Margaret Thatcher descended the stairs, greeted me, and led me into the house. There were two sofas in her office with a table between them. I sat down and she sat down opposite me. Somehow, we ended up sitting very far from one another. There were three men—me, the interpreter, and the prime minister's chief adviser—but suddenly Mrs. Thatcher got up and by herself dragged her sofa right up to the table so as to be closer to us. We hadn't even managed to lift a finger. Her action was so simple and yet so serious, and so quick and energetic that I hesitated slightly, then got up and dragged my own seat closer, realizing that it was quite heavy.

Mrs. Thatcher is really very original and natural. We were now sitting face-to-face and spoke quickly and animatedly. She was interested to know what the main opponent of her favorite, Gorbachev, was thinking. An inherent thirst for new impressions compelled Thatcher to keep asking questions, to formulate her own position in reply, and then ask questions again. I, of course, was enormously fascinated with the train of thought and the logic of one of the most powerful politicians of the West.

One of the most interesting moments in our conversation came toward the end of our meeting. I implored the prime minister: "Mrs.

Thatcher, I want to convey to you the most important point, that there is a new reality in the world now—Russia. Not just the Soviet Union, with which you have good relations. Now there is also Russia. It's important that you know that. Are you prepared to make contacts—trade and economic ties—with the new free Russia?"

During our entire conversation, Thatcher had instantly answered any question I delivered. This time she paused and reflected for a while. Then she replied, "Mr. Yeltsin, let's wait and see. Let Russia first become new and free. And then . . . anything's possible." She smiled.

When I left Downing Street, I thought to myself, well, at least she didn't say no. For a first acquaintance and first meeting, that was already quite good. But I did not doubt for a moment that Mrs. Thatcher, and many, many politicians of the world along with her, would soon learn of the appearance of the new Russia. As Mrs. Thatcher walked me out to my car, I saw that her aides were whispering frantically to her. "That's not according to protocol." She waved them away and came down to my car, and we said good-bye. Everything was very human, warm, and touching. That is the kind of mark Mrs. Thatcher made in politics—original and sincere. A woman who broke the political mold of men. Thanks to this first lady, candor in behavior became a component of diplomacy.

For me, Margaret Thatcher is also important as an example of how politicians can remain true to themselves for many years despite their ordeals. Priorities changed, the country suffered a whole range of political crises, and how many times did the prime minister of Great Britain have to endure the harshest battles in Parliament? With practically each new law passed, especially taxes, passions ran high; there were press campaigns and demonstrations, yet the government stuck firmly to its course. And Margaret Thatcher was able to accomplish all this with her invariable smile, which grew more and more charming in a womanly way with each passing year.

When I called Helmut Kohl "my friend Helmut," I am not being overly familiar. Recently, at my invitation he and I took a vacation together on Lake Baikal. I found it very interesting to watch how he caught fish, how he laughed, and how precisely and effortlessly he formulated interesting ideas. I took him to a Russian *banya.* On the banks of the Angara River there is a wonderful Russian *banya* constructed of huge century-old logs; the atmosphere in the steam room is wonderful as only a real village *banya* can be. Since the *banya* is right on the riverbank, after the steam bath, Kohl and I ran into the water, which is so cold it stings. That was when he and I had a nice long conversation. He was amazed at the extraordinary natural beauty of Baikal.

Kohl and I have been fortunate to meet in famous buildings. One of the most important meetings for me was during his short stay in Moscow in early 1993. We met at a government mansion in the southwest of Moscow, well known for having previously belonged to the KGB. This was the place where Kryuchkov held his most secret meetings when he was plotting the August coup. Kohl was amused by that story and began animatedly to look all around.

I wanted to discuss with Kohl a matter of fundamental importance for me: if I were to restrict the activity of the parliament, how would the West react? The confidential nature of our conversation was quite in keeping with the historical traditions of the place where we were meeting. It was clear to me that some basic democratic values existed for the West. In this specific case, I would be infringing on one of these values. Nevertheless, I wasn't afraid of asking the chancellor of Germany this question as our relations were candid and open. I also knew that my intentions would not be misconstrued by Helmut Kohl.

He supported me and expressed confidence that other leaders of the Group of Seven (the United States, France, Canada, Great Britain, Germany, Italy, and Japan) would sympathize with the harsh but necessary measures for the stabilization of Russia. Several months later I was able to confirm Kohl's prediction. In September–October 1993, Kohl himself and all the leaders of the Western countries unequivocally supported my actions to bring Russia out of a severe political crisis.

Kohl and I did not talk only about politics. I would share my recollections with him from time to time. In May 1986, while still a member of the politburo, I had been invited by the German Communist party for an official visit to their Congress. After the forum was over, I was taken on an excursion to a factory in the Ruhr. After touring the shop floors I came to a workers' break room. I was simply amazed. How hard I had fought in Sverdlovsk to establish decent conditions in such break rooms at factories, lounges with a sauna, armchairs, and music. But the German version was beyond belief. I was struck with the stark thought that we would never live like this.

It was not merely a question of wealth. It was a habit of doing everything with intelligence—a habit peculiar to the Germans in particular, who are our antipodes, so to say, in their scrupulousness and attention to tiny details, daily existence, and the practical side of life. When it seems to me that even our country is starting to change in that direction, I always remember Mr. Kohl.

As for the Americans, by seniority and by the chronology of our relationships, I should put them in the opposite order—George Bush and Bill Clinton. But Bill Clinton is now president of the United States. So let me say a word about him first. So much in international politics depends on him that I sincerely empathize with him.

Clinton is very unusual. He is young and handsome, looks wonderful for his age, and he impresses the women. Perhaps the figure of Clinton means some kind of new breakthrough for America.

I am impressed with the way these Americans do these things. During the election campaign, there was a rather harsh debate going on between Bush and Clinton, or perhaps it could be stated even more strongly—a confrontation. But as soon as the elections were over, as soon as it became clear who won, Bush began to help Clinton, and Clinton helped Bush. In our country, they would have remained mortal enemies for the rest of their lives. But Bush and Clinton gladly talk on the telephone to each other and consult with one another. For example, I would be talking to Clinton, and he would say, "I not only support the treaty, I congratulate you and Bush together for this enormous victory you have won." (We were speaking of the signing of START-II in January, two weeks before Bush was to leave the White House and two weeks before Clinton was to assume the presidency of the United States.)

During the election campaign I was told that Bush was under severe stress. The story was that he would sit immobile for several hours staring into space. I called him to try to cheer him up. I knew that feeling of acute loneliness all too well. Sometimes your body cannot handle such stress. It's the constant internal concentration and strain. You just need to clench your teeth and take yourself in hand in order not to wilt, quit, retire—whatever. Therefore I think I do understand Bush.

In the fall of 1989 I made my first trip to the United States. Afterwards, there was a notorious campaign of vilification in our media against me. In America, I had said in an interview that when I flew over the Statue of Liberty, I felt a greater internal sense of freedom myself. This provoked a huge commotion in Moscow. A special parliamentary commission began to investigate my trip. My aides and friends, Ilyushin and Sukhanov, dragged me to the *banya.* It was an ordinary neighborhood *banya,* rather unattractive, but they knew how much I loved a steam bath and they wanted to diffuse some of the stress.

So imagine this scene. We walk into the steam room and it's packed to the gills, about forty people. The political discussion really heats up, like a street rally. Everyone's naked. They're all shouting and waving their birch branches around and lashing each other's backs.* "Boris Nikolayevich, hang in there!" they cried. "We're with you." Then they gave me a real thwack on the back. It was a colorful sight. The fact that this occurred in the *banya* was symbolic for the *banya* is a place of cleansing. All feelings are pure there, and people are naked. It would be interesting for me to know now: what would those guys in the *banya* say to me now?

That moment in the *banya* was when I changed my world view, when I realized that I was a Communist by historical Soviet tradition, by inertia, by education, but not by conviction. The scene in the *banya* remains vividly in my mind.

I thought that Bush would be reelected, that American conservatism would kick into gear. The Republican party would always get its campaign started later but would finance it more energetically. This time that failed to work.

George Bush was at the summit of power for virtually three terms, as vice president during the Reagan era and four years as president. Twelve years is a long time. (Incidentally, when my presidential term has expired, I will have spent eight years at the summit of politics, or counting from my politburo days, ten years.)

I must say an interesting metamorphosis has taken place with George Bush. It was obvious that he was suffering during the election campaign, and the Republicans were always behind. Bush spoke in every state—a tremendous amount of effort. And when he wasn't reelected, it was almost a load off his shoulders, some sort of

*It is the Russians' custom to beat each other with bunches of leafy birch twigs in the steam bath.—Trans.

defense mechanism switched on. He suddenly had a surge of energy, and we achieved START-II.

George Bush and I established very friendly relations. Barbara Bush also calls now and then. I hope that she will come to visit, and Naina will host her well, and she will have a wonderful time. Bush and I agreed to play tennis. It's sure to be a very tough match.

Turning to the former Soviet empire, I met many times with Lech Walesa, president of Poland, and Vaclav Havel, president of the Czech Republic. I will say there are certain psychological difficulties in communicating with them. Hanging over us is the cursed legacy of the USSR, which was a self-styled "Big Brother" to the other countries. Havel and Walesa are obliged to keep a certain distance in dealing with Russia—they owe it to their peoples. I understand that. But we are, after all, linked not only by a common history—the East European camp, socialism—but we are also bound by the fact that for the first time such former dissidents have bravely stepped into the international political arena, dissidents who were hounded and persecuted in various ways.

Havel was imprisoned; he was a participant in the Prague Spring and a writer. Walesa fought for many years as the head of Solidarity, the workers' union. They are political leaders as well as popular leaders. At some point their entire societies united behind them, and they became symbols of major historical events. Now they face great difficulties.

The appearance of such figures in international politics is interesting. Every country has a *nomenklatura,* that layer of people who make up the government and who hold the key posts. They preserve stability, but sooner or later new figures break through this layer. This process does not tend to be so unsettling in the West. Even so, in almost all the countries of the Group of Seven, there have been major shake-ups at the top. Perhaps the world is subconsciously preparing for some new, very serious changes.

My first visit to Poland was extremely strained. One of the Poles' basic positions at the talks was that our military trains running through Poland to withdraw troops from East Germany caused losses for Poland's economy. Therefore, Russia should pay some compensation.

I thought long and hard over the reasons for this harsh offensive on the part of Walesa. Of course, the presence in the world of such a large and cumbersome entity as the USSR was not a simple matter. You could change the name "USSR," but you couldn't change the problems that had accumulated over the years. The Poles had lived all these years with the feeling that the USSR undermined the country's prosperity and economic potential. This national sense of themselves led them to express these demands, so difficult and so hard to understand.

But my second visit to Poland went quite differently. I was able to discern—as I always try to do—a painful area, a secret wound in the history of our relations. It was well known that the KGB tried to manage the crackdown on the trade union Solidarity. I brought Lech Walesa a copy of the documents of the Suslov Commission (Mikhail Suslov was the "shadow" leader of the Brezhnev politburo in charge of ideology), an entire dossier on Solidarity. The Polish and Soviet secret police analyzed with a fine-toothed comb everything there was to know about the leaders of the workers' movements. At times this file was terrible to read, so relentless was the KGB's X-ray vision. I thumped the file and said, "Here's everything. Take it." Walesa turned slightly pale.

Walesa told me that the Polish parliament would be having elections again, the Constitution allowed for it. Noticing my avid interest in this topic, he joked, "Why don't you disband your Supreme Soviet and elect a new one around them. Let those old deputies sit there and go on meeting and playing parliament. Everyone will very soon forget them." I smiled at this appealing idea.

There were old debts to pay in Prague. The admission that the invasion by the USSR in 1968 was an act of aggression was extremely important for Vaçlav Havel, and for the entire Czech people. Havel wanted to show me the old part of Prague. We sat in a tavern, drank some beer, and I suddenly thought, here we are, tired people who are no longer young, just drinking beer like nice friends. It was even possible to relax for a moment. But soon we would leave, and once again all the problems would rain down upon us, problems that brought with them an era of change that would shatter everything and everyone. What a hard road we had to travel, we, the first leaders of the post-Communist world.

Everyone knows that we Russians do not like to obey all sorts of rules, laws, instructions, and directives—any kind of previously established regimentation of behavior. We are a casual sort of people and rules cut us like a knife. People often ask me if I was bothered by all the niceties of protocol—where to step, where to stop? How did I manage it all?

In the beginning, I was unsure of myself and didn't have a protocol officer, which led to numerous blunders. Should I stand to the right or the left? Step forward or back? Come to a halt next to the flag and *then* turn my face or simply bow my head? I tried to catch on to the proper behavior by looking at what my neighbors were doing.

In conversations and talks my feelings sometimes lead me astray. I took too much of an active lead in negotiations. It's important not to spend more time talking than your counterpart. Otherwise, the negotiations will be over before your opponent has managed to get a word in edgewise. I have to watch this tendency and restrain myself.

Though it did initially, it no longer surprises me that almost everything on an official visit involves some sort of protocol and planning. Even what seems casual and spontaneous is usually carefully controlled. For example, photos and television images of Bill Clinton and me strolling lazily on the beach at our Vancouver summit meeting gave the appearance of the two leaders as friends, communicating easily and naturally. In fact, the entire route had been thoroughly checked in advance by security people, our walking time estimated, and our path precisely marked with tiny blue ribbons that were invisible to everyone except the two presidents.

But the lessons learned on these foreign trips are much greater than mere rules of order and decorum. As I said earlier, travel enables you to learn much about yourself and others.

I recall an episode that happened at Camp David. We were in negotiation with the top American government officials—the president, the secretary of state, the national security adviser, and four or five other people. In a corner of the conference room where the talks took place, there was a little table with pitchers of juice and a coffeepot. I noted how at home James Baker looked wearing a turtleneck and a jacket with leather patches on the elbows. I recall how Dick Cheney called to Mr. Baker, "Jimmy, pour me a juice, will you please." "Jimmy" poured some juice for himself and Mr. Cheney, in an absolutely relaxed and natural way, without any affectation or airs. If the meeting had been in Russia, we would have definitely had a young man in a tuxedo and bow tie serving, the bosses would have been sitting formally in their seats, and the server would have bowed and brought them juice on a tray.

I thought to myself at the time: why are Americans like this? I realized it was because they were absolutely independent people—even from the president himself—and therefore they could work for the sake of ideas, for the sake of a cause.

We are still too dependent upon one another, and on power. We are dependent on dachas, cars, special government telephone lines, and armored doors—the perquisites of power. Ridding ourselves of this dependency is an uphill battle.

Well, then, upon what does President Yeltsin himself ultimately depend? Or upon whom? First, I am obviously dependent upon my ego, on the image that I created and that those around me have created—that of a willful, determined, strong politician. Second, I am very dependent upon the opinion of people I respect, and there are quite a few of them. Not every opinion influences me, but it happens that a word said in passing or a line in a big newspaper article will sometimes force me to change my train of thought completely. Finally, I am dependent on my notions and principles, which, like the majority of normal people, I can't do anything about. Such beliefs are absorbed in childhood, and they are stronger than we are.

After Midnight

Once I was nearly crushed to death by love—the love of a crowd that bunched up and pressed against me. This sort of scene occurred frequently when I ran for president. Tens and hundreds of thousands of people would gather, and it was impossible to get to my car. The ring of security men couldn't keep people back. The crowd would first crush the security men, then me. Thankfully, there were never any bad consequences. There were never any assassination attempts, although there are constant threats. That's common everywhere.

Sometimes for curiosity's sake I see how our security people work compared to the Americans or Canadians. In my view, no one knows how to behave in a crowd like our guys. Sometimes they literally get into a horizontal position, their arms pushing against one human wall and their legs holding back another. What a knack they have for these sorts of things.

I usually get out of my car very quickly—it's a peculiarity of mine, a deep-seated feature of my nature, something I can't do anything about. I jump out of the car because when I see people on the street I'm interested in them. I don't have any sense of danger, none at all. I simply don't believe something bad will happen. My security people are particularly careful to watch my back. After my accidents, any kind of pushing, especially an unexpected shove, could cause me a great deal of pain. My men walk along very close behind me, in my footsteps, almost stepping on my heels.

For me, my security service is not merely one of many presidential services. Before the August coup, there were only a dozen or two poorly armed security men, and I truly came to appreciate them.

Alexander Korzhakov, my chief of security, and I have been inseparable since 1985, when I moved to Moscow. Korzhakov and I worked together when I was a central committee secretary, and later first secretary of the Moscow party city committee;* at the time, Korzhakov served in the KGB's ninth directorate, which is responsible for guarding government officials, and was one of the people "assigned" to me. When I was kicked out of the politburo in 1987, they also fired all my guards. Nevertheless, Korzhakov remained with me. He called and, just like that, asked if he could come over and keep guarding me, without pay. And he came. When I was elected as a people's deputy to the Soviet Congress in 1989, he drove me around in his own car, a Niva. On our days off, I sometimes visited him in his quaint little native village outside Moscow, which he affectionately called "Buttermilkton." There wasn't enough room for us all in his small cottage, so we set up a tent outside, and went fishing and swimming in the river.

To this day, Korzhakov never leaves my side, and we even sit up at night during trips together. He is a very decent, intelligent, strong, and courageous person. While outwardly he seems very simple, behind this simplicity is a sharp mind and an excellent and clear head.

There is another person who's been with me for many long years, Viktor Ilyushin, my aide from my Sverdlovsk days as head of the regional Communist party office. He has an amazing memory and an incredible capacity for work. He is very erudite and knowledgeable about a broad range of issues. He knows how to debate and

*The chief party official responsible for Moscow who was automatically made candidate member of the politburo.—Trans.

defend his own opinion. Seemingly dry and pedantic and focused only on his work, to many people Ilyushin gives the impression of a cold bureaucrat. But that is just because very few people manage to make contact with him and see him in any another way.

I start every day in this fashion: at 8:30 A.M., Ilyushin comes into my office. He places a file of the most urgent documents before me, we discuss the schedule for the day, and together make some changes. In the evening, sometimes very late, right before I leave the Kremlin, Viktor appears once again and hands me a thick folder with the documents he has prepared that day. That's my homework for the night.

Ilyushin piles on the work and sometimes he overloads me. I occasionally become irritated because not every meeting can fit into his scheduled slot of five to ten minutes. But Viktor won't give me any more time. I begin to get nervous and angry, and as chief assistant, he is always the one to bear the brunt of it. He patiently hears out my exasperated tirade and then leaves the room. Soon he returns to remind me that it's time to go on to the next matter, since my angry speech took up several valuable minutes.

Once I asked my pilot to land the president's helicopter near a river I fancied. We were coming back in the chopper to Moscow from one of our provincial tours. I thought such an impromptu landing would be possible, but it violated protocol, for one thing, because it meant losing contact with the nuclear button. It was decided we could stay, but no longer than an hour. The antiaircraft defense system could keep an air corridor for our helicopter open for only two hours. Security was always tight. I was never allowed to fly in the same helicopter with the prime minister, for example. We had to be in different aircraft—just in case.

The main problem with being president is the constant sense that you are inside a glass bowl for everyone to see, or in a kind of barometric chamber with an artificial atmosphere where you must stay all the time. Someone is always trying to take you by the arm, to suggest something, to make things comfortable, more comfortable, and still *more* comfortable. A kind of psychological numbness sets in, unnoticed by those around you, and soon you have the sensation that you are swathed in cotton. This is a simple elementary thing, as easy as ABC. Why make some sort of big deal out of it? All presidents live this way. That's how our lives are.

6

SHOCK THERAPY

Editor's Note: Yeltsin describes his decision to free prices and introduce market economic reforms, and tells about the men he selected to lead the policy. The process is painful and the consequences for the country are a period of turmoil. He also writes of his relationship with his wife Naina.

Not a single reform effort in Russia has ever been completed. The purpose of Peter the Great's reforms, for example, was to create "Russian Europeans." Obviously, that was an extremely ambitious goal that could not be achieved within one generation. In a certain sense, Peter the Great's reforms have not been achieved to this day. Although we have become Europeans, we have remained ourselves.

If we look at the reforms of various ages, everywhere radical reform has been attempted, there is a rollback, a sharp backlash. This is particularly true of the twentieth century. In Russia, not two land reforms, three revolutions, Lenin's new economic policy, Stalin's industrialization, Khrushchev's thaw, or Kosygin's quiet reforms changed anything fundamental in Russia.

I suppose there have only been three decades—the last quarter of the nineteenth century and the twentieth century—that were truly reformist in the sense that trade, industry, and society were developing, although this was accomplished under the banner of "czarist oppression" (as the intelligentsia believed at the time).

The goal I have set before the government is to make reform irreversible.

The power and might of economic progress must be synchronized with the enormous political changes. Then we will be unstoppable. Then other people will definitely come after us who will finish everything and move the country toward prosperity.

I never believed that Yegor Gaidar was a physician who could cure our sick economy, but I didn't think he was a quack who would finish the patient off, either. To continue the medical metaphor, I remember the morning in the Spanish hospital when almost immediately after the operation I was told to get up and walk, without crutches or assistance. Gaidar's role consisted of raising our paralyzed economy to its feet and forcing its vital centers, its resources, its organisms to work. Would it get up or not? It was a quite brutal but necessary policy. While the other "doctors" were arguing over treatment plans, Gaidar dragged the patient out of bed. And I think the sick patient took a few steps.

I draw this conclusion not on the basis of economic indicators; they are objectively poor. They are the indicators of another economy—the old Soviet economy—that no longer exists. Rather, I am making this analysis based on the fact that people with an entirely new psychology have emerged in our country. They have the psychology of the *muzhik*, the sturdy Russian peasant, who does not expect anyone to help him and doesn't rely on anyone—not the government, the parliament, or Yeltsin. "A plague on all their houses," says he, and quietly goes about his business. If you look around, you will see that there are such people now, mainly young people, in business, the media, the arts, science and culture, indeed everywhere. For the time being, they are not so conspicuous; they are too busy. But they exist. To put it bluntly, normal people—the kind of people who used to be crushed by the state—have begun to appear in our country.

I believe the reason for this is precisely the same as the painful, shocked reaction of a body when all its forces are mobilized, when the patient acquires confidence and focus. I think that in the development of society this model can be used to some extent. This approach, however, can lead to catastrophe, to complete collapse when it's a question of survival, when a person simply becomes enraged, losing his human traits because he fears losing his means of existence. But we have a rich country with a gigantic, although backward economy. We just have to remember that.

Russia's trouble was never a shortage or an abundance of reformers. The trouble was an inability to adhere to a consistent policy. Whether czar or general secretary, everyone wanted to distinguish himself in history. All of them took on an extra load, aware of their unique mission, and they turned the wheel of government sharply, about 180 degrees.

In the history of Russia in the last centuries, there were only two rulers—Alexander III and Leonid Brezhnev—who in practice, by virtue of their personal blandness and mediocrity, hewed to a purely conservative, even distinctly antireformist line. In their dominion, society lived under a very strict ideological notion of the state. Naturally, dissent was persecuted.

Both Alexander III and Brezhnev were in power for an unusually long time. Both departed this life scorned by all their thinking contemporaries. Why?

Indisputably, Alexander III made a great leap forward in industry. He didn't bring prosperity to the people; otherwise, there wouldn't have been revolutions afterward. But under Alexander III, a middle class at last appeared in Russia; a material base was prepared for the flourishing of art and science. The Russian state finally entered the family of civilized nations.

And it's true that under Brezhnev, the inhumane Soviet system was preserved, and political persecution continued. The USSR was headed for a dangerous military confrontation, but another tendency could also be observed. Despite the outward curtailment of reforms (as in the era of Alexander III), Brezhnev did not turn the country around 180 degrees, as many thought at the time. The essentials of Khrushchev's reforms were preserved. An obtuse, but admittedly very consistent administrative hard line allowed some favorable tendencies to build. Brezhnev's notion of "developed socialism" and the "steady increase in the workers' prosperity"—ridiculed thousands of times under perestroika as utopian—did have a certain reasoning behind it.

As we see now, the Socialist system made great inroads into popular psychology. Obviously, there was no prosperity. With no butter or meat in the stores, this slogan seemed a mockery. But in fact, when a certain parity was achieved in international affairs, the people were not, as they always had been before, required to throw all their efforts into stoking the state, to give their utmost in sacrifice for a common goal. Step-by-step through the terrible rusty grinding of a bureaucratic system, the Soviet people began to come close to achieving the Western standard of living. They got their own apartments, electrical household appliances, social security, a small plot of earth to garden—even private automobiles. There were more or less bearable conditions for the "little man," the ordinary citizen, in both culture and education. I do not want to deal with the complex processes under way in society in that era, which spanned the mid-1960s to approximately the mid-1970s. I merely want to emphasize this tendency of a gradual, unnoticeable increase in certain creature comforts. Understandably, this almost unnoticeable improvement was achieved at the cost of a barbaric squandering of the country's resources, and not through normal, efficient work.

Then the leader became decrepit. The dilapidated *gensek* (general secretary) became a symbol of the dilapidated economy: huge, even gigantic, but muddled.

I remember how much criticism was provoked back in the Gorbachev era with a new government ruling authorizing enterprise and the removal of restrictions on the activities of middlemen. "The black market is flourishing with a vengeance in Russia," the press complained. And it was true: no matter what metro station in Moscow you came out of, mobs of peddlers were hawking "colonial wares" (as our witty columnists dubbed them)—imported vodka, cigarettes, candy, and so on. It's an eyesore, and nothing more.

Let us recall the classical texts. When has the capital of traders ever had a reputation for being pure as the driven snow in Russia? The works of the nineteenth-century playwright Alexander Ostrovsky are brimming with financial ruin, intrigue, and mountains of debts. Today, these are true-crime stories from the police blotter. The history of great Russian industry, the history of Russian capital before the revolution, began with tales of the wild era of the famous merchants of the Zamoskvorechie region. This doesn't mean that we're eager for swindlers to prosper. That is why the police and the procurator's office exist, to combat this hard reality. There should be only one limitation to profiteering: the law. Unfortunately, the law-enforcement agencies are adapting very slowly and poorly to this new crime phenomenon. That's the typical Russian style.

In September 1992, I looked at the economic figures for the preceding nine months. They were cause for alarm. The country was steadily creeping toward hyperinflation, the collapse of industry, the disruption of trade among large plants and branches of the economy. There was just one sign of hope—the consumer index was way up. Within a few months, the shortage of goods was eliminated, by all indices, except for the cheapest items (for which people still have to wait in line in Russia). Now there's a completely different kind of shortage in Russia—a scarcity of money. Gaidar had, in fact, warned of this.

In an interview for Russian television, the famous exiled writer Alexander Solzhenitsyn asked a rhetorical question of the host, which was directed as well to the viewers, the whole country, and the president: "Would you treat your own mother with shock therapy?"

Our mother is Russia, and we are her children. It is truly brutal to treat your mother with shock therapy and is not something a good son would do. Yes, in some sense Russia is our mother, but at the same time Russia is us. We are its flesh and blood, its people. I would use shock therapy on myself, and not just one time. Sometimes it takes a sharp break or rupture to make a person move forward or even survive at all. By choosing the path of shock therapy, I did not choose it for some immature Russia or some abstract people. I chose this path for myself as well. The first person who would have to suffer this shock—and suffer it repeatedly with savagely painful reactions, having to strain all resources—would be me, the president.

The debilitating bouts of depression, the grave second thoughts, the insomnia and headaches in the middle of the night, the tears and despair, the sadness at the appearance of Moscow and other Russian cities, the flood of criticism from the newspapers and television every day, the harassment campaign at the Congress sessions, the entire burden of the decisions made, the hurt from people close to me who did not support me at the last minute, who didn't hold up, who deceived me—I have had to bear all of this.

This is to say nothing of the October coup.

The next portion of this chapter will deal with the political technology, so to say, of economic reform—the behind-the-scenes effort. Readers of my book should be exposed to this as well. Yet I wouldn't want these motifs to obscure the main subject: the need for a determined move forward after the breakdown suffered by the country. It is a moral human imperative.

The situation in the country as we embarked on reforms was not a happy one. Having lost stability, society braced itself in fear for the start of radical reforms, realizing the danger of price hikes and unemployment. By the autumn following the August 1991 coup, the rationing of virtually everything had reached its limit. The shelves in the stores were absolutely bare. In many cities, people were issued thick stapled booklets of coupons they could use to make purchases, since everything—salt, sugar, bread, matches—was in short supply. The political atmosphere was also quite gloomy. The former Soviet republics regarded each other, and especially Russia, with grave mistrust. It was at this very tense and critical moment that I received the first wake-up call from Alexander Rutskoi.

On December 18 (that is, two weeks before the start of the January 1, 1992 reforms), Rutskoi published a piece in *Nezavisimaya gazeta* [*Independent* newspaper] saying that the government was an unruly disorganized hotbed of intrigue; no one knew where we were headed or what our ultimate goal was; the president was trying to govern unilaterally and despotically; and if the liberalization of prices scheduled for January was not canceled, he, Rutskoi, would resign.

Persistent rumors began to circulate among foreign observers that the military people, unhappy with the collapse of the Soviet Union, were plotting a new coup, with Rutskoi supposedly as its political leader. The situation was far from a coup; nevertheless, Rutskoi's name was invoked, with good reason. On a trip around the defense plants of Siberia, Rutskoi had scathingly labeled the team of reformers in Gaidar's government "little boys in pink shorts." The precedent for crudeness in politics was set, and Ruslan Khasbulatov soon picked up the baton with enormous glee.

I first became acquainted with Gennady Burbulis when we worked together in the interregional deputies' group.* Even then he

*The liberal caucus in the Soviet Congress of People's Deputies formed in 1989 and led by Yeltsin, Andrei Sakharov, and other prominent deputies and numbering several hundred.—Trans.

made a strong impression on me with his erudition as a professional philosopher. I quickly realized as well that Burbulis had never been a bureaucratic theoretician or a compliant executor for the bosses, that is, the soft, elusive type of person he seems at first, and in fact the way most intellectuals are. On the contrary, he was a driving, energetic person with a very strong will.

We had not known each other in Sverdlovsk since we moved in different circles. Nevertheless, those common roots, the memories of Sverdlovsk, also meant a great deal in our relationship. Finally, there was the fact that he had seriously played soccer in his youth on the army team, and loved sports as much as I did.

His first immediate duty as my aide was to head the campaign office in Sverdlovsk when I ran for election to the Russian parliament in 1990 (and later for the office of president of Russia in 1991). Soon afterward, Burbulis was officially appointed "as plenipotentiary of the chairman of the Russian Supreme Soviet," a kind of special assistant at large for the speaker of the parliament. Such a job title had not previously existed; it was created specially to fit Burbulis in order to highlight his special status.

Gennady and I were in particularly close communication during my time working at Arkhangelskoye in 1990 when I was speaker of the Russian parliament. In general, I loved to spend time there and I must admit that my conversations with Gennady inspired me with new ideas during that period. He knew how to look far into the future as well as give current events a strategic, global interpretation. As a result, a conception of a new politics, a new economy, a new state system and way of life for Russia began to take shape more distinctly.

I made my final selection, however, in September 1991, in Sochi, when both Ivan Silayev and Burbulis came to visit me on vacation. During these stressful days after the coup, I had the opportunity to compare once again the cautious compromising older Silayev with the young Burbulis, who was full of vitality and energy. I had an urgent need to share the total responsibility of running the country with someone, to assign to someone else the long-term planning and selection of courses of action and personnel, leaving me free to conceive all the tactics and strategy of the immediate political struggle.

At that moment, I was counting on Burbulis to fit the job description. I not only admired his original thinking and drive but I also liked his ability to assess other people's ideas and his familiarity with the young politicians and practitioners of his generation. He would be able to tell me the people upon whom we could rely, and, fortunately, I wasn't mistaken on that score. For example, Gaidar and Andrei Kozyrev, who replaced Shevardnadze as Foreign Minister, who were Burbulis's finds and whom he vigorously promoted during this period. So, Gennady Burbulis became state secretary* and first deputy prime minister of the Russian Federation. The press often dubbed him the éminence grise of my administration. That's nonsense, of course. For there to be such a character, the figure in the president's office would have to be utterly spineless, soft, and apathetic (which is how I see now, with the perspective of time, the relationship between Suslov and Brezhnev).

Burbulis had two serious minuses—an overweening pride and an inability to present himself to the public, which at times reached absurd proportions. For example, television commentators would invite Gaidar on a talk show, and Burbulis would find out about it and come in Gaidar's place, sit himself down, and start spouting boring pompous commentary over the air. That is of course an isolated example, not indicative. Nevertheless, I must admit that all of Burbulis's attempts to become a shaper of public opinion were unsuccessful.

At the top of the agenda during the first few days of 1992 was the question which newly independent state would control the Black Sea Fleet and the Crimea†—Russia or Ukraine? The potential future of CIS hung in the balance.

At first the Ukrainian Defense Ministry and the Ukrainian Supreme Soviet unilaterally pressured the personnel of the Black Sea Fleet to take an oath of allegiance to Ukraine. Then in poor judgment, the Russian Supreme Soviet retaliated by invoking the

*The Russian *gosudarstvenny sekretar'*, state secretary, is roughly the equivalent of a national security adviser although not responsible for foreign affairs per se.—Trans.

†Although the Black Sea Fleet had technically been passed down from the Soviet Union to CIS, it had historically belonged to the Russian empire, based on the Crimean peninsula in the south of Russia on the Black Sea. The Crimea itself was an area of contention; Khrushchev had made a gift of the Crimea, which had been part of Russian territory, to Ukraine. It was a favorite resort area of Soviet leaders. To add to its complex history, the Crimean Tatars, a Muslim ethnic group, were seeking to return to the peninsula, their historic homeland before Stalin deported them on false accusations of treason during World War II, and declare the region their own republic.—Trans.

illegality of Khrushchev's transfer of the Crimea to Ukraine in 1954. The incident was explosive because it proved the Ukrainian government and parliament were prepared to use vigorous strong-arm tactics on the Black Sea Fleet without any coordination with us.

The timing for such a squabble couldn't have been worse. The Ukrainian parliament knew perfectly well that Russia was bracing itself for economic shock reform with the freeing of prices. After the formation of CIS, various local ethnic problems began to make themselves felt. There was the issue of Volga German autonomy, for example; the Baltic demand for the immediate and unconditional withdrawal of Soviet troops; the efforts of oppressed peoples in the Caucasus for historical retribution and a return of their autonomy—immediately and unconditionally; and so on.

Everywhere, people were using the term "the disintegration of the army," although in fact it was merely a question of the former Soviet republics creating their own armed forces.

A list of actions we took to settle the Black Sea Fleet dispute over the course of two years would fill several pages in a book. There were endless delegations, consultations, meetings at various levels, and finally some interim agreements, press conferences, and statements.

Before my speech to the UN Security Council in early 1992, I flew directly to the Crimea to meet the officers of the Black Sea Fleet on the navy vessel *Moskva,* bound for the port of Novorossisk. The officers of the fleet urgently needed this rather unusual meeting more than anyone. The sailors felt it was very important to eliminate their sense of isolation and distance from Russia and its leaders. After spending some time on this mighty fighting machine, awed by its power and vastness, I sensed that *I* also needed this meeting with the sailors. The worried faces of the sailors have stayed in my mind, seemingly asking me: will Russia remain a naval power? Do we sense ourselves to be a strong country? Indeed we do.

Why am I writing about the problem of the Black Sea Fleet in a chapter about shock therapy? Because it was artificially created by the Ukrainian parliament's desire to demonstrate its independence. No one was intending to move the ships from one base to another (nor would they have been able to); no one had given (nor could have given) any orders to the fleet, which is armed with nuclear weapons, to set their sights on Russian targets. Nevertheless, within a few days, the media was spreading the powerful myth of an alleged danger! Approximately the same happened with "spiraling hyperinflation," "massive unemployment," and other horrors like the "impoverishment of the people" to come from Gaidar's reforms.

The psychological shock from reform exceeded many times over the actual harm to individual families. The devil you know is less frightening than the devil you don't.

From the very first days of the reforms, the Gaidar government was operating under terrible mental duress as the press and the parliament let loose a hailstorm of criticism and kept up an incessant drumbeat of protest. Gaidar and his people were cut virtually no slack and were never given even a modicum of freedom to maneuver. According to their plan, realistically, inflation was inevitable but would stop in 1992, or perhaps the first half of 1993.

Who prevented Gaidar and his team from curbing inflation? Let us investigate.

People often say they don't understand why a figure from the old democratic elite was not included among my close aides. By "old democrat," they mean prominent advocates of democracy from the perestroika era like Gavriil Popov, dean of the department of economics at Moscow University, or Anatoly Sobchak, a lawyer who is now the mayor of St. Petersburg, or Yuri Afanasyev, rector of the Historical Archives Institute (subsequently renamed the Russian University for the Humanities). All these figures were in the Soviet parliamentary opposition known as the interregional deputies' group.

It was true that in 1989–1990, these people were authentic leaders of the popular wave of democracy, but then what happened? Popov and Sobchak were strong independent politicians. They went their own way, and the outcomes were different in each case. Popov made a very smart move soon after his election as mayor of Moscow; he appointed Yuri Luzhkov as his first deputy. Luzhkov was an experienced economic manager and deputy of the chairman of the Moscow City Executive Committee, that is, deputy to the official who was roughly the equivalent of mayor in the old Soviet system.

Luzhkov at first seemed a rather bland figure, overshadowed by Popov's vivid personality. Then suddenly Luzhkov blossomed in a burst of color. After the August coup, there was a clear crisis of faith in the democratic government. The kinds of qualities Luzhkov possessed—experience, reliability, the ability to manage the complex organism of a modern megapolis—propelled him into the ranks of the politicians people trust and from whom they expect a great deal. Gradually, step-by-step, the new Moscow mayor got the executive branch of government at the Moscow regional level to function efficiently. He brought into the mayor's office two young deputies who were just turning thirty years of age, and more experienced people who had known Moscow for decades. Luzhkov proved that democracy was not to blame for the severe problems of the post-Communist era. The municipal government could function normally even under a new social system if it had the right leadership.

Meanwhile, Popov was able to get himself out of the hot seat at city hall just in time. He returned to his teaching and theoretical politics and remained the same Gavriil Popov as people had known him. The same cannot be said for Anatoly Sobchak who, in the job of the St. Petersburg "town governor" (as the mayors used to be called in old Russia), was forced largely to change his former image as a liberal. From a well-respected politician and professor of law, he turned into a harsh, authoritarian administrator.

As for Yuri Afanasyev, well, he's the eternal opposition member, which is why, by the way, I have an enormous fondness for him. Such people are very necessary in society but not in government. They are better off somewhere to the side, or on a hilltop, where the view is better.

Of all my colleagues in the interregional deputies' group of this caliber, Burbulis was almost the only one who could assume such a great load of work—not staff work, but political work.

Burbulis became acquainted with Yegor Gaidar in the fall of 1991, when Gaidar was director of the Institute of Economics in Moscow. Burbulis immediately asked him to prepare a position paper for my report on the economy. In general, Burbulis prefers to work with teams of people. When he met Gaidar's team at a dacha outside Moscow, he couldn't help but like them. They were a very close-knit group of people, congenial both professionally and personally, a circle of fellow believers. Burbulis and Gaidar's people clicked, and their cooperation was off to a good start.

Yegor Gaidar was born into a family in the Soviet literary elite, a very interesting family indeed. His grandfather was Arkady Gaidar, a famous author of children's books, a legendary but complicated figure. Yegor's great-grandfather on his mother's side was Pavel Bazhov, the famous storyteller of the Ural Mountains known for his great mastery of the Russian language. Yegor's father, Timur Gaidar, was a rear-admiral and prominent journalist who worked for many years as a foreign correspondent for *Pravda*. As a boy, Yegor lived with his father in Cuba and later Yugoslavia, completing his high school education in Belgrade. In 1978, he graduated from Moscow University's Department of Economics with honors, never having once received a failing grade, nothing but As. His dean at the university was Gavriil Popov.

For a time Gaidar worked in academic institutes and then at the central committee's journal, *Kommunist*, and as an editor in the economics department of *Pravda*. By the time we met, Gaidar had acquired a Ph.D. in economics, was head of an academic institute, and had three children—all at the age of thirty-something. Much later, Gaidar was to write in an article:

> We began the reforms in a very interesting situation when you could have listed many absent preconditions, making reform impossible to implement at the time. I myself could have given a perfect explanation of why in 1992 the reforms should not have been launched. There was no stable support in the parliament; there were no normal functioning institutions of governance (the army, customs, the police)—they were still staggering from the crisis of power that had begun in the early 1990s.
>
> There were sixteen central banks instead of one; there were no traditions of private enterprise; there was no strong private sector as in Poland. There wasn't a kopeck to be had of hard currency or gold reserves, nor the opportunity to attract free investment from the international financial market. But aside from all that, we couldn't wait any longer. We couldn't just keep doing nothing, or keep explaining why it was impossible to do anything.

Once I had grasped Gaidar's concept of economic reform and then met the author himself, I had to agree with Burbulis. Several days later, I signed a decree appointing Gaidar deputy prime minister and economic minister. Several of Gaidar's close colleagues were appointed along with him to key economic posts in the government.

For Gaidar's team, Burbulis's authority at that time was absolutely unimpeachable. The ministers would clear all matters requiring my involvement through Burbulis. They would either come to his office in person or, if necessary, he would punch a button and speak to me on the direct line.

At the time few people realized that Gaidar was potentially no less strong a political figure than Burbulis. Gaidar's ministers and Gaidar himself basically took this position with us: your business is political leadership; ours is economics. Don't interfere with us as we do our work, and we won't butt in on your exalted councils, your cunning behind-the-scenes intrigue, which we don't understand anyway.

Burbulis had been appointed first deputy prime minister, technically a rung lower than Gaidar, who was deputy prime minister. Even so, Burbulis was at that point the de facto head of the Cabinet of Ministers. In order not to stir up political machinations around the selection of a candidate for prime minister, and so as not to have to put the candidate to a vote in Congress, Burbulis came up with the bold tack of delegating the leadership of the government to me during this transitional period. The idea took hold.

On Tuesdays, the economic section of the Cabinet of Ministers would regularly convene with Burbulis chairing the meeting. The atmosphere was informal, and Gennady, much beloved by everyone from the days of the interregional deputies' group, would decide over tea and sandwiches both strategic and tactical issues as well as matters of personnel placement. This was how a certain Valery Makharadze, a former local government official from the city of Volgograd who had not distinguished himself in that post, was made a deputy prime minister. Aleksei Golovkov, a former junior researcher from the same institute where Gaidar and Stanislav Shatalin had worked, was put in charge of administrative affairs for the Council of Ministers, although this job required an incredible amount of purely technical initiative and experience. As a result, the office work began to pile up or go astray.

Why am I going into all these administrative details here? Because they are indicative of Burbulis's style of work. He hated the bureaucracy as a class, scorned the apparatchik's work, and loved the way Gaidar's ministers would just crash through everything as if they wanted to tear apart with their bare hands the entire decrepit system of rank and top-down management. Only later did I realize that unlike Burbulis, Gaidar was perhaps a great statesman. His ministers, however—not all of them, of course, but some—were done in by their inability to implement even their own programs. When they collided with the harsh reality of putting theory into practice, at some point they lost their heads and could not overcome their frustration. Burbulis was of no help because of his inherent antipathy to the dirty job of staff work. Meanwhile, Gaidar had not yet understood his own role nor found his footing.

If, for example, Pyotr Aven had still been heading the Ministry of Foreign Economic Relations approximately a year after his resignation; that is, if he had managed to fit into the current Russian economic scene, he could definitely have been entrusted with any economic position in government. He has a brilliant mind, great international contacts, and all the necessary accoutrements for the job. But Russia resisted all the experiments of these reformist ministers. Although it's very hard to create anything in Russia, it's even harder to destroy it.

Soon it became evident that the Gaidar government, which was rapidly making one decision after another, was in complete isolation. Gaidar and his people never traveled around the country to take the pulse of the nation. From the outset, these ministers perceived the Khasbulatov parliament as an instrument of pressure on them, as a symbol of everything that was reactionary, everything that had to be fought. That was their attitude to Rutskoi, the vice president, as well.

This state of affairs deteriorated before the next (the Sixth) Congress of People's Deputies. By that time it had become obvious that the Gaidar government was perceived not as an independent economic group but as Burbulis's team. And Burbulis himself began to have first cool and then rancorous relations with all the parliamentary factions: with Rutskoi, with my office, and so on. It was a kind of childish infantile division of people into "ours" and "theirs"—those on "our team" and those on the "other team." It was here that Burbulis's jealousy and ambition to remove fierce rivals came into play; in short, all the features of an oversensitive, arrogant nature.

Now people are telling me that Burbulis turned out to be right in the end! That is true. In retrospect, looking at this negative side to Burbulis's behavior, I would have to say that his childish desire to take sides and keep score was a fatal disservice at the time. Many months later, Rutskoi griped to people that he was being frozen out, left without anything to do. There was a certain bald truth in this. Perhaps if that energetic comrade could have found something to keep him busy, some outlet for his energy, everything would have turned out differently. Instead, to occupy himself Rutskoi was forced to write a groundbreaking paper on agriculture. Even that didn't divert him for long, and he adopted other causes—as we can see now all too clearly.

To sum up what preliminarily went wrong with reform: Burbulis found people to implement the new economic policy of the Russian government. But the implementers turned out to be more talented than himself. Still, by sophisticatedly refusing to "dirty their hands with politics" and leaving all political initiative to their chief, the Gaidar team made a tactical error that cost us all a great deal.

In my view, if Gaidar had had just a little more time, he would have broken down the prejudice against him, his team, and his program. He and his government were rapidly gaining experience. They began to travel around the country. Gaidar, for example, met with factory directors in the auto industry town of Togliatti. His alienation was eroding. Also vitally important was Gaidar's and his team's failure to work well with the deputies, although an improvement in the perception of Gaidar had occurred in the parliament as well. All he needed was just a little more time.

I began to notice that features in Burbulis's character which previously had seemed incidental to me were in fact related to his whole system of behavior and relationships with other people.

Burbulis was the first of the new Russian *nomenklatura* who came to power after the August coup to order a government limousine (a ZIL) for himself. He provided himself with a large security retinue. I think he experienced a special thrill when the escort car raced ahead of his ZIL, its lights blinking and siren screeching. This was the typical love of the provincial for the attributes of power in the capital. Burbulis could walk into any meeting in the Kremlin or anywhere else without invitation, regardless of the agenda or degree of formality, and sit at the right hand of the president. Furthermore, he knew that I wouldn't reprove him for it.

That was a purely personal mistake on my part. Why the formal outward trappings of power were so important for him remains a mystery to me. After all, Burbulis was an intelligent person who in reality controlled the strategic lever of government, possessing enormous powers. Some mysterious feature prevented Burbulis from realistically matching his tasks with his abilities.

I won't hide the fact that at a certain point I began to feel an irrational weariness with this man. It had been building up subconsciously. I got tired of seeing the same face in my office, in meetings, at receptions, in my home, at my dacha, on the tennis court, in the sauna. It was understandable that people wanted access to the president for the sake of the cause, for one's own ideas, but they had to know the limit! This wasn't persecution mania on my part. As easily as Gennady had walked into any meeting, he began to come to me in person all the time. He overstepped some boundary in our personal relations. Well, it happens.

Despite these revelations of his character and the strain on our relationship, I continued to have a very high opinion of what Burbulis was doing for Russia. That hasn't changed, but work is something else. It is slave labor, day in and day out. There are times in the life of a talented creative impulsive man of the moment when he is capable of such slogging—these are extreme moments, so to speak. But then they pass, and there remains only the wish to appear to be as he was in the past, a wish not always comprehensible to those around him.

After Midnight

In *Against the Grain,** my first book, I described in general terms how Naina and I met and married. Sometimes in the middle of the night I reminisce about our life in Sverdlovsk in order to somehow relieve the stress, to shift gears, to forget myself. When I worked as first secretary of the regional party office, Naina would come home from work very upset. When she would come into the hall during the lunch break at her job, people would immediately strike up loud, obvious conversations around her—look at how terrible everything is, they don't rent out housing fast enough, there's no butter in the stores, and so on.

"Borya," she would say, "I really do go to the grocery stores in the center of town and there are all sorts of things missing. And that's in the center. What about the suburbs?"

What could I do? The region was an industrial one, and I myself had to lobby over the telephone for almost days at a time for train deliveries of meat from agricultural regions. As a builder, I tried to push construction because a home is the most important thing for

*Published in Russia in 1990 as *Ispoved na zadannuyu temu* [*Confession on an Assigned Theme*] and in the United States as *Against the Grain* (Summit Books, 1990).—Trans.

people. We assessed a fee from the major plants for construction and were able to build and rent many homes.

My wife takes everything to heart. I remember when she learned that Gaidar had been removed, she simply couldn't get over it and called him at home. When she heard his calm voice, she burst into tears.

Oddly enough, we never had any jealous scenes over work. I pushed myself to the limit, to complete exhaustion, even back in the early days on the construction sites. I would be buried in my work until late at night, even when I worked as a foreman. She made her choice then. This didn't mean, however, that our life was barren—on the contrary. Sometimes I would hurry home after some meeting at the party office and we would pick up our wailing infant daughters at eleven o'clock at night and take a taxi to some friend's birthday party.

She really loved my surprises. When she was about to give birth to our daughter Lena, I drove her to a maternity hospital in Beryozniki, so she could live with my mother after the delivery. I was working in Sverdlovsk at the time and could not be with her. After she had given birth, they brought her an enormous bouquet of flowers with a note and poem from me—something she had never expected. (I had prepared it all in advance.)

Naina remembers our engagement as something of a surprise. After we graduated from the institute, Naina and I parted after vowing that we would definitely meet within a year, on neutral territory—neither her hometown nor mine, which seemed more romantic. Then there was a regional volleyball competition in the city of Kuibyshev. At first I was going to call to invite her, but then I thought—what if she didn't come?—and sent a telegram. I racked my brain trying to think of what to write. Finally, I decided to send a message that would completely guarantee that not only would she come, but she would hop on the next direct flight. The message was, "Please come. Boris has a heart condition." I didn't sign it.

Although Naina knew I was capable of pulling a prank, she really did almost break her neck to get there, found our hotel, and saw me right away. Our engagement took place when we spent the whole night strolling around a park. Now she says she can't imagine how it was possible to spend the whole night walking around. I think Naina had not really been prepared for receiving that crazy telegram and making this crazy rendezvous, which had become such a sharp turn in her life. But after that meeting I actually went to visit her in Orenburg, her hometown, then brought her to register our marriage in Sverdlovsk, then took her immediately to Beryozniki, to meet my parents.

When Naina and I studied at the institute, we lived for several years in neighboring rooms in a dormitory. But we didn't have a love affair in the modern sense of the word. In fact, at first I liked another girl in her group. Then I fell in love with Naina. But it was difficult to start up a real romance in our communal living quarters. We lived a life brimming over with vigorous collective activity. We dubbed our two rooms of girls and boys the "collective farm." I was chosen "chairman" and Naina was made "sanitation engineer"—the most spic-and-span there ever was. We had one girl as treasurer, and pooled our money to share meals. We would all joke around together, go to the movies, have parties—in short, just lived our lives together. Of course there were sports, endless volleyball, with me on the court and Naina on the bench at matches and at practices—I can see her face even now, quiet and radiant.

In those student days, we lived in an atmosphere of pure friendship, of a happy and slightly frantic romanticism that now seems simply impossible to imagine. I don't recall ever seeing such fantastic energy ever again—and all against the backdrop of the half-starving, almost ascetic, barracks existence of the Soviet Union in those days. The object of our romanticism and emotions were global issues—outer space, communism, the virgin territories, where young Soviets were being sent to work the land. It was all something incredible and immense.

In other words, my relations with Naina were platonic and somewhat secretive, which was the norm in the spirit of those years. Perhaps other people had other experiences (most certainly they did), but we did not. Therefore, the store of feelings we had before our wedding was far from exhausted. That was the style of my generation—easy and open.

I remember my tortured smile in the maternity hospital when our second daughter was born. I stood and looked through the window where I could see Naina's face, and I was distressed deep down somehow. She, too, was suffering; she knew that I had wanted a son. Only later did I understand what a great joy it was to have two daughters—the elder takes after me and the younger takes after her mother.

Recently my grandson, Borka, returned from a tennis competition in France. I said to him, what, you lost two matches? He replied, so what, I won on the total score. But wait a minute, I explained, that means you can't discipline yourself at the right moment, if you first lose and then win with the same opponent. Go take a cold shower, I told him. You have to condition yourself, you need hard tempering for total self-discipline. He seemed to take off for the bathroom but suddenly he came back and said tauntingly, "Hey, Gramps, didn't you ever lose?" Then he added in embarrassment, "In sports?"

In the first years after my marriage to Naina, I would run home after work. Those were happy days. We initially lived in a room in a communal flat, a two-room apartment in Khimmash. Then when Lena was born, I was already the head of administration and was given a two-room apartment in Vtorchermyot—both districts of Sverdlovsk in those days, with the grand-sounding names of the industrial plants that so reflected the spirit of the giant Soviet projects of the time.* The happiest period of my life was undoubtedly in that communal apartment (as it was for many of my contemporaries). There were so many little feasts and happy celebrations and wonderful sleepless nights. So many friends came to visit.

Then began the long period of my career in the regional party committee, the local government office responsible for running the Sverdlosk area. At times I didn't know where it was taking me; I came just as an ordinary person but a person of power, throwing myself into a party career as I had once thrown myself into spiking a volleyball, and then succeeding at my construction work. The wife of such a person has an unenviable fate.

There are probably some qualities in me Naina likes and that let her forgive me everything. Even so, there are things she takes badly, such as the subtle, gradual pressure by various means of those around us on the wife of the number-one man, as happened in Sverdlovsk and of course continues now. It is pressure for very mundane purposes—people are simply lobbying for their own interests. I think this style of pressuring, whereby people try to get something through the wife or relatives of the ruler, has always been widespread in Russia and was particularly strong under Brezhnev, given

*Khimmash is chemical machinery plant, and Vtorchermyot is scrap iron works.—Trans.

his nature. Unfortunately, as I see it, this practice was further encouraged by Raisa Gorbachev.

I do not want to gloat or to say any offensive words to her "after the fact." But I know perfectly well that it was in the Gorbachev era that our women became particularly irritated with the First Lady. Now Naina is inevitably compared to Raisa.

When Gorbachev came home to the dacha after work (the guards told me about this), Raisa used to meet him at the door and take him for a walk—once, twice, or three times around the house, which was her way of relaxing him. During these walks he would tell her his whole day, literally by the minute. Gorbachev's wife was not just informed; she was given a total briefing. Sooner or later, this could not help but have an effect, and did have one, on Gorbachev's attitudes toward people, toward staff appointments, and toward politics in general. When I come home, my wife and daughters are sometimes wound up from watching television, and bombard me with questions and exclamations: Papa, how could it be? How could he do that? How could you . . . And I would have to be rather abrupt in stopping them—give me a break. I don't need politics at home.

As for the lobbyists, the people who give Naina requests for favors, notes, plans, etc.—she simply can't explain to strangers that her husband won't listen to her.

The Sixth Congress of People's Deputies that took place in April 1992, eight months after the coup, was the first aborted attempt by the antireform forces to roll back our "rapid improvement" policy (that may be an inept definition of the Congress, but it's a short one).

I must admit that I feel different now about the Congress than I did then. To put it bluntly, I was much more interested in it after my experience of the earlier Gorbachev-era Soviet congresses, and the Russian congresses in which I took part; I had an image of the parliament as being a truly nationwide forum. We cannot forget how, after the Brezhnev years of boring rubber-stamping legislatures, these new parliamentary sessions were enormous events in our country. Night after night everyone was glued to the television set, waiting to see how his elected representatives would perform. I had no idea back then that these congresses would hound me.

Because of my initial respect for parliament as an institution, I took very hard the sharp criticism by the government that dogged those first three months of our reforms. By then I was receiving reports from several different analysts, who also had nothing good to say. Although an inexperienced politician, Yegor Gaidar kept giving assurances that stabilization was just around the corner. I was in turn forced to mimic his confidence. But in April and May, the first lifting of price controls on energy resources was due. This would be the second round of inflation after the January price liberalization (there was a third round to come that summer), yet so far no stabilization at all was foreseeable in the near future. The mood in the government was one of concern, if not depression. The only reassuring note was the promise of the Group of Seven to rapidly provide major financial aid. At this point we grew dependent on several experts who said one thing one day and another thing the next. Such ambiguity was not at all encouraging.

Since I had no intention of parting with my government, I began to approach the Sixth Congress with the attitude that I had to give it a good horsewhipping. That's putting it crudely, but it's exactly what I had to do.

It had a completely unintended effect, however.

I was unhappy with the work of some of the ministers. Consultation with factions in the first days of the Congress revealed that the deputies, too, were identifying the same figures as problematic—Vladimir Lopukhin, minister of fuel and energy; Edvard Dneprov, education minister; Anorei Vorobyov, health minister; and Pyotr Aven, economics minister. I naturally passed this list on to Gaidar through Burbulis, since I considered it premature to meet with the government at this time. Gaidar's team took my suggestions for some changes in the cabinet extremely badly. They had been convinced that their flanks were absolutely covered and I think many of them were simply in shock. I spoke personally with Gaidar and named these four people. An emergency meeting of the government was called and apparently the possibility of a collective resignation was raised even then. But it was hard for Gaidar's ministers to make such a decision at the very height of reform, at the most critical juncture. Their next move was to request an emergency meeting with me.

I realized that I was demoralizing them with the four proposed dismissals, but I had my own troubles. The Congress was planning to issue a negative review of the government's performance. If the Congress passed such a resolution, it would mean that emergency amendments to the Constitution would be passed at this or the next session.* That would spell the end of a reform that had never even gotten off the ground. I tried to speak calmly, very calmly, so that my decisions would not look like those of a typical angry boss. But these proud young people perceived my calm as chilliness and distance. The next day, Gaidar came to the Congress, asked for the floor, and submitted the government's collective resignation. This was like a punch in the face.

First, I must point out that for once, Gaidar had made a major political decision completely independent of Burbulis. No one expected it, although it was outwardly so logical, simple, and normal that I cannot understand now why the deputies were so upset.

Second, I had not expected the whole government's resignation because it had not been coordinated with anyone. Initially, it was an unpleasant surprise, but soon I came to appreciate Gaidar's move. It was a very important watershed. Gaidar had intuitively sensed the very nature of the Congress: it was a large political spectacle, a great circus where only the most dramatic and breathtaking tricks and turns could carry the day.

The victory was total: Congress withdrew its resolution calling for the resignation of the four economic ministers. Amendments were made to the Constitution granting additional powers to the president. The next Congress was postponed to the fall. The resignation of Gaidar and his ministers was rejected.

However, as I noted, some definite modifications in the government's work was something I, as its leader, was calling for myself. This was not merely a matter of pressure from the deputies. A month after the Congress, I revisited this issue. Convening the Cabinet of Ministers, I announced the dismissal of Lopukhin.

I remember two faces: one was scarlet, almost crimson—that was Gaidar; the other was as white as a sheet—that was Lopukhin. It was hard to look at them. The young ministers probably thought

*The amendments concerned the relationship and powers of the president and government vis-à-vis the parliament; the use of popular referendums to decide important issues, including constitutional principles; and the federation treaty with Russia's constituent republics.—Trans.

that, like a mean teacher, I had been saving up something nasty and was now taking them out for a whipping with the birch rod in punishment for their disobedience. That wasn't the case at all. There was a very concrete reason for Lopukhin's dismissal. Using him as a battering ram, Gaidar was putting pressure on me to release prices on energy resources simultaneously with other prices without any restrictions. Future historians will determine which one of us was right, but I will always remember Lopukhin's deathly pale face.

At what point in our relations did Rutskoi's famous anti-Yeltsin speech occur? Evidently Rutskoi had very early on cultivated an overly familiar style—the swaggering style of holding "meetings with the public," "telling it like it is, no matter how painful." Then one day I remember an assistant came running to me, wide-eyed, with a cassette of Rutskoi's speech. Nobody had hidden a recorder in Rutskoi's pocket; the tape was simply made from television, over which he had broadcast—to put it politely—his invectives.

"What do you think I should say to the president—give me your wallet. Here's three thousand rubles. Go see if you can survive on that!" These were the kinds of things Rutskoi—*my* vice president—said on television. I could forgive him if he just didn't understand Gaidar's program. I could even forgive him for wanting to score points, wanting to sound off in front of an audience in order to pump up his own belligerent spirit. That I could see. But what I couldn't see was why Rutskoi would look me straight in the eye and vow eternal loyalty. Why did he hint at webs of intrigue, behind-the-scenes scheming, when it was all so obvious that *he* was the problem? After all, there were tapes and transcripts of his talks blasting the government. Still, I concluded at the time that this was merely the honest blustering of a military man who just didn't get the subtleties of politics or economics. It happens. I had not yet realized that in fact it was treachery.

The media constantly raised the issue of some economic lobbyist putting pressure on the government and on me personally. I found these contrived articles somewhat humorous. I don't know the details of how lobbying works in the West, in America, for example. I imagine the lobbyists deploy their full arsenals, starting with indirect payoffs and ending with campaigns in the press.

People in our country talk about the military-industrial complex as being behind everything. They invoke the name of Arkady Volsky,* the directors of defense plants, the generals, the party apparatchiks—and you begin to imagine some sort of secret plot, a shadow Cabinet.

In fact, it's quite easy to lobby in Russia, even against such an inflexible prime minister as Gaidar. The fact is that I myself worked for decades in the Soviet system of economic management.† It has no secrets from me. I know just what terrible shape things are in and what real life is like in both the large and small industrial enterprises. I know the best and the worst features of our plant directors, workers, and engineers. Despite the fact that I am a builder by profession (and that has unquestionably left its mark on me), I am well acquainted with both heavy and light industry. As a party official in Sverdlovsk, I had to become deeply involved in this political cauldron.

So if some middle-aged industrialist comes to me and says in a worried voice, "Boris Nikolayevich, I have worked for forty years in the petroleum industry. What is your Lopukhin doing? Such-and-such is happening. There are such-and-such statistics. It's a nightmare; everything's going to hell in a handbasket," of course I lose my patience. I feel I have to make some changes.

My first attempt to add Yuri Skokov or Vladimir Lobov, two seasoned former factory directors, to the government for the sake of balance was haughtily rebuffed by Gaidar. Still, seeing that the young government was up to its neck in problems (I had been meeting with the ministers at a mandatory official session every Thursday), I was forced to bring in some energetic plant directors.

*Volsky was an aide to Andropov when he was general secretary and was a central committee official who occupied a number of important posts in the Soviet era. He now heads the Russian Union of Industrial Managers and Entrepreneurs, essentially a lobbying organization for large government-subsidized industries. In the December 1993 elections, Volsky's party, Civic Union, a centrist group favoring gradual reform to protect the large industries, took less than 5 percent of the votes and therefore gained no seats in parliament. Nevertheless, as recent government appointments suggest, at least some of the industrialists have considerable influence. Volsky has been portrayed by both the Soviet and the Western media as a dark figure who influences the government behind the scenes with his extensive contacts in the military-industrial complex.—Trans.

†In a planned Socialist economy, such figures took the place of executives of corporations in the West.—Trans.

What is a plant director in Russia? First off, he's the man who gives you a job and makes it possible for your family to live, who can fire you or promote you on the career ladder. It doesn't matter whether he runs a government factory that has privatized by forming a joint stock company or a factory still subsidized by the state. The fact is, the actual director of the factory is the one who decides your individual fate.

After consulting with the appropriate parliamentary committees, two people were nominated for government positions: Georgy Khizha and Vladimir Shumeiko. (Several months later, Viktor Chernomyrdin was brought forward.)

What was behind all these Cabinet reshuffles? I will speak of Lopukhin as a separate case. He was a talented economist, one of the most capable ministers in Gaidar's government. But obviously, the gas and oil industry was critical to our entire pricing policy. Would energy prices be free or controlled? Any blunder here would reverberate through the whole economic system of the country since every branch of industry depended on energy. I made a deliberate decision to remove Lopukhin from his post and put Chernomyrdin (whom I knew from my days in the Urals) in the government. I also saw that reform was going full throttle: it was creating entirely new economic realities—raw materials and commodities markets, a securities market, a revived and renewed banking system and stock market in Russia, which was turning Russian trade upside down. There had been nothing like it since the days of Lenin's New Economic Program.

When I realized these results of reform, I wanted to to guarantee this new policy a long life with some strong new driving figure. In time I was proved correct. Chernomyrdin came into play much later, but his appointment ensured continuity in the government's economic policy, given the parliament's reactionary storming of the government early in 1993.

The story with the ministers of health and education were completely different, but in some ways their fates were similar to Lopukhin's. Health Minister Vorobyov came to the government with Gaidar, and Education Minister Dneprov was appointed approximately a year before that. Both were middle-aged, mature, original thinkers and major specialists in their fields. Dneprov is famous for being a mutineer in the hide-bound Academy of Pedagogical Sciences. He put together his own team in the Ministry of Education and developed a whole new plan for revamping the post-Communist Russian school system. Vorobyov came to the government with fresh ideas for reforming the health care system. The difference was that Dneprov had come in a year earlier, when the old regime was still in place and the rigidly hierarchical system still worked and people obeyed their bosses. With this type of subordination, he was actually able to put some new education policies into practice. But by the time Vorobyov came, the health care system of which he was to take charge was collapsing.

No one could keep track of the changes or go along with them for a very simple reason: the staff of the ministry simply ceased to function. The health care system was a very sore point in our society in both the literal and metaphorical political meaning. As soon as some incomprehensible reforms began in the system of free neighborhood clinics, turbulent discussions erupted about out-of-pocket medical expenses, and people really had second thoughts. Although private schools with tuition were fairly rare (they irritated everyone for some reason, although I could never understand why: if you don't like them, then don't go to them), talk of fees for medical care made everyone nervous. Vorobyov's advocacy of private doctors in a new health care system gained the most attention and gave it negative publicity; the positive prospect of wealthy clinics and highly paid doctors was ignored—and with good reason. Unlike economic reform as a whole, any health care reform leading to paid treatment would have to be done in planned stages over a number of years.

The parliament's selection of which targets in the government to shoot down was most likely finalized on the eve of the sixth Congress, and showed the hands of those who had made the deal for the resignations with the parliamentary factions. Volsky's Civic Union set its sights on the Fuel and Energy and Foreign Economic Relations ministries since the new policies in these areas were feared to be most detrimental to their industrialists. The alliance of Communists and Russian nationalists, known as patriots, focused on the social issues like health care since their constituents were keen to retain the free social services they had enjoyed under the old Soviet system. At this stage of the game, the appetites of these lobbies were not especially large.

Reforms in education and medicine were not premature; on the contrary, they were long overdue. The story of these failed ministers, although fairly localized and not terribly significant, is a clear indication of another vulnerability in our overall program: it was too hard to conduct reforms in all areas at once.

In early and mid-1992, people talked of nothing but the coming wave of strikes. Economists predicted that the fall of production would lead to massive unemployment. The political opponents of reform in the parliament said the population would not endure the avalanche of price hikes and would go into the streets to demonstrate, banging their empty pots and pans. Suddenly, there was a terrible shortage of cash, and whole regions did not receive their wages or pensions for months. But in 1992, none of these scary predictions came true. In reality, only two groups of the population really began to make their demands—teachers (along with day-care workers) and miners.

The plight of day-care workers was indeed deplorable, and even in Moscow, their wages were ridiculously low. Only their human sense of responsibility for the fate of little children kept the workers, young girls and women, from staging an unprecedented action—a strike in the day-care centers, which would have caused terrible losses throughout the entire economy in every area where women worked.

The same was true of the plight of schoolteachers, although it was perhaps not as egregious. However, the problems of the teachers and caregivers could not be taken in isolation from government employees in general, whose wages came out of the state budget. The rise in prices, spiraling inflation, and the tail-spin economy placed whole groups of the population in total dependence—literally for their survival—on what kind of social welfare policy we could devise. Despite some isolated actions by teachers in various cities, on the whole, they did not seek open confrontation.

We prepared a single pay-rate system for state employees, including teachers, throughout all the branches of the economy. Salaries were increased. Of course raising the minimum wage bounces the whole wage structure, and it is not as flexible and as efficient as everyone would like. But I hope we'll live to see stable times.

Everyone knew that the miners had a special relationship with me, ever since the days in 1989 when the interregional group called for a general strike and they responded with one of their own political demands: the resignation of Gorbachev. To be sure, as part of Ukraine, Donbas was now on Leonid Kravchuk's conscience. Vorkuta and Kuzbas were coal-mining areas I had visited a number of times and to which I would certainly return. Their demands were harshly formulated at times, and they expected a great deal from me, but they supported me during the tough reforms.

We have a saying in Russia that when you chop wood, the chips fly. Although Khasbulatov tried his best to portray the miners as economic chips flying from the Gaidar team's woodcutting, their demands did not fit the picture. These miners were not against reform. Nevertheless, they did try to defend their economic interests, insisting that such hard work should be rewarded with part of the overall profits from the industry. Unfortunately, we did not have precise mechanisms to turn such enterprises as coal mines into joint stock companies. There were long, hard negotiations under way constantly.

I must say that in the spring and summer of 1992, when the word *stoppage* resounded throughout the country (the work stoppage on trains with coal, the stoppage on factory floors, the stoppage of transportation), my aide Yuri Skokov very courageously conducted the negotiations with the miners.

I met Yuri Skokov when I worked at the Moscow City Executive Committee. He was director of Quantum, a large defense plant, and he had run for elections to the Soviet parliament against Vitaly Korotich, a prominent writer and journalist who at the time was editor in chief of *Ogonyok* [*Little Flame*], a pioneer of glasnost. Due to various backroom deals and party scheming (described in *Against the Grain*), Skokov won the election and proved himself to be a disciplined party protégé.

Skokov is an intelligent man—that is the first thing that must be said about him. And very hard and taciturn. Many people were asking what his role was in my inner circle. It was a legitimate question. Skokov was actually the "shadow" prime minister whom I had always had in mind. Both Silayev, under whom Skokov chaired the Supreme Economic Council,* and Gaidar, on whose watch Skokov became chairman of the Security Council, sensed a latent threat

*Formed in October 1991 under the USSR Supreme Soviet, or legislature, to set policy.—Trans.

emanating from Skokov. They both had numerous arguments with me about him.

I have not yet mentioned Skokov's role during the August 1991 coup, and it was significant, perhaps more important than some of the official and public leaders of the White House defense. As my representative, Skokov met with Pavel Grachev and Boris Gromov, who represented the army and the Interior Ministry, respectively. These top-secret meetings were crucial and played a decisive role, psychologically at the very least. Skokov kept a low profile at the time, and that certainly impressed me. Nevertheless, I realized that Skokov's overall political views, not to mention his position on economic reform, were distinctly different from mine, from Gaidar's, or even from Burbulis's. This discrepancy was also of concern to my supporters. I think Skokov realized that in today's Russia you had to work for a strong government, not against it. Indeed, what was wrong with that? Although only a shadow prime minister, Skokov, who had long enjoyed political authority among executives in the party and economic system, was a thorn in the side of the real prime minister. (Incidentally, Skokov is the only politician from the executive branch who was provided a large office in the White House by the leadership of the Supreme Soviet.)

By the end of 1992, Skokov began to behave strangely. Whenever we would meet, he would so fervently and so frequently claim "Boris Nikolayevich, I'm the only one who is loyal to you; all the others around you are enemies" that it started me wondering. Perhaps he was the one with a persecution mania.

I think that this very strong person found it quite difficult to throw in his lot with us. Long a figure with considerable clout, Skokov's service in the new democratic government of Russia was surely a marriage of convenience to preserve his influence. Such adjustments come hard. Knowing of the resistance gaining in parliament and privy to a great deal of information from various sources, Skokov could not make up his mind and finally take a side. That demolished him, or at least caused him to break.

Perhaps we'll see this semiofficial shadow prime minister in politics again. I hope so, but as a person who is more straightforward.

In the summer of 1992 before my trip to the United States, I made an announcement at the airport that Yegor Gaidar was now appointed acting chairman of the Council of Ministers of Russia.

This meant that the real prime minister's office would not remain vacant for long. Both Burbulis and Gaidar himself put me in a rather tight spot. The old model—having a political figure to head the cabinet while the first deputy was really the one to run the economy—was out the window. Not a single one of the deputy prime ministers appointed to positions in the Gaidar team could aspire to leadership. But Gaidar himself was increasingly taking the reins of government into his own hands, and he began to be feared and respected even in parliament, despite a continuing barrage of criticism from Khasbulatov.

By this same summer of 1992, another economic issue moved to the center of politics—the IMF's [International Monetary Fund] granting of large loans and the creation of a fund to stabilize the ruble. Western experts had always assumed Gaidar would play a key part in this effort. Given these realities, I made my choice to upgrade Gaidar seemingly under the pressure of circumstances, unexpectedly and rashly. Gaidar's opponents were at least prevented from organizing a massive attack against him. They missed the moment; many people were already receiving the news of Gaidar's appointment with happiness and hope.

By the end of the summer, the economy was obviously cracking along two fault lines. It was impossible to attempt any economic measures or plan an economy when prices on everything were constantly jumping. And it was impossible to hold down inflation without any strategy to freeze wages; that is, with a supreme soviet that wanted to have wages keep pace with prices. This inflationary period was threatening to go on for years. Inflation meant that whole groups of the population were slipping below the poverty line, and with the sharp stratification of society, the wealth of some contrasted with the poverty of others.

The country was entering into a difficult period of social alienation. This was the depressing picture that we discovered after conducting the initial analysis of the economic reforms. Could all of these troubles have been avoided? I don't think so. Every country has to go through a patch like this, through an economic isolation ward, a cordon sanitaire on the way to prosperity. Even America, the richest of all the richest countries, had its Great Depression. The Americans' path to a high standard of living was long and hard.

But Russia, as always, is an entirely special case. Having embarked on the path to the market at the end of the last century, it is setting off on this route at the twilight of this century. It is making the transition even after Argentina and Poland, Chile and Brazil, Hungary and Singapore. The enormous system of the world economy has virtually been formed already, and Russia has not yet found its niche in it. The departure from the civilized world for seventy-five years, during which an enormous Socialist industry was built, kept us from progressing naturally into the market. Nobody is waiting for us there now. Repeatedly in our history, we have had to break into it ourselves, to reject the chimera of stability, the stability of a semi-free and semi-impoverished life. Once again, we've got to catch up, strain every muscle, and make super efforts merely to become like everyone else. The parade of these grand Russian leaps must end at some point. We must admit that despite whatever economic problems we have in common with any other country of the world, we have a different destiny. After seventy-five years of socialism, it is doubly different.

A country of large plants, large institutions, large agribusinesses, large enterprises (and even entire factory towns) will inevitably reproduce the type of relationships established under serfdom: the style of a solid, traditional interdependence. Opposing this old world are ephemeral commercial organizations that are still not safe from any kind of robbery, and which cannot guarantee their partners anything, although they are very flexible. It will take a long time for these two worlds to graft together and interpenetrate. I think it will be at least a few years. Until that happens, employees can flow easily back and forth from the state to the private sector, protecting themselves and their families from the worst with this mobility. But we shouldn't impose our priorities, our binding obligations in this subtle matter. A strong state should extend a hand to citizens where it is treacherous and frightening, where trouble looms.

In turn, the state also needs a great deal from society. Besides democratic guarantees and the correct international policy, it needs decency and discipline from its citizens. This is not the American model, and not even the same market that possibly was expected in Russia in early 1992. Russia's special nature has made itself felt in the last two years in all its entirety. We have only to listen to it carefully.

And then everything will be all right.

A second summer in a row of economic reforms was again turning into a troubled winter full of gloomy predictions. Could such an outcome have been predicted? Could we have foreseen that Gaidar's reform would not bring what was expected—that is, rapid stabilization? Of course we could have. If people, especially those in high positions in the government, are mature, they should be realistic about changing their plans and how ideas are actually implemented in practice. But the economy was hostage to politics.

The fierce attack on the reforms by one party, and the backlash of propaganda and agitation and the rigorous defense of the Gaidarites by the others, prevented the government from functioning normally. It must also be admitted that the Supreme Soviet desperately resisted the stabilization measures when inflation had not yet reached the boiling point, when wage controls and tighter credit could have made a difference. Meanwhile, the parliament was mindful of the opportunity to seize control of the executive branch and demanded the replacement of the government with a new coalition government.

In and of itself the change of the government did not presage anything terrible. What *was* terrible was losing people's trust, conducting an inconsistent policy, and beginning to vacillate. What I did not see before me was a normal government with a leftist Socialist orientation. That I could have understood. Instead, there was a coalition government, which in our politically charged atmosphere would be explosive and, frankly, deadly. Did that mean we had to have a technocratic government made up of the former directors of large plants?

At some point I began to waver. A very serious meeting was held with Yuri Skokov, and he gave his consent to replace Gaidar in this crisis situation (the Seventh Congress of People's Deputies was approaching). I could not withstand massive pressure from parliamentary factions, parties, political movements, and economic schools, agricultural managers, and entrepreneurs. For different reasons, they demanded that Gaidar be replaced, and kept demanding and demanding.

The opposition's gloating over the Gaidar government's unfulfilled promises* threatened to escalate at the Congress into the usual

*I.e., to curb inflation, establish certain fiscal policies, and regulate mutual payments.—Trans.

harassment campaign, which would destabilize the country and undermine the authority of our policy and our ideas. What could possibly help us to avoid vacillation and stick to the radical economic program? I will try to answer.

On June 12, 1992, the first anniversary of Russia's new independence day,* hysterical followers of the neo-Communist leader Viktor Anpilov tried to take Ostankino Television Center by force. Anpilov, leader of an extremist neo-Communist movement called Working Moscow, formerly worked as a correspondent for Gostelradio (the Soviet state television and radio) in Nicaragua. People said that he was obsessed from his early youth with the idea of revolutionary romanticism. In real life he chose a rather dangerous role for himself: a street leader, a general of the barricades. Working Moscow was constantly demonstrating on the squares of central Moscow. Anpilov's role was dangerous both for himself and for those of us around him because he personally never had to risk anything, whereas society was to learn the first lessons of organized Russian terrorism—Anpilov was not above inciting violence.

It was particularly despicable of Anpilov to draw belligerent old people to his demonstrations. I could understand their feelings and their gut reaction to what was happening around them during Russia's reforms. But to turn them into demonstrators, to push them in front of policemen's billy clubs, and then pay them a little something to stretch their pension for this? That wasn't revolutionary romanticism—that was just cynicism.

Nothing of this kind ever occurred during the larger rallies of democrats, millions strong. There were no calls to violence and no victims. Order prevailed throughout. The people's deputies took complete responsibility for the safety of their marches and, if necessary, dispersed them with the help of OMON after first making an agreement with the authorities.

Anpilov's militants, however, had a completely different attitude. They were out for blood. Violence would prove that the authorities were incapable of handling the situation, and would be a sign of trouble and anarchy. So they strove to shed blood at any cost.

*June 12, 1991, was the day the new Russian Constitution was ratified and Yeltsin was elected as the first Russian president.—Trans.

Then the true nature of these "popular expressions" came out, as the Supreme Soviet and its speaker, Khasbulatov, would call them. Despite the large number of elderly people and the revolutionary red banners and other trappings of communism, these demonstrations used the purely fascist ploy of the sudden savage attack, one that neo-Nazis all around the world have used. Anpilov followers massed around Ostankino, and as middle-aged women and technicians left work at the television station, they shouted crude swear words and filthy anti-Semitic curses at them. They beat up video engineers on their way home after the night shift. As young policemen formed a ring around the demonstration, the demonstrators beat the cops on the head, trying to cause them permanent injury.

It was obvious that these were dangerous people. Or actually, dangerous people were behind these virulent demonstrations—provocateurs who perhaps enjoyed the secret support of influential government officials. Without strong backing, it is impossible to instigate a violent situation like this in Moscow. It simply cannot be done. After I watched the television footage for ten minutes, my heart sank with awful dread. I was struck by the faces of those demonstrators outside Ostankino. This was not some spontaneous explosion of outrage but a well-orchestrated attempt to put pressure on the government. They were trying to probe the "populist Yeltsin's" main sore point—dependency on people's moods, on the public's sympathy. Someone had decided that this artificially created popular explosion would be a very precise and fitting one.

I sensed that there were people somewhere trying to frighten me. I sensed that these pseudopopular uprisings were a crude hoax. I sensed the hand of my old friends, the KGB.

After Midnight

Who were my real friends? Although it seems simple at first, that was a very difficult question. I am a fairly open person by nature; I love to be in a group of people, a circle of close friends, with joking, partying, and singing. But all of my real "classic" friends, so to speak, the friends of my childhood, remained in Sverdlovsk, a city in the Ural Mountains, which has now been restored to its prerevolutionary name, Ekaterinburg. The friends of those days were named Misha Karasik, Yasha Olkov, Andrei

Mogilnikov, and there were other kids. I shared everything with them when we were young. Out of that circle, out of the people of my generation, my wife has remained with me, and is very close to me. She and I are the same age and the start of our life stories was very similar. She is probably the only person who really understands me completely.

People often cite the names of officials from Sverdlovsk, various people whose acsension to power was supposedly made possible due to personal affiliation with me. These include my aide Ilyushin, and Burbulis (whom I didn't even know at all when we were in Sverdlovsk) Lobov, and Petrov, another assistant. My relationships with these people are not those of childhood friends. They are the relations of team players, partners, built on a recognition of professional qualities and a striving to select a strong group of people who shared my thinking.

Incidentally, when I fell out of favor in 1987, as I wrote in my first book, it was my Sverdlovsk friends from my student days who came to visit me. By contrast, my deputies from my party work in Sverdlovsk behaved rather reservedly during that time, and some even tried to avoid me altogether. I never held a grudge against them, however, because I realized that rationality rather than emotions dominated our relationships. Without nursing any grievance, I summoned some of them back to work with me again when the time was right.

For more than thirty years now, I've been a boss—that's exactly what people of my social class in Russia are called. Not a bureaucrat, not an official, not a director, but a boss. I can't stand the word—there's something about it that smacks of the chain gang. But what can you do? Perhaps being first was always a part of my nature, but I just didn't realize it in my early years.

I remember how disgusted I felt when I was transferred from Sverdlovsk and made head of the construction department in the party's central committee in Moscow. It was a minor post in the central committee that seemed a let-down after running such an enormous region like Sverdlovsk. But how the atmosphere changed when Gorbachev was "installed in Moscow" and we could really get down to work. In fact I can feel alive only in a demanding situation on the job.

There are numerous bugbears in the profession of politician. First, ordinary everyday life suffers. Second, there are many temptations to ruin you and those around you. And I suppose, third, and this is rarely discussed, people at the top generally have no friends. You develop a kind of insularity and exercise incredible caution in dealing with people. All of this is true of me—the insularity, the caution in speaking with new acquaintances. Even so, I do have some friends.

I first met Shamil Tarpishchev in the summer of 1987 in the Baltic resort town of Jurmala, Latvia. He was coaching the national tennis team training for the Davis Cup match to be held in Holland (he was a senior coach at the time), and he invited me to a match and brought tickets. We spoke of how tennis is poorly developed in our country, wondering why it wasn't as popular here as elsewhere in the world and what was needed to make it so. I asked him to visit my office at the party committee, but he didn't come. Instead, when some other sports official came in his place, I was impressed with Tarpishchev's modesty—he hadn't tried to personally take advantage of our acquaintance.

A year later I accidentally ran into him again in Jurmala, literally nose to nose, when I was in disfavor. He and the people he was then coaching were playing soccer on the beach. He ran after the ball and ran smack into me, and put out his hand in surprise. We were both happy to have this chance meeting, and exchanged a few words. He asked what I was doing and wondered whether I would like to play some tennis. Shamil asked me to play doubles with him. I declined. I don't know how he had guessed that I was still learning to play tennis. I had never spoken to him about it; apparently, he figured it out when I watched him for a long time teaching some boy how to play. That was how it all began.

Then we met at the Friendship Athletic Complex in Moscow where Shamil had brought his kids for training. Finally, in the fall of 1990, when he was president of the Tennis Federation (I even joked that he was already president and I wasn't yet), I invited Shamil to visit me on vacation in Sochi, to do some coaching and to play some tennis. The first thing I experienced in playing doubles with him was a wonderful emotional relaxation. There is no monotony. Each person opens up in the game in his own way, and that is a great feeling—when there is an almost silent dialogue as you hit the ball. When you oppose an individual and his character, it's good to know that next to you another man is lending you support. I instantly felt in Shamil a real understanding, without saying anything.

When I became president, I immediately offered him a job as presidential sports adviser. After he accepted my offer, he refused to make any contracts in foreign currency or accept any lucrative foreign work. There were so many miserable athletes—both famous and unknown—in our country's sports. How many peoples' lives had been broken under the Soviet style of competition? Shamil decided to take on all these problems, not as a bureaucrat or an official but as a former professional athlete. Shamil often has a hard time in this job. He sometimes gets frustrated from his lack of familiarity with the customs of government bureaucracy and the psychology of officials, and yet he must deal with them every day. I try to help. Not as the president, but as a friend.

Rumors circulate constantly during a tennis game, or at the steam baths, or in some informal gathering that certain people, unknown to the public, some dark anonymous types, manage to worm their way into the president's confidence, to influence him and prod him to take certain decisions. These rumors are persistently spread among ordinary people. I don't think it's an accident. Exploiting my dislike for public appearances on television, someone is trying to project an image to the public of a weak politician subject to pressure.

I have tried to show in this chapter how various decisions are made, and how difficult and burdensome that can be. Whether they are right or wrong, they are always the result of a very difficult choice.

7

A ROUGH PATCH

Editor's Note: Yeltsin tells of his growing battle with parliament, culminating with his decision to call a referendum to reaffirm his leadership. His feud with Rutskoi and parliament speaker Ruslan Khasbulatov assumes overwhelming importance, gradually eroding the momentum of reform. Yeltsin characterizes this as the most difficult chapter of the book for him, leading to a crisis he portrays as "so bitter, so insane."

I have called this chapter "A Rough Patch" with good reason. The events of October 3 and 4, 1993, which shook the world, belong to that bad stretch in the road when the country was constantly being jolted by congresses and Supreme Soviet sessions, when the front pages of the newspapers ran polls on the public's confidence in me, when a lawful instability declared by the legislature engulfed the country. Outwardly, this seemed like a triumph of democracy. Now, like Italy, we had a protracted government crisis, attempts by the parliament to replace the prime minister, and attempts by me to reach an agreement with the parliament. We were "just like everybody else"—everything was normal.

This period of open confrontation started with the April 1993 referendum, in a civilized, lawful manner, as it seemed to me. It was just a matter of hammering out an agreement for new elections; but that was not to be, and it was impossible to end this story peacefully. The White House was stormed. That meant we weren't "just like everybody else." That meant this wasn't just an ordinary parliamentary struggle—a fight for this or that law, this or that government, this or that policy.

No, this was a fight against me, first a subterranean opposition, then a more and more open conflict. This was a fight to change the foundations of the state. To define it even more precisely, this was a long, carefully orchestrated attempt to overthrow the government. If I had realized sooner that this parliament would not pass a new Constitution under any conditions, that it was incapable of coming to any agreement or of creating laws, there wouldn't have been any bloodshed. There wouldn't have been any innocent victims. There wouldn't have been that moral shock we all felt. There wouldn't have been the schism among the democratic groupings in society that threatened to escalate into a new crisis.

What brought us to this rough patch, when the chief forces were taking shape and the major players of the future coup were coming to agreement? First, it was the constitutional crisis. Although the president had taken an oath to the Constitution and a constitutional duty, the Constitution totally restricted his rights. Second, there was the August 1991 coup syndrome. The new Russia had come in spite of the state of emergency, brought into being by the defense of democracy. But to break the law? That was a serious moral and psychological barrier, not only a legal one.

Third, only by observing from very far away could it seem that the president and the parliament were eternally fighting like gladiators in the ring. Many deputies had left parliament to come over to the government, taking fairly high posts.* The work of parliamentary committees and commissions yielded much that was useful, but in fact these laws were not always passed in the same form they were drafted. The political schism did not happen all at once, but gradually over time. It was a very complicated, subtle, and sometimes elusive process.

A number of factors influenced the logic of events. One rather significant factor was the Russian *avos'*—a little word translated as "perhaps," "just in case," or "what if." By the way, I do not use this ancient Russian notion to mean the carefree, light-minded, or lazy attitude that might be interpreted as the dreamy Russian "what if."

*For example, Sergei Filatov, formerly Khasbulatov's deputy, who came to work as Yeltsin's chief of administration.—Trans.

Rather, it is our national trait of an inherent belief in something better. It is a hope for a happy ending, the faith that "God sees everything" and everything will be all right. In contemplating this national trait, I thought to myself: will we really take up arms, after seventy-five years of Soviet rule, so agonizing and protracted, to prove who is more important, the parliament or the president? Were all those constitutional amendments, congresses, resolutions, and votes designed only to shake the country, and undermine the stability we had achieved with such difficulty?

Were there really people who wanted a revolution?

Every day, for a year and a half, people watched the parliament on television. For a year and a half, the deputies spoke at these congresses and sessions, and most of their speeches were blatant attempts to discredit me and my policy, to prove that I was incapable of running the country. But if these many months of agitation had not been enough to damage me, if the April 1993 referendum had confirmed the president's authority, what question could there be? We should come to an agreement about new elections. We should think of what to do next.

None of it worked out.

Journal Entry, November 6, 1992

On the eve of the traditional celebration of the October Revolution (November 7), I met with Khasbulatov in the Kremlin. The meeting lasted from 6:30 P.M. to 11:30 P.M. We did not have some kind of systematic discussion, but touched upon a variety of issues. Khasbulatov sat, incessantly smoking his pipe, practically not taking it out of his mouth the whole time. He began to turn green from so much tobacco. We were drinking a dry white Georgian wine called Tsinandali, and we also discussed our personal lives. He told me about his domestic cares—his mother was in Chechnya, his homeland, an autonomous republic within the Russian Federation. Lots of his immediate relatives were there as well. General Dudayev, the region's dictator, was essentially holding them all hostage.

I asked Khasbulatov why he wasn't getting along with Filatov, his former deputy who was now my chief of administration. He blamed Filatov for everything, although I think that Khasbulatov was absolutely wrong here. Filatov is a very reasonable, decent person who just couldn't tolerate Khasbulatov's despotic manner.

I recall the moment back in 1990 when I settled on the choice of Khasbulatov as nominee for the position of deputy speaker of the parliament. Unfortunately, there was a real element of accident in my selection. I hadn't known him at all in the past, and when the nomination of reformist lawyer Sergei Shakhrai failed to pass three successive votes (the conservative part of the Congress refused to accept him), I convened a reconciliation commission. Many candidates were named by this commission—about fifteen people. I understood that we had to find some compromise figure, some little known deputy who wouldn't be proposed by either democrats or conservatives, which would only lead to a deadlock. That was how Khasbulatov emerged as a candidate. As a non-Russian, a Chechen, the other non-Russian republics of Russia supported him. His background was quite ordinary: he was an academic who had taught political economy.* On the whole, the reconciliation commission supported Khasbulatov and his nomination passed easily when it was put to a vote. When I worked as chairman (or speaker) of the parliament, Khasbulatov supported me very enthusiastically, sought my advice on every issue, and did not interfere in larger political matters.

Our conversation sometimes took a rather harsh turn. I have known Khasbulatov now for a while and have studied his Oriental nature. He always prepares several opinions on the same issue, then expresses only one of them aloud, keeping the others up his sleeve to pull out if necessary. On the surface, there seemed to be ordinary, businesslike conversation, but the internal dynamics of the encounter were incredibly tense. Each of us wanted to be leader, but for him, it seemed to me it was some kind of innate passion.

I had begun our meeting with a harsh reproach: you say one thing to my face, and then you go and do something else behind my back. Recently at a seminar in the city of Cheboksary in the Chuvash region, where the heads of Russia's legislative and executive branches had assembled, I had attempted to resolve the conflict between parliament and the government. I said to the Supreme Soviet: let's cooperate. I extended a hand and met them halfway.

*For many years this had amounted to lecturing from a Marxist perspective.—Trans.

Then, when the session opened, I tried to make another gesture. The response was utter silence. How could that be?

Khasbulatov said yes, we were wrong; we should have reacted to your gesture immediately and officially, and I'll do that in the next few days. We'll pass a political statement at the Supreme Soviet, saying that we support the president, and his statement in Cheboksary, and the parliament will show that it, too, is ready to meet halfway . . .

It is an abnormal situation when two branches of government cannot get along. Nevertheless, it was important to remove people's tension, and therefore I agreed to his proposal. It wasn't so terrible that the statement would come a month later than it should have. The main thing was to defuse the atmosphere before the Congress.

Let's not bring shame on ourselves and squabble in front of the Russian public and the whole world, I said to Khasbulatov. That is, if there are nonparliamentary forms of behavior on the part of the deputies or any of the groupings, as chairman you should immediately put a stop to such things, turn off the microphone, and tell the troublemakers to go sit down.

Khasbulatov seemed to agree.

It's high time to cut short this entry. Khasbulatov also talked about the constitutional amendments, and the most difficult subject, the composition of the government. We went over each name on the list. Khasbulatov's list consisted of ten names and coincided with the proposals of the industrial lobbyists in Civic Union. Plus there was this little ploy: let's leave Gaidar, but bring in new ministers under him. That was an outrage! Gaidar would never agree to it. I tried to steer clear of any discussion of Burbulis.

Only now do I understand that Khasbulatov deliberately dragged me into this exhausting, debilitating relationship. That was his chief modus operandi: to threaten resistance and force me to withdraw, to make concessions, and then to cut off my tail piece by piece. Finally, he would push me into a blowup. Surely, he didn't seriously believe I was afraid of this rather passive, amorphous parliament that at the moment was controlled only by Khasbulatov's will, indeed by a mere flick of his eyebrow? Surely, he didn't think I would be so frightened that I would drastically change the political strategic course? In short, this was not a search for a compromise—something in which I believed at the time—but a playing at compromise, a mere pretense.

Once I was riding in my car past a rally of either nationalist patriots or Communists—I don't remember which was the larger group since they often demonstrated together. I think it was the Communists. I stopped and saw a middle-aged Russian woman carrying a large red banner on a pole, mechanically waving back and forth like a pendulum, as if she were a marionette on a string. She was swooping the banner in lazy circles up and down, monotonously chanting all the while: "Down, down down . . ." I asked Korzhakov to go up and ask her: down *with whom?* She told him to go to hell.

Unfortunately, Khasbulatov was someone who was born to jerk the strings of people like this woman with the flag.

Khasbulatov should be viewed outside the context of the Supreme Soviet. In principle there are people with heads on their shoulders there, people who actively draft laws, budgets, and domestic and foreign policies. But in the years that Khasbulatov has been speaker, these thinking people—although they apparently had nothing better to do—could not come up with a plan for Russia's development. Khasbulatov pumped up the political opposition for two whole years, but all they could come out with was hot air. All they could do was shout or scream scary things with glassy eyes.

This was a severe and bitter moral lesson, and I sincerely feel sorry for our first parliament, but it must be admitted: Khasbulatov's leadership stunted its growth and turned some of the normal deputies into a political machine. It's too bad.

There is an opinion that our former parliament was a freak in the wonderful family of parliaments of the world, all of which were intelligent, decorous, and utterly democratic. But that's not completely the case. The words *congressman, deputy,* or *senator* in various languages is not surrounded by such a glowing halo. We have only to recall Mark Twain to realize that this elected body has long been associated in the minds of Western people with corruption, official sloth, and an inflated and empty self-importance. While this claim may be disputed, no one can deny that parliamentary activity is constantly beset with scandals and exposés.

The Congress conceived by Gorbachev was a horse of a different color. In fact, the Soviet Congress was not even a parliament with all the attributes of such a legislative body. The Congress created during perestroika was supposed to reflect the structure of

Soviet society—the Communist party had the best seats; the trade unions, athletes, and stamp collectors had specially set-aside seats,* along with the artist unions, and so on. Most notably, however, this parliament was filled with the former bosses of the Communist system. The problem is that at the time of the elections, no other figures had ever really been involved in political life, so people voted for them.

Russia is a large country, of course. But when you have fifteen hundred people in a hall, that's not a parliament or a senate but a popular assembly. It's difficult to make any decision because there are numerous factions trying to recruit adherents, plus a huge number of independent deputies. It's an arena of ruthless political scrapping, spasms of little groups forming, personal ambitions being flaunted. Most of all, it's hysterics, overheated emotions, and a matter of who can shout the loudest. It's pointless to speak with a quiet voice; the laws of large auditoriums and the psychological factors of speaking to a crowd (in this case, a crowd of popularly elected representatives) begin to operate. Not just I, but any president would be forced to put some gravel in his voice in order to get decisions passed, to move the agenda forward, to make an attack, and so on.

Everyone has an issue to raise. First it's an ethnic problem, then an economic one, then something to do with foreign policy. Sometimes these issues have nothing to do with the agenda. It's just that a deputy gets a burr under his saddle and takes on the whole parliament all by himself.

At the Seventh Congress in December 1992, the confirmation of a permanent head of the government was to be on the agenda, and I was supposed to nominate a candidate. The battle was in earnest, so in addition to the work at the sessions, I had to meet with faction representatives, individual deputies, and regional heads of government. In other words, I poured an enormous amount of effort into the Seventh Congress—and all for only one purpose: to persuade the deputies to take my candidate. I begged, I pleaded, I prevailed upon

*The Soviet Congress of People's Deputies, elected in 1989, had set-asides for official Communist bodies as well as Communist-dominated quasi-public organizations like the stamp collectors' association or the society for the blind, which enabled apparatchiks ostensibly nominated by these interest groups to gain still more seats for the Communists in the parliament.—Trans.

the deputies not to demolish the reforms in Russia so that Gaidar could remain, and the Russian government could function normally.

Everyone expected that the draft of the new Constitution would be discussed at the Seventh Congress, but they were later disappointed. Everything was moved to a completely different plane—a discussion of amendments to the *old* Constitution still in effect.

On the surface, amending the Constitution seemed like a normal, logical course of action. We had originally adopted that plan when I had been chairman of the Russian Supreme Soviet. Through amendments, we introduced the notion of sovereignty, the post of president, the fundamental concept of private property, and so on. There was no time to pass a new Constitution. We were hurrying with economic reforms and left the political reforms for later. That was an oversight.

From a legal and political perspective, we could not go on forever jerking the Constitution around; this process of amending had to have some sort of logical limit. The amendments were already snowballing out of control and beginning to contradict each other. We began to get the chaotic effect of what scientists call Brownian motion: the amendments unsystematically piled up on each other, there was no logic, and no one understood anything. Instead, there was legislative anarchy.

The Congress was demanding oversight of all basic political and economic actions. That is, the bulk of the amendments I proposed for review were rejected by the Congress. That was all I had to show for a long and torturous battle, of all these anxious and exhausting discussions, all of this debate about amendments imposed by the Supreme Soviet.

When I could calmly reflect over what had happened, I realized that the parliament was suffering from collective insanity. Such a body cannot run a country. It was already smelling of a revolutionary situation. And the predominant scent of revolution is blood.

After Midnight

Today is November 7, the anniversary of the Great October Revolution. Although it has been overtaken by events, people go on celebrating it by habit, some snickering cynically as they look at the red banners. However, I have a certain strange attitude toward this holiday.

When I lived in Sverdlovsk, November 7 was always one of the most stressful workdays for me. Organizing public celebrations in a city the size of Sverdlovsk with a population of millions was a very demanding and exhausting job. Once on the eve of the holiday, I was on my way home there, with about sixty kilometers to go, when the driver veered off the road, and got royally stuck in a ditch.

What to do? It was dark out and nothing was visible. There was no telephone in the car, and it was impossible to get in touch with anyone in the city. We looked at the map and saw that it was eighteen kilometers to the next village. It was 11:00 P.M. at night, and I had to be in Sverdlovsk by 9:00 A.M. If I, the chief city official, did not appear at the November 7 celebration, the main national holiday, if I was not seen on the dais viewing the parade, it would be a catastrophe. This simply couldn't happen. People would think that either I had died or had been removed from office. But I hadn't died, no one had removed me, and I spent an hour and a half trying to pull the car out of the ditch. Around 1:00 A.M. it became clear we weren't going *any*where in that car. What would happen later that morning in Sverdlovsk?

November 7 in Sverdlovsk was not celebrated as it was in Moscow, where only representatives of collectives marched on Red Square and the demonstration lasted exactly one hour and forty minutes. In Sverdlovsk, people marched with their families, the entire town turned out, and the demonstration lasted four or five hours. I closed my eyes and imagined those endless columns of smiling people, carrying flags and flowers.

So the driver and I, up to our knees in snow in the pitch-black darkness, slogged toward the nearest village. I knew from experience that a person walking rapidly can make five kilometers an hour on a good road. Which meant that in this snow, we would shuffle up to the village long after the parade was over. It was about ten degrees below zero, but the steam was coming off us from exertion. The main thing was never to sit down, then you don't get tired . . . just *never* sit down. After a few hours, however, we were falling down from exhaustion. If we couldn't hold out any longer and sat down, in that one moment of relaxation we would be drawn toward sleep, and it would simply be impossible to get up again. So we kept walking along the plowed fields, not even on the highway.

Somehow, we made it to the village sometime after 3:00 A.M. As bad luck would have it, everyone in the village was dead drunk. No matter what door we knocked on, the residents were passed out cold. We kept asking for a telephone or where we could at least find a tractor, but nobody could answer. Obviously, they'd all had a head start on celebrating November 7.

Finally, we found a tractor. We took a tractor driver, who was drunk as well, and put him in the cab of the tractor with us. While we had been wandering around looking for help, it had gotten to be 6:00 A.M. I began to shiver. Show me where there's a telephone! I shouted to the tractor driver. Where's the telephone! He was completely out of it. In the end, some people managed to open the door of the rural government office where there was a phone and we reached the regional police chief. I told him that he must mount an operation and execute it rapidly and accurately as only he knew how. First, send a helicopter immediately. We'll drive on the tractor to a designated spot on the highway, where you can have someone meet us. Send a sober driver to replace the drunk one, so that he could drive the tractor back to the village. Think up a route through the city, so that I could get home from the airfield. (Traffic was already stopped at the start of the parade route; the columns were marching by now. I lived literally three minutes away from the main town square.) Go for it!

I had to be on the parade stand by 9:30 A.M., or at the outside no later than 9:40 A.M. By 9:00 A.M., we had reached the designated meeting place without incident, driving the tractor along the highway. The helicopter was already hovering overhead. By 9:15 A.M., an ambulance and a traffic police car were waiting by the helicopter as we landed. The traffic police worked beautifully, speeding through the city in a few minutes. The police stopped the parade for a few seconds, cutting it in half so we could slip through, and then the columns resumed their progress. With sirens blaring, we reached my home at 9:45 A.M. I already should have mounted the parade stand to speak at that moment. Everyone at home had been warned I was coming, and when I opened the door, the whole family threw themselves at me, each carrying a suit, a shirt, or a tie. I shaved while everyone dressed me. As the clock struck 10:00 A.M. on the dot, there I was on the stand. I had made it!

Today is November 7. People of the older generation or even of middle age have a strange feeling on this day. Who is Red and who is White?* Who were the heroes? Maybe there were no heroes. You couldn't tell. And who were we in our history? Slaves, cannon fodder? Was that all? Whatever the case, we cannot escape our destiny.

The incident of the highway breakdown was the kind that keeps haunting you, even in your dreams. Suddenly, you are seized by a feeling of utter helplessness—as we were in that snow, where we were stepping through the darkness into the unknown, into that village, which seemed to be under an evil spell. For some reason, it was absolutely necessary to get to that parade stand and not to bring shame on myself or to seem to have disappeared. It was a terrible anxiety.

Perhaps there was something mystical and symbolic about that episode. I think there is good reason why this scene replays in my dreams many times over. In the end, as in the original story, I always come through. But whenever I have the slightest feeling of helplessness or frustration, I am seized with the memory of that anxiety.

That was how it was during those difficult months.

Journal Entry, December 9, 1992

I came back to the dacha from the Congress in a complete trance. This was probably the first time in five years, since my expulsion from the politburo in 1987, that something like this had happened to me. I don't think that everything was accidental at that Congress, that everything was a coincidence, that my Achilles' heel could have been so carefully discerned.

I cannot stand public beatings when everyone gangs up on you and pounds you from every side. It's not so important what the fight is about. Even as a person ascends the speaker's platform, I can intuitively sense in his step a savage desire to strike a painful blow, an attempt to whip himself up, a purely negative, terrible impulse to hit. I understand these aggressive emotions in a battle, in an uncompromising fight; but when people gang up on one person, punching and kicking in a parliamentary debate, and there you are and you can't do anything about it . . .

With hindsight I saw that my feeling about this parliamentary drubbing was a repeat of the psychological blow I suffered after the

*The Russian Revolution led to a civil war between Reds, or Communists, and Whites, who opposed the Bolsheviks.—Trans.

plenum of the Moscow party city committee. Then, at Gorbachev's command, I was brought right from my hospital bed and stomped on for several hours in the best party tradition. (I wrote about that in my first book).

I took one look at my wife's and children's eyes and headed straight for the *banya* and shut myself in. I lay down on my back and closed my eyes. Frankly, my thoughts were in a whirl. This was not good . . . this was not good at all. Alexander Korzhakov was the one to drag me out of this pit. Somehow, he managed to open the door to the *banya,* and persuaded me to come back to the house. All in all, he helped me out as one human being does another. Then, as always, Naina absorbed the main blow herself. Gradually, I recovered from my depression.

One of my relatives then came up with an interesting suggestion. I should ask people to pick whom they wanted: me or them. The public would understand everything perfectly. I latched on to those words. Political scientists and legal scholars had long been suggesting a referendum to me. But the issues were couched in terms of deciding the fate of the Congress—should it be dissolved or not? I was not prepared to go that route. Here was a suggestion for an entirely new phrasing of the issue: do people want to go on living with the president or with the Congress? That evening, God himself inspired one of the people closest to me with this idea.

I immediately asked to be put through to Ilyushin. That night, I brought Shakhrai and some speechwriters in on the job. Besides me, four other people labored over this short speech. At the heart of the referendum idea was my conviction that during such terrible moments, I very much need the support of the simple people, the people from the street, the randomly selected people. Only from them do I draw vital strength when things are difficult, when everything has reached its limit.

Someone suggested that after the speech, an excursion to the Lenin Komsomol automobile factory or to a ball-bearing plant should be organized. I chose the auto plant.

I slept for two hours and then got up and went over my speech, working until morning. Even so, it was still too unpolished.

I recall who introduced me to Ruslan Khasbulatov. It was Sergei Krasavchenko, chairman of the Soviet parliament's committee on economic reform, a former member of the interregional deputies' group. When Khasbulatov left his office, Krasavchenko had this to say to me: "Boris Nikolayevich, you better watch yourself with that man. You can't turn your back on him for a second, he's that kind of man. You always have to make sure he's still behind you, don't you see?"

Only later did I recall these mysterious words, which then, frankly, had had no meaning for me. At that time, Khasbulatov seemed intelligent and reasonable. And unassuming.

His reserved quality was the main thing I noticed. In Professor Khasbulatov there was none of that obnoxiousness so repellent to my nature, that brutish, loutish energy typical of many party workers.

Valery Zorkin was one of the members of the constitutional commission. In fact, he was the most modest and unassuming of them all. When it came time for the Supreme Soviet to choose a chairman for the new constitutional court, it was decided to settle on Zorkin's candidacy as the most compromising one, a figure who would suit absolutely everyone! He wasn't left wing or right wing. He was objective. A professor and legal scholar. A quiet decent member of the intelligentsia.

What then happened to these people? Where did their insane drive for power come from? I don't know how the lives of these ordinary Moscow professors would have turned out if the new political era had not unexpectedly swept them to the top. Apparently, there is some mystery in every such "quiet" person who carefully and calculatedly presents himself as quiet and loyal to those around him. Perhaps as a child Zorkin wanted desperately to be a leader, to be head of his group, but someone crushed and humiliated him. Maybe it was the constant feeling that people around him did not appreciate him, did not understand what a great person he was—in school, at the institute. Or the girls were perhaps inclined to pay too much attention to outward appearances and could not look deeper inside . . .

Or else is it that we cannot fathom the depths of a purely rational mind, where everything is subordinate to common sense? We can read the tea leaves forever, but I have only one thing to say: the last years have convinced me that knowledge of people, experience in dealing with them, a kind of street smarts means nothing in politics today. Even the experience gained in such corridors of power as the central committee of the party simply doesn't help! Even there, the relationships between people were simpler, Soviet-style. Now in the new era, some other very strange mechanisms have begun to operate. Perhaps I will learn to figure them out.

The Khasbulatov–Zorkin tandem was very much in evidence at the Seventh Russian Congress of People's Deputies. Frankly, it was a sharp and unexpected blow. I had expected only an objective view of things from a judicial body, a neutrality, without mixing in politics. Experience dictated otherwise. The appearance of Zorkin on the speaker's platform signified a completely new era in the relations with the Congress. It was the beginning of an attempt to legally remove the president from office.

After Midnight

It seems that no matter what form of transportation I would take, I would end up in an accident—whether in planes, helicopters, cars, trucks, even on horses. Once when I was riding a sleigh as a little boy, a horse raced downhill and threw me out of my seat so hard I almost seriously injured myself.

The next accident to come along was far more serious—it was a train wreck. I was studying at the Ural Polytechnical Institute at the time and I used to travel home to visit my parents during the summer. Sometimes you wouldn't be able to get a ticket, or you'd buy one for a few stations away, merely to get on the train. You just had to know the art of avoiding the conductors.

That particular summer, the train was going at a good clip as it approached the next station. The car was reserved, with open upper and lower sleeping berths and a third luggage shelf "for students," as it was called since young people would wedge themselves up there. Opposite the berth was an open window, and I was standing below it in the corridor. Suddenly, I was thrown against the wall and the car began to tumble. One after another, the cars were falling, first those up ahead, then on down the line, each one pulling the other down the hill, a fairly steep slope.

It was hard, but I managed to get a leg up and jump out the window of our car, which was almost on end. I rolled downhill with my head tucked in and my arms outstretched. I rolled and rolled and finally landed in a swamp. At first I was frightened, but I managed to collect myself. I was unhurt except for some bumps and bruises, but there were dead and wounded people inside the train. I helped pull them out, yanking apart the twisted metal. It was a horrible accident. I didn't make it home until late at night.

It always seems as if someone is rescuing me. I've even begun to believe that I'm under some mysterious protection. It can't be that so much could crash on the head of just one person at every stage of his life. Literally every stage! And each such crisis could have ended in death.

Am I afraid of death? I don't know why, but for some reason I'm not, no matter how much you bang me around. I read in some magazine that an astrologist predicted a violent death for me during the year 1993. Well, let them predict.

Journal Entry, December 15, 1992

What compelled me to take the step of having a rating vote? After the speech I gave on December 10, 1992, I could have changed the situation drastically. Frightened by the threat of a referendum, the Congress backed off and made concessions. An agreement was made between the Congress and me under which the parliamentary factions could nominate candidates for the post of chairman of the government or prime minister, as many as fifty names if they wanted. I would select five people out of that list and present those names to the Congress for a "soft" rating vote, to see what simple percentage of votes each candidate would receive. Out of the three people who won a simple majority of votes, I would then select any one of them and offer this candidate to the Congress for approval.

This idea of a soft nonbinding vote was not mine: some lawyers suggested it from international practice. It was an extremely clever and unexpected move, and indeed soft. Instead of putting a candidate to a binding vote immediately, with a rating vote you were in fact conducting a poll of the deputies—whom did they support? Who was the most popular? What were the nuances among the nominees? This type of vote also left me the option to choose, which was the most important thing.

After that December speech, I breathed more easily all around. I started to see the light at the end of the tunnel. It's possible to make concessions, but not when your back is up against the wall. Then it's not concessions but execution by firing squad. The reconciliation commission was already an improvement. I forced the Congress to stop the confrontation, forced it to fear the voice of the people. A rating vote was okay as long as the president retained the right to make the final selection. That acknowledged his stronger position but left him a way to make a dignified exit from the stalemate.

I will get ahead of myself in the story. At the next Congress two months later, the deputies realized what a mistake they had made in allowing this vote. They realized they should have twisted my arm to stop it. They saw that whether Gaidar stayed or went, reform would not stop and I would not be broken. But it was too late; the light was already visible up ahead. I sensed the logic of my actions.

In point of fact, the choice was not between Gaidar and some other prime minister, but between one tactic of battle and another. Either dissolve the Congress immediately or quietly follow the path of least resistance so that the compressed spring would gradually uncoil and finally collapse, until the public finally understood that the president was the head of state even in this constitutional deadlock. I chose this second alternative.

The parliamentary deputies' factions nominated twenty names for prime minister, among them Yegor Gaidar, Yuri Skokov, Viktor Chernomyrdin, Vladimir Kadannikov, Vladimir Shumeiko, Yuri Petrov, Georgi Khizha, Nikolai Travkin, and others. (A faction of Communists supported Petrov, and although he was my chief of staff at the time he never warned me of this nomination. That is, once again, commonly accepted ethics were clearly violated.)

Out of this range of figures I selected five: Skokov, Chernomyrdin, Gaidar, Kadannikov, and Shumeiko. As they say in chess, the positional game started. The voting began. Two—Skokov and Chernomyrdin—came out ahead with the highest take, having received 637 and 621 votes. Gaidar, who garnered 400 votes in favor, had one more vote than Kadannikov and therefore became the third candidate. I could have proposed Gaidar as a candidate to the Congress, but I didn't do that. My reasoning was as follows: if Gaidar's share was twenty to thirty votes more, that is, if he'd had a solid third place among the three preferred candidates, there would have been no questions. I would have nominated him, given him the floor at the Congress, and we would have tried to persuade the deputies to go along. Although as I now see it, we would have been likely to fail.

I summoned the three candidates for a private conversation in the winter garden of the Kremlin. At first, of course, I spoke with Gaidar alone. He came to me with his usual diffident smile. He already understood and had foreseen my decision, even though he was naturally upset. It was not an easy conversation, but it seemed to me that he understood my doubts and my desire to act in this fashion rather than another. If I had nominated him at that point, it would have led to a terrible crushing failure at the next Congress. I couldn't take that route. When I asked him about Chernomyrdin, he reacted instantly, which meant he was prepared for it. That is, like the intelligent fellow he was, he had rehearsed the whole conversation ahead of time. He said that Chernomyrdin would support reform and would not kick out the team that had been established, but there was a note of bitterness in his voice. He said good-bye and then went to give an interview to the press.

A conversation with Skokov ensued. His attitude was that since he had taken the highest number of votes, he had the most right to be nominated. I told him that because we had known each other so long, I would speak candidly, and he ought to understand me correctly: there was absolutely no way he could be nominated now. "You oppose the democrats in the government," I told him. "Your name is linked with the military-industrial complex. In short, I can't do it." He seemed to take this calmly. "That's your prerogative," he said. Still, a person's face gives him away. Skokov took my decision extremely hard, and I had trouble looking at him. I felt sorry for him. He was too proud a person to be subjected to such a conversation.

Finally, came Chernomyrdin, who did not hesitate for a moment when he heard my choice.

I know that the reaction of the West and in our press to the nomination of Chernomyrdin was fairly chilly. He was called a typical party apparatchik, in spite of the fact he was not a party worker but a manager in the state-run economy who had worked all over Siberia and the Ural Mountains region. He'd been through the school of hard knocks, and had seen the view not from the regional party offices but from the ground up. I had seen Chernomyrdin in swamp waders up to his knees in mud—that was part of his job in the petroleum and gas industry, and it was indeed a hard one.

President Bush called me before the Congress to ask me to fight for Gaidar and Kozyrev. In Gaidar, the Western governments saw a guarantor of economic reforms; for me that was no secret. It was one thing to look at our situation from over there, however, and another to actually be here. Gaidar had no chance of being approved by the Congress, so, given the reality of the situation, I settled on Viktor Chernomyrdin.

Once again, he seemed to be a compromise figure, a nomination of a candidate with whom everyone could be happy. It was dictated—let's face it—by regrettable necessity. We had already seen many times what comes of such choices—nothing. This time I believe the gods smiled favorably upon Russia. This time everything turned out different; the dire predictions did not come true. Why?

First, Chernomyrdin had worked for a time in the Gaidar government. He saw the magnitude of what was going on. He understood the logic of actions not from the outside, but from the inside. He had taken a good look at people and had tried to ensure the smoothest possible personnel transition.

Second, Chernomyrdin's promotion was not some unexpected ascension by a member of the *nomenklatura,* a sudden career takeoff like Rutskoi's or Khasbulatov's. Chernomyrdin had doggedly worked his whole life toward such a position. He knew all too well that there couldn't be mistakes, that he would have to answer for every step he took.

Third, Gaidar's reform had led to macroeconomic improvement or, to be more precise, to the destruction of the old economy. It was achieved with terrible pain, not with the flash of a surgeon's scalpel but with a rusty ax, hacking out worn parts and mechanisms right along with the good pieces, but achieved nonetheless. There was probably no other way to do it. Except for Stalinist industry, adapted to modern conditions and a Stalinist economy, virtually no other industry existed here. Just as it had been created, so must it be destroyed.

Gaidar never fully understood what industry was all about, and in particular the steel, petroleum and gas, defense, and consumer industries. All of his knowledge was rather theoretical in nature, which was potentially quite dangerous.

Chernomyrdin knew industry. But if he were to get in over his head with the macroeconomics, if he were to miss Gaidar's strategy, that would be even more dangerous—a hundred times more dangerous. Furthermore, Chernomyrdin was faced with an extremely difficult job: not just maintaining the former priorities but also implementing what Gaidar had promised—a stabilization program. Roughly speaking, he had to create a national hard currency that would float as before, and float for a fairly long time without turning into a meaningless pile of paper.

As far as his personal qualities, Chernomyrdin showed himself to be as I had expected—solid and reliable. He did not let me down in a single critical or tough situation. I was impressed with his taciturnity and reserve, his very sober thinking, and his tough masculinity.

Between the Seventh and Eighth congresses I made a number of tactical moves: I removed several people from the government who had become intolerable to the Congress. These were Press Minister Poltoranin, State Secretary Burbulis, and Yegor Yakovlev, head of television, a well-known journalist who had previously been editor in chief of *Moscow News* in the glasnost era.

Poltoranin and I had agreed much earlier that we would create a completely different organization also to be financed by the government, aside from the Ministry of the Press, which would retain its customary oversight and subsidy-allocation functions. Its mandate would be to guarantee the press freedom from lies, falsifications, and distortions; from the financial influence of business and other lobbyists; from pressure by the security service; from some individuals; and so on. It would be a federal information and analysis center, somewhat of a mixture of an academic research institute, a news agency, and a sociological study center. Poltoranin was quite suited for such a serious position. To the public, however, it seemed as if Poltoranin was being forced to resign before the Congress from his post as minister. I therefore quickly signed a decree about the creation of this information and analysis center.

A vacuum had formed between Burbulis and me, both in our work and personally. At the Seventh Congress, I had found myself completely alone, so I proposed that he take a break from government for a while, to take some time to think and look around.*

The most difficult case was Yegor Yakovlev. He later explained his dismissal as revenge for his independence and self-assurance, for not "running with the pack."

Yakovlev had perestroika to thank above all for his rise to the top. The Gorbachev era had propelled him to public prominence, like many others at the time, such as the former editor of *Ogonyok*, Vitaly Korotich, the historian Yuri Afanasyev, the lawyer Anatoly

*Burbulis is currently running the nongovernmental Strategy Foundation.—Trans.

Sobchak, and the economist Gavril Popov. Yegor Yakovlev had edited the weekly *Moscow News*, and after the coup, after clearing it with me, Gorbachev had appointed him head of Ostankino Television. When Gorbachev resigned in December 1991, Yakovlev remained as head of central television. I was quite happy with this. I was ready to work with an independent strong, and talented person, especially one in such a position as television.

The first draft of the decree on Yakovlev's dismissal was harshly formulated: for disorganization in work and mistakes in the policy of coverage of such-and-such . . . It sounded like the denunciations of the good old days. I really was angered by the fact that because of one careless broadcast, the president of North Ossetia, Akhsarbek Galazov, was attacking the president of Russia—how much effort we had spent to establish good working relationships with the Caucasian autonomous republics!*

I had to change the wording of the decree, of course, and it was not as eloquent, but I suddenly realized that I was not going to cancel his dismissal. The decision had subconsciously been building in me, even though I had no public disagreements with Yakovlev. Evidently, I was chiefly influenced by the shock I had experienced from the June 12, 1992, storming of Ostankino when neofascist and Communist demonstrators had mobbed outside the television station and harassed the staff, leading to some injuries and police dispersal of the crowd. I realized that Ostankino was almost like the button to the nuclear missiles since it was such a tremendous magnet for political grandstanding. I also realized that the person in charge of this button could not be a nervous intellectual type but had to be a person of another temperament, of more straightforward organizational ability.

I was criticized a great deal for Yakovlev's dismissal. But to be honest, after he left, little of fundamental importance changed on Channel 1 of state television. There were the same serials, the same politics, and the same commercials.

The only thing I curse myself for is not finding the time, or really the strength, to meet with Yegor Yakovlev and talk to him in a normal human way. Personally, I have retained very kind feelings toward him.

*Galazov was insulted by an alleged pro-Ingushetia position taken in a broadcast. He was in a dispute with the neighboring republic of Ingushetia, also within Russia's Federation.—Trans.

In principle, the Eighth Congress was foisted on me by Khasbulatov and Zorkin. I had not planned it, had not "ordered" it, so to speak. I felt as if a rubber band were stretching, ready to snap. But you have to get back in the ring and fight the second round. I had to fight for my constitutional amendments, for my ministers, for additional powers, for the referendum. All these decisions had to be taken.

Once again I began meeting with factions, deputies, and political movements. The meeting with Civic Union was very chilly. I sensed that the members were talking from a position of strength and invoked their contacts with the military-industrial complex. I came away from this meeting with the unpleasant impression that I had stood before them like a schoolboy giving an account of some transgressions.

The meeting with the bloc of democratic parties went very differently. Here I somehow listened more calmly and easily, even to the criticism. Intonation is very important to me. Let them criticize, as long as they do it decently, and see you not as a function but as a person. The proposals were most drastic: don't wait for the Congress to open; impose presidential rule immediately. Well, that was not the way to frame the issue. For the time being, the government was still strong enough to intercept any anticonstitutional moves, malevolent attacks by gunmen, or neo-communist terrorism. That wasn't the problem. It was that the Congress had brought us to a deadlock.

I also had a general meeting with the deputies, for once without any vicious tones, rudeness, or aggression. Those who came spoke fairly calmly. So what, then, was the reason why at the Eighth Congress the deputies finally cast in their lot with Khasbulatov to the end? Was it that my speech was a failure? Was it that our press campaign seemed orchestrated and provoked a counterreaction? Was it that Khasbulatov was able through intrigue to group some forces together? It was all three of these things, but there was also a fourth. To understand the context, we must go back to the previous Seventh Congress.

Everyone remembers from his childhood fistfights how effective it can be to look someone directly in the eye, keep your hands in your pockets, and your shoulders calmly thrown back. A show of potential force can have an effect. But when we grow up, we often forget another important detail from the ethics of healthy relations, quite relevant to our lives as adults.

Strong-arm tactics are too often used in politics, which is a dangerous thing. Such forceful methods quickly become devalued, and then force easily turns to weakness. This is particularly true of a gesture like leaving and slamming the door. Or leaving the Congress, where sometimes you feel like getting up and walking out almost every minute. God, it really is unbearable.

I have described how Yegor Gaidar performed at the Sixth Congress. His threat of resignation en masse was an absolutely targeted and unexpected ploy—it looked as if in one moment the Congress was responsible for depriving the country of a whole government. The deputies put their foot in it themselves.

At the Seventh Congress, the deputies forced me to leave the hall. They simply compelled me to do this, this time for a different sort of reason. A large majority of the Congress voted against the second and seventh items of the resolution concerning the referendum on support for the president and additional powers for the president. Their solidarity was almost total. Everything I had worked for, all my efforts, all my attempts were in vain. A peaceful agreement was not to be had. In such a situation, it is hard to walk out—it looks as if you have practically been ejected.

It would have been better to sit it out and then to stand up quietly and leave as if nothing special had happened—they voted and that was it—and then take action later. When deputies who are snickering, confident of their absolute impunity, are looking at you, either point-blank or furtively, it's hard to react correctly and appropriately. You cannot imagine how difficult it is. In this kind of situation, I feel better the first moment after I've acted. My nervous system rallies, and I even begin to breathe easier somehow. Apparently, I am poorly adapted to waiting, exercising cunning, and playing dirty. As soon as the situation is exposed with complete clarity, I'm a different person. This is probably both good and bad.

At the Seventh Congress, I made the wrong decision. I should not have left the hall, thereby abruptly embarking on confrontation. I had no idea at the time of the consequences of the move.

After I walked out, everyone in the room was seized with horror: what next? Now what? For some reason it seemed to me that the

'amily. Away from the turmoil
›litics there remains the
ility and emotion of family life:
›rating my sixtieth birthday in
nograd with my wife Naina and
ghters Tanya and Lena, other
nbers of the family and old
nds from high-school days, 1
uary 1991 (*above*). Burying my
her at Novokuntsevo cemetery,
cow, on 23 March 1993 (*right*).

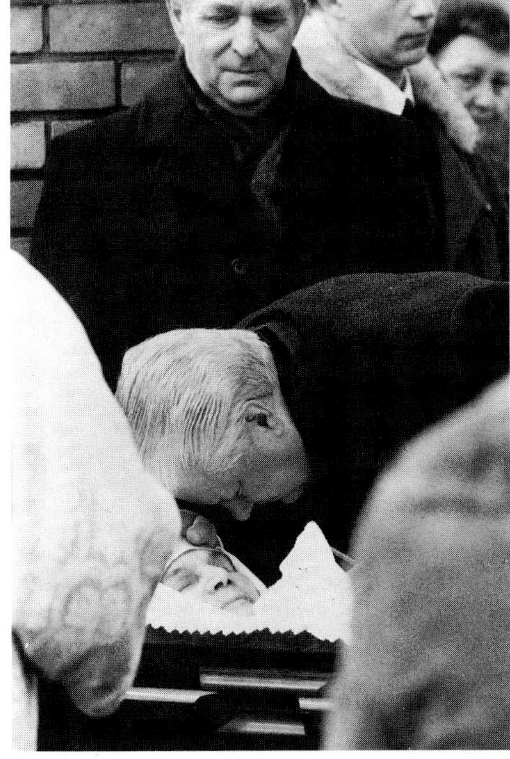

The Yeltsin Clan. My children and grandchildren are the fixed point in my world. Above, left to right, are Borka, Katya and Masha. Below, my women – from the left, Naina, Tanya and Lena.

ıvincing the Citizenry. I spent
ch of the summer of 1991 in
eria, negotiating with striking
lminers (*below*) and touring
region's vital industries (*right*).

The Second Putsch. After the failure of the coup they orchestrated, Vice-President Rutskoi (*above*) and Chairman of Parliament Khasbulato (*left*) are taken, under arrest, to Lefortovo Prison – from which they were to be prematurely released, under amnesty, in February 1994. Outside the charred White House, the coup's footsoldiers look defiant in surrender (*below*).

ew Broom. After his appointment in
:ember 1992, I introduced the new
ne minister of the Russian Federation,
tor Chernomyrdin, to the world's press.

Keeping the Faith, March 1994. As long as the Russian people show that they need me, I shall continue to serve them as best I can.

Congress would immediately split in half, and that in itself would be an object lesson.

Unquestionably, there was a certain hastiness in my exit. I didn't give even my supporters time to make sense of everything and react; some of them were just left sitting in the hall.

Am I a strong or weak person?

In emergency situations, I'm strong. In ordinary situations, I'm sometimes too passive. Sometimes I don't look anything like the Yeltsin everyone has grown used to seeing. I mean, I can fly off the handle in a stupid way, like a child. That is probably a weakness. Other people say my weakness is that I create obstacles so that I am forced to make a terrible effort to overcome them heroically later. That's not true. The obstacles find me on their own. Always. I don't go looking for them.

I was faced with a serious choice after the Eighth Congress. Either the president would become a nominal figurehead, and power would be transferred to the parliament or he would have to take some measures to destroy the existing imbalance of power. A group of lawyers with the presidential council headed by constitutional expert Sergei Alekseyev prepared some background materials for me. There had been similar parliamentary rebellions in international practice, and it was no accident that Gorbachev had talked about presidential rule. The president either temporarily restricts parliament's rights or he dissolves it, and the Constitution once again begins to operate in full force after new elections.

A select group of my aides—my speechwriters Pikhoi and Ilyin; my chief aide, Ilyushin; Sergei Shakhrai; and Yuri Baturin, the presidential legal aide—drafted an appeal to the people. I want to emphasize that although my assistants did the writing (they took the idea and incorporated it into a text), I myself made all the cardinal decisions independently.

Shakhrai's and Baturin's signatures of consent were on the draft decree. I outlined some talking points and made a taped television speech. The taping was scheduled for noon and was due to be broadcast at 9:00 P.M. Prior to the broadcast, I spoke with Rutskoi. I had to find out his position, so I asked him outright: how would he regard tough, determined actions by the president, such as a state of emergency? Rutskoi's reply was firm: yes, it was long overdue.

As for Yuri Skokov, he had raised this course of action a number of times in private discussions, citing intelligence reports that claimed a plot against the president was quite likely, and we shouldn't wait any longer.

When I actually signed the decree, however, there was a certain pause. Ilyushin is the one who really performs the job of issuing decrees. He insisted that before the decree was published, Rutskoi and Skokov must sign off on it. "Why?" He replied that there shouldn't be any discrepancies, that very grave actions were being taken, and a situation of chaos could not be tolerated where some were saying one thing and others were saying another. These two figures in the president's team should not just support verbally a decree that would fundamentally alter the balance of power in the country. Without signed consent, the decree must not be released.

I immediately perceived that Ilyushin was terribly upset and could not conceal his anxiety. It's hard to talk to a person in such a state. His agitation didn't spread to me but evoked a feeling of protest in me. I reined myself in and tried to instill in him, as usual, a precise and clear logic. Yes, Ilyushin was right, there was a point to obtaining the signatures of Rutskoi and Skokov.

Ilyushin took the copy of the decree and sent it to Skokov at the Security Council. Filatov, the new chief of staff who had replaced Petrov, went to Rutskoi. That was in the afternoon.

Soon I received word that both Rutskoi and Skokov had refused to sign the decree. Meanwhile, the time for the broadcast was approaching. Something had to be done. Either it had to be canceled or I had to summon Rutskoi and Skokov to try to persuade them, or something else.

I reached Judge Zorkin, head of the constitutional court, on my car phone. He had already been briefed, and I think he probably had a copy of the draft decree on his desk. His reply was evasive: yes, Boris Nikolayevich, we have to weigh all sides of this measure; examine what the consequences could be. There should be a judicial opinion on the constitutionality of the decree.

Sergei Shakhrai went to see Rutskoi, made ten emendations to the text of the decree. Finally, after long negotiations, it turned out that he would not sign the decree after all under any circumstances. Skokov also declined to approve the decree. His argument was that the country was not ready for it. One of them must have made a copy of the document, with the signatures of consent on the back, because by the next day, the constitutional court had subpoenaed Baturin to provide testimony about it.

To be honest, these aspects of Zorkin's behavior came as the greatest shock for me. He had thrown himself into investigating the provenance of the decree like a hard-boiled prosecutor. What was extremely unpleasant was that the chairman of the constitutional court was being misleading, to put it mildly. That evening on television he had said that the president had not spoken to him, and that he had learned about the decree only from my address on television.

Perhaps for the first time in my life I was abruptly putting a halt to a decision that had already been made. It was not that I was vacillating; it was just that I hesitated. You could even say that I stopped for a while. The reaction to the decree indeed gave me pause. It did not contain even a hint of any kind of oppressive measures against the deputies. There was no call to dissolve the Congress. There was not even a watered-down version of a state of emergency.

The "special" or "emergency" measures mentioned in the text referred merely to the legal procedural side of the decree and were distinct from a full-blown state of emergency. I was banning any decisions by parliament and the Congress that would limit the powers of the president of Russia.

Later on, at about 11:30 P.M., there was a television broadcast of a joint statement of reaction by Rutskoi, Yuri Voronin, deputy chairman of the Supreme Soviet, and Zorkin. It was obvious that they were declaring war on the president. A clear outline of their next tactic emerged from their verbose speeches: to convene the Congress and declare the president in violation of the law. Power would then be transferred to Rutskoi.

It was yet another severely stressful development, but the worst was yet to come.

Politics means struggle. I knew that the decree had helped me to reveal the line of political resistance, and now their hand was utterly exposed. While pretending to defend the law, Rutskoi and Zorkin were in fact launching an attack against the president.

Although practically signed, the decree was halted, and again people began to revise it. The phrases about the "emergency measures" were removed.

After Midnight

On Saturday evening, March 20, my mother had sat and watched television with the whole family. She saw my statement about declaring emergency measures, came up to me, kissed me, and said, "That's my boy, Borya," then went to her room. On Sunday, Mama died at 10:30 A.M., though I was not informed until that evening. In the morning, I had passed by her room at least three times, either looking for papers or on my way to make a phone call. That last time, our security man had seen Mama come out of her room and call something to me. I didn't hear her and had kept walking. That Sunday there was a session of the Supreme Soviet as well as a rally of the liberal democratic Russia movement and demonstrations by the Communists in the squares of Moscow. I was busy taking care of matters, preparing the next steps, receiving information about the parliamentary session, constantly on the phone to the security ministries, speaking to Chernomyrdin . . .

When I was told at midday that Mama was feeling poorly, I said, "What are you waiting for? You should take her to the hospital." I was told that the doctors were seeing her, that an ambulance had been called. I was somewhat reassured.

I lay down for a moment because I had just about reached my limit, having spent the previous night without sleep and having been under a lot of stress even before that. I was very worried about Mama, and asked several times how she was doing, but no one told me anything. They only said she was in the hospital. Despite everything, I didn't sense that it was the end. My thoughts were all distracted with the damned Congress.

That evening, about seven members of the government came to visit me. They had already learned of my mother's death—I was the only one who didn't know. Such powerful figures had come together, apparently very much fearing how I would take the news.

I remember asking everyone to leave, and then lying down.

That was it. Mama was gone.

Why did she die on this day of all days? Was it some sort of sign? Her death was like a blessing, like some kind of sacrifice, as if to say to her son, that's it, I can't help you anymore on this earth. She died quietly, painlessly, in her sleep, not changing her pose—that's what the doctors said.

The funeral was Tuesday. It wasn't terribly pompous nor terribly modest. It was a Christian funeral with a church service. Mama was buried at Kuntsevo Cemetery in Moscow.

I didn't like the press making much of the fact that Rutskoi and Zorkin had come to my mother's funeral. Of course, the sight of them was unpleasant for me but nobody made any jabs or statements, or passed any notes. They just came, and the less said about it the better.

At the Congress, however, there was no reaction, either official or unofficial. In fact, I didn't want the Congress to have anything to do with my mother's death.

I had given instructions back on March 9 to start a scheduled repair of the Great Kremlin Palace of Congresses. They had already taken apart the tables and were painting everything. The drapes had been removed from in front of the statue of Lenin,* and the scaffolding was still in place. To be honest, I could no longer make the mental effort to look at that monumental statue of Lenin. Sometimes I would ask myself: where am I? When is this all happening, in the past or present? What's all this nonsense with the statue still being up? Then there were other voices saying let Lenin stay, the whole country will see the Congress on television, and with that enormous Lenin in the background of the Great Kremlin Palace, they will simply give themselves away. Everyone will see who was really gathered in the Congress. The newly repaired hall was a very convenient excuse to force their hand, but in the end, we dropped it. What difference did it make in which hall they met?

Our analysts had run simulations over and over on the computer, using different methodologies. It seemed that there wouldn't be enough votes for an "impeachment." There would be 618 votes, plus or minus 1. And that's how it in fact turned out. At the time I had little faith in all that clever arithmetic. The parliament was incensed and out for blood. I remember how Khasbulatov's voice had reached a shrill pitch at the Eighth Congress when he started yelling something at

*After the August coup, the giant statue of Lenin that stood in a recess at the front of the hall was covered by curtains, and the Soviet hammer-and-sickle was replaced by the Russian tricolor. The Lenin reappeared again during the impeachment hearings.—Trans.

Chernomyrdin. His yelling was so unexpected, because I had become accustomed to Khasbulatov's having a quiet voice. But with him, nothing is accidental. Even at that moment he was deliberately playing a part, switching on a collective reflex in the deputies, who had grown slack. It was as if he were saying to them: front and center, go get him!

Still, what if there *was* an impeachment?

Why is the word *impeachment* so terrible? After all, if the Congress passed such a motion it would have no legal force. A popularly elected president could not be removed from power by the Congress, especially this Congress, which had long ago lost the people's trust. Furthermore, the subjective factor is not important here; what's important is the legal substance of the issue—the Congress does not have the power to remove the president because it did not elect him. Any schoolchild could understand that. But the Russian word *impichmyent,* borrowed from the English "impeachment," had been pronounced, and for our people the word itself had a mystical, sacred meaning, especially *because* it was foreign. That's the kind of psychology we Russians have. I wasn't afraid of impeachment, but rather the more ordinary-sounding Russian-language verbs *remove, dump,* or something even more biting.

Sometimes inexplicable factors operate in history, however, and must be treated very cautiously. If they dumped the president, that would mean there was no authority; everything would be permissible. Somewhere along the line, opposition forces had begun to amass, anarchic, aggressive—even terrorist—yearning for release. Then something snapped, and the subsequent scenario became irreversible. The security agencies would be obliged to go into action. Would they break the law so as to preserve order? Only for a time. But how long? This is what I feared.

What in fact should be done if I were removed from power after all? I was not afraid of this possibility. I was ready for it. If the parliament was to pass such a resolution, I saw only one way out: to appeal to the people. The people would not let me down, of that I was absolutely certain.

While the votes on the impeachment motion were being counted, I was in the Kremlin. And I believe it was vitally important that at the moment of the vote, the deputies were also seated in the Kremlin.

It was not the pomp and circumstance of the Kremlin palace that influenced them, but still there was a certain magic to the place, the magic of the air of history. Certain defense mechanisms subconsciously kick into gear, the mechanisms of genetic memory: people realize that in spite of everything, this is the Kremlin, this is Russia, this is my country. How can the leader be attacked? These mechanisms are what suppressed the aggressive impulse my enemies were counting on, the impulse of the herd beating up on one person, the vengeful blood brotherhood. The motion for impeachment did not pass.

I went out to speak to an impromptu rally on the lane winding downhill below St. Basil's Cathedral off Red Square. The weather was chilly, but it was easy to breathe in the steamy air, filled with hot camera lights and people shouting. There were lots and lots of people, a whole sea of people below St. Basil's. At first it seemed there was nothing to celebrate. We hadn't won yet, had we? It was just that we hadn't lost this round, this match. It was then I realized it was going to be all right. Once again, for the umpteenth time, my life's tactic had worked—play to win. Play only for the victory. Don't be afraid. Don't turn back.

When I walked up to the microphone I wasn't embarrassed to chant this word: *victory.*

As I reread these words, I can still say I am not embarrassed by that scene. It *was* a victory, although on the other hand, it was also a defeat. In the global, strategic scheme of things, all through this entire rough patch that had lasted from the Seventh Congress to the referendum, we had been losing. We lost because we allowed ourselves to be dragged into this massacre, this battle, this war with Pyrrhic victories and artificial defeats. When I say "we," I mean the president's team.

True, I wasn't the one who started this fight. It was started by those who decided to test the stability of presidential power. Society was the one that suffered. The people were the victims, regardless of "who started it first." I knew that. And I tried to put an end to this silly confrontation as quickly as possible, this fistfight so mortally dangerous to democracy. The amendments to the Constitution hadn't passed, so I proposed a new prime minister. When the new prime minister did not suit them, I raised the issue of a referendum. However, even this idea, a referendum, which had seemed incontrovertible to me, was rejected out of hand by the Congress. The members acquiesced to it only after the failed impeachment motion.

All of my efforts, all the frantic energy of these months was spent on trying to exercise restraint, trying not to be tempted to solve the problem of the parliament with force, to go beyond law and order. Now that I was so close to decreeing restrictions on the rights of the Congress through an act of will, once again I backed off. I was hoping for a peaceful, decent, honest outcome to the fight—*after* the referendum.

I was mistaken. Our disagreement was in fact not about tactics. Nor was it even about politics, I think. No, what this was about was employing a democratic instrument—the Congress—in a pitched battle to destroy the presidency. Only I realized that too late.

After the preliminary results of the April referendum were reported, almost the first words out of Khasbulatov's mouth were about the "Poltoranin–Goebbels" television station. To compare Poltoranin, now the government's new information agency head, with Joseph Goebbels was simply an insult in decent society. This was one more example of the speaker's "purely metaphorical" characterizations.

Crude pressure and overkill are not what it takes to run a public relations campaign—that only provokes a reaction of antipathy in the public. What is needed is an idea, a concept for such a campaign. I think we found such a concept. We won against our opponents precisely because of the honesty and openness of our campaign ideas and our positions.

First, the parliament itself formulated all four questions posed in the referendum. We were therefore playing on their field by their rules. I coined a slogan for the campaign: *Da, da, da, da!* Answer yes four times! People had always liked to say *Nyet,* no, in our country—no to war, no to imperialism, no to the whole world of violence we will destroy.*

*The questions were as follows: 1) Do you support the president of the Russian Federation? 2) Do you support the social and political policies of the government? 3) Do you advocate early elections for the president? and 4) Do you advocate early elections for the parliament? The results were as follows: 64.05 percent of the population voted; 1) 58.5 percent in favor; 2) 52.88 percent in favor; 3) 32 percent in favor; 4) 41.4 percent in favor. Yeltsin advocated a "yes" to each question, even concerning his reelection. The democratic opposition advocated a "no" to the third question, in order to protect Yeltsin.—Trans.

People were sick and tired of trying to understand complicated propaganda slogans, and they had become fed up fifty years ago, not just now. We have to say: *yes!* Yes to a normal life without all this squabbling, without all these exhausting congresses, without the eternal political infighting. We have to say *yes!* to the president. This affirmation, which served as a counterweight to the parliament, which always negated everything, seems to me to have been a success.

Second, we had the support of prominent people. Many criticized the television host Elder Ryazanov for a show about me and my family, thinking it was indecent and that he was sucking up and trying to find favor. But it wasn't a suck-up—he really was fighting for democracy to win. Frankly, Ryazanov is no less popular among the people than I am. He spoke with his inherent tactfulness and respect and from the outset, it was a conversation between equals. Everyone has forgotten that part.

I can say the same about all the other artists and writers of Russia who supported me: I never sensed any hint of social obligation in their tone of voice. These are people of such high caliber, of such exalted rank, they can indulge themselves in saying anything they think—even about the president.

A cursory glance at the press clippings from this period will verify my point. *Moscow News, Stolitsa* [*Capital*], *Ogonyok,* and *Literaturnaya gazeta* [*Literary Gazette*] all carried very pointed debates during those weeks about the attitude toward me as a political figure. Many Russian émigré writers, including Vladimir Maximov and Alexander Zinoviev, were harshly critical of me. They did not have faith in Russian democracy. For them, Gorbachev, who had "forgiven" them and allowed their works to be published again, would always remain a nicer, more treasured figure. Evidently, the feeling that you can return to the motherland, that you had ceased to be a pariah was one you never forget. So I was an alien figure for them because I hadn't been directly involved in their rehabilitation. Yet surely they'd had no shortage of articles in the press and television interviews of late, and this émigré reaction was only a smidgeon of the criticism I got before the referendum.

The most unexpected response was in the answer to the second question of the referendum which really amounted to a referendum on shock therapy. Somewhat more than half—but more than half, just the same—of the people who had voted in the referendum (and that was a very decent percentage of the working population) answered yes to reforms, new prices, privatization, and so on. My opponents had not expected this.

Their only trump card had been their belief that the population would vote for me merely to preserve social peace, but that they couldn't stand my reform policy. With the affirmative response in the referendum to market reforms, this ace was whisked out of their sleeve.

For the first days after the referendum, the opposition was in terrible disarray and could do nothing but sputter about "propaganda." Or they would blatantly juggle the facts, saying that only two thirds of the voting population had participated in the referendum and that of this group, only half had voted for market reform—which meant a minority of the whole population. That meant the majority was against me! That was rather amazing logic on their part, as if they'd spoken to each person who didn't turn out for the elections. How many of those who failed to get to the polls were just people who decided to go to their dacha on a Sunday? How many simply hadn't made up their minds and didn't want to vote in vain?

Even so, how can the results of the second question be judged? Essentially, the referendum was a second presidential election two years after the first. Usually by the second year, a crisis of faith in the elected head of state or party sets in. People expect much more from politicians than they can give; they want some immediate changes in their own lives! Otherwise, they reason, why did I bother voting? But change takes a long time. So what can we expect from voters in Russia, where for so many years people were fed the promise of infeasible reforms, perestroika, an overhaul, that kept getting bogged down in various areas of life? And where, even before that, they were simply lied to every day from the television screen, told that their standard of living would keep steadily rising, despite the shortage of consumer goods?

In theory, any person who would undertake such painful reforms, with such price hikes, should inevitably be crunched to bits. The opposition was counting on this, on the people's reform fatigue. I even saw a cheery little poster about the referendum on a fence with a pejorative nickname for me: LET'S EAT YELYA ALIVE ON APRIL 25. It turned out, though that people weren't voting merely for me. By myself, I wasn't perhaps so important after all. People were voting for something to happen. I think that was the chief moral of the referendum story. Perhaps people will change their minds and vote for another government. Perhaps.

Today politicians must be concerned with the public's greatest expectations. This yearning for concrete action—action that can be debated, and may be disappointing, but is action nonetheless—had not died down in people even into the second year of reform. It was not to last forever.

There were some areas where the voting returns were not at all reassuring, primarily in rural regions of the country. That's understandable. First, the peasants are conservative by nature and take a long time to become accustomed to anything new. So far, the reforms hadn't done a thing for them; they were just a big headache. Second, there were a number of regions with their own complaints against the government. The governor was arrogant and fueled corruption and the mafia, or had promised to resolve some local issue and hadn't budged on it (like the closing of a nuclear power station or an environmentally unsafe factory), or else had failed to put up some new buildings.

Third, there were the regions where the referendum became a reason to think about the future: what country are we living in, Tatarstan or Bashkiria? The politicians of these republics would very much like to become heads of independent states. But do people want to live in such an "independent" state, where geographic or cultural or economic independence can never be fully achieved, although it will be the official ideology? I doubt it.

The status of the regions of Russia, including the traditional national enclaves in the north, the Volga, Siberia, and the Caucasus, is still not clear. Work on the new Constitution should elucidate it.

Now this chapter, the most difficult one of the book for me, is done. Ahead is the epilogue of all these events, so bitter and so insane. The great moral victory of the referendum was devalued by the rivers of blood, by people's deaths, by the awful truth of a civil war. For the sake of what? Why? Why do our parliamentary battles end in the salvos of tanks? Whose evil will is this? Whose malice aforethought?

After all, members of parliament get their noses punched in other countries. But it never ends like this.

It's true, I'd rather not have a victory like this. Still, it had to be achieved, even at a terrible cost, in order to preserve at least the basis for stability in society, some hope for order. For peace, even if only external and fragile, but peace nonetheless.

It had to be done for our children, our parents, and all our nearest and dearest, so that no more blood would be shed, so that the insanity of a coup could be prevented.

That is how I evaluate my actions on the terrible night of October 3–4. I hope that the majority of my fellow citizens will see it the same way.

Now we must analyze how this happened, how we got here, and what we should do now. Meanwhile, the referendum represents an impossible hope for authentic civic peace.

Was there any historical meaning for this failed stage in the history of Russian democracy? Of course there was. Who knew five years ago what a referendum was in our country? What was "impeachment"? How a parliamentary system differs from a presidential system? What legitimate versus illegitimate authority meant?

Besides a few legal scholars, I doubt that anyone knew. Now people are learning bit by bit to figure out all these constitutional subtleties. The very word *constitution* was a strange dish for us to taste. We seemed to have had a Constitution, but it was almost as if we didn't, so invisible was its presence in the society of the Brezhnev and Gorbachev.

The attitude among the common people was: there are some bosses up there, and thank God for it. By nature, our people are seemingly law-abiding, quiet, unhurried. As Russians like to say, we're agreeable. At least until pushed. But what was this law-abiding nature built upon? What laws? Or was it founded only on fear? On the terrible fear of the bosses?

In short, thanks to these events, some sort of notion of a structure for society is being instilled, some kind of code of basic regulations and laws, some kind of system of relations among various state institutions. With this notion, people are gradually gaining some comprehension of their role in this mechanism, the mechanics of living.

8

A HARD SUMMER

Editor's Note: As the crisis with parliament deepens, Yeltsin focuses on the rampant corruption in high government circles, including an episode in which his security minister brings him together with an émigré businessman whose activities lead to the minister's dismissal. Russian reform becomes entangled in scandals.

It was Saturday, July 24, 1993 and the sun was shining—I had certainly missed it this rainy summer. The air was easier to breathe and at last I was on vacation. Although the cares in Moscow would still reach me at my dacha, I felt I could use some distraction from them. That day, however, I sensed that my vacation at Valdai,* only just begun, was already drawing to a close.

Each news report out of Moscow was more hysterical than the one before. Although the constitutional process had supposedly been set in motion, it was suddenly bogged down again. In my absence, Khasbulatov had refused to recess the Supreme Soviet and let the deputies go on vacation. Alone in the city and tired from lack of rest—and all the more angry for that reason—the deputies began to quarrel among themselves.

The democratic parties held emergency meetings and passed resolutions demanding that I return from vacation. Sergei Filatov called me several times a day, hinting that I should return, that without me the situation was getting out of control. That evening, Naina

*A resort area in the north of Russia about a five-hour drive from Moscow.—Trans.

watched *Vesti,* the news program, and could barely wait until the next day when we sat down to breakfast to give me an emotional account of current affairs, interrupting her narrative with cries of "But, Boris, they can't do that, can they!" I had already known about everything she was telling me. At 6:00 A.M., as usual, I had reviewed all the material coming in from the Security, Interior, and Foreign ministries, had reviewed the situation analysis from my experts, and had seen the press clippings. So when Naina started in on me, I made a face at her and said, "Oh, please, don't, at least not at the table. Let's not talk about politics; let's have a break." Naina stopped dead in her tracks, even though she wanted to discuss the news, smiled, and said, yes, you're right, enough about politics, let's go pick berries. She then went off to the woods dressed like a serious berry picker, wearing boots and carrying a basket.

I envied her. I couldn't go on a walk in the woods then. The monotony would irritate me, and the silence of the forest would compel my thoughts to return to Moscow. So I got on my bicycle and went off to the gym to play tennis with Shamil Tarpishchev. At such moments, the enthusiasm, exertion, and active struggle of tennis forced me to forget unpleasant things, even those involving politics. We played two full sets, and I was sweating and totally spent. The feeling of exhaustion from sports is like nothing else; it seems as if you can't even lift your arm or leg. You sit with your eyes closed and sense every cell in your body, and gradually, slowly, your strength returns. As if you were born anew.

After a steam bath, we headed for home. Naina was waiting for us with a full basket of berries. She was terribly proud of her accomplishment, which actually was quite amazing since within three hours, she had picked enough blueberries to fill several gallon jars of jam.

It was time for lunch. Naina and I were joined by Shamil Tarpishchev, Alexander Korzhakov, and Valentin Yumashev, whom I had invited to Valdai so that he and I could work on this book. The conversation was light and bantering. Suddenly, one of the staff people came up to Naina and whispered something in her ear. She excused herself and left the room. Normally, we are not bothered at the dinner table, only in extreme circumstances. In fact it was just such an emergency.

Five minutes later, Naina returned with a worried face. Before even sitting down, she asked, "Borya, what happened, what have you done, what's this money exchange all about?" I remained silent, but everyone at the table was instantly upset. What was this exchange? What money? Naina related that our daughter Lena had just phoned. It seemed that she and Valera had set off the evening before on a hike in Karelia, a beautiful northern area of Russia bordering Finland. Valera had received his vacation pay yesterday; as a pilot, he had a high salary. Then suddenly it was announced this morning that only new ruble notes would be accepted as legal tender, and the old ones—up to thirty thousand worth—must be exchanged at savings banks. Valera had received all his vacation pay in the old banknotes. Now what was he to do? He and my daughter were on vacation, but with all their money useless, they had nothing for travel expenses. Naina exclaimed once again, "Borya, what's the big idea? Did you at least know about this?" All eyes were on me.

I did know about it. About a month and a half ago, four of us had met—me, Chernomyrdin, Finance Minister Fyodorov and Viktor Gerashchenko, chairman of Central Bank of Russia. We had come to an agreement that in the future, we would coordinate financial matters. No single party—the president, the government, or the bank—could initiate any unilateral actions that could lead to financial havoc. After that meeting, we managed to stick to this very important agreement, even though there was constant pressure from all sides. Everyone needed money—the Supreme Soviet, the regions, the plants, agriculture, the army. We were constantly forced to turn people down. Sometimes it was simply impossible not to give out something, but if such a decision was made, we would coordinate it with one another.

Before heading off for vacation, I'd had a conversation with Chernomyrdin about the banknote exchange. I knew the date when the regulation was to go into effect. The reason for the exchange was that as soon as new banknotes had appeared, old money from the former Soviet republics flooded into Russia. It was simply impossible to stem such a tide. The central bank and the government made a decision to withdraw the old notes from circulation. Boris Fyodorov had always in theory advocated having our own Russian ruble zone, therefore Gerashchenko believed him to be an ally on this matter.

Chernomyrdin and I had agreed that Gerashchenko would work out the specific details of the exchange. A minimum of people were to be involved in this operation since information of this nature was extremely sensitive—we didn't want panic or embezzlements. And naturally I requested that none of Prime Minister Pavlov's stupidities be repeated.* Geraschenko's implementation was clumsy.

The day for the exchange came. We had supposed that citizens would easily and effortlessly part with their old bills with Lenin's portrait, and gladly change over to the new money with the Russian flag. But the whole country went into an uproar. People were furious—not at the actual fact of the exchange; most were fairly calm about that. But it was the *way* in which people were being asked to make the exchange that caused them to explode. Even the family of my elder daughter had been affected.

Our lunch interrupted, Naina asked me to tell her what to say to Valera. They wouldn't be able to get back home from vacation; they wouldn't have enough money.

"Borya, you could have had least told us about this!" my wife spluttered. I couldn't contain myself now and bellowed, "*What?* Nobody is supposed to know, but my family knows! Thirty thousand rubles is enough for him to take on vacation. They shouldn't go on a spree anyway!"

I was angry but my wife also felt she had said too much. While I cooled down, I reflected mournfully that once again we had done something stupid. Something that would have to be fixed with a terrible uproar. Of course, 30,000 rubles per person was too small an amount to exchange at one time. The other great inconvenience was the strict deadline—two weeks—allowed for the exchange. What if a person was on a business trip, or got sick, or was on vacation? He would not have time to make the exchange. We ourselves would drown trying to deal with such situations, since if we made an exception for some, we'd have to make them for everybody.

The scandal continued to heat up back in Moscow. Fyodorov, who happened to be in the United States at the time, made a hard-hitting call for the immediate resignation of the Central Bank chairman. Newspapers and television hurled themselves with such fury at the government that the sparks flew. The exchange fiasco united every-

*In January 1991, Pavlov ordered the immediate withdrawal of all denominations of 50 rubles and higher, causing panic and the depletion of people's savings.—Trans.

one—the opposition, the right-wing, the left-wing, and the centrist publications. They all forgot about their differences since the exchange had touched everyone to the quick. To be sure, the democratic press indulged in speculation that I did not know about the "provocation" being prepared with the banknotes, that this grandiose idea had been instigated by Gerashchenko and Khasbulatov in order to set the popular masses against the president.

People standing in lines at the savings banks cursed me, Chernomyrdin, and the entire moronic Soviet government. The Council of Ministers held an emergency session and reconfirmed that the exchange operation was in Russia's interests. The directors of the central bank explained to infuriated citizens that the banknote exchange would not infringe their rights, all earnings would be exchanged in the end, and no one should worry. But no one wanted to wait for that end to come; people were carrying packets of old bills around—their entire savings for the future—worried that they had become a pile of worthless paper.

Clearly, I had to step in to handle this enormous scandal now rocking the country. I told Korzhakov to ready the helicopter for the morning; we would be returning on Sunday to the city. Naina gasped, and muttered, more for her own sake than mine since she didn't expect a reply. "Borya, once again, you're not rested." She realized that I would be physically unable to stay in Valdai on vacation, fishing, reading books, and playing tennis. I would simply champ at the bit and that would be a lot worse. So Naina bowed her head and went obediently as always to pack my things. I called Chernomyrdin in Moscow and asked him to come see me the next day, regardless of vacation.

I had no doubts that we had to barricade ourselves off from the truckloads of old rubles flooding in from the republics, that we could not bear such a burden. I made the decision, however, to modify the unacceptable features of the exchange. First, I raised the sum for any undeclared exchange to 100,000 rubles, and, second, I extended the deadline for exchanges to one month.

Valera and Lena, themselves victims of the ill-thought-out economic reform measure, had gone on their vacation anyway with the old money and somehow managed to get through until their return. When you're young, relaxing, and taking a swim, the lack of money isn't a problem. I wish I had had such problems . . .

Despite the troubles caused by its clumsy implementation, the exchange measure still bore some fruit. In August, September, and October, the exchange rate of the ruble stopped plunging and even grew stronger against the dollar. The rate no longer jumped wildly by tens of percentage points, but settled into a normal fluctuation. There was hope that inflation (and with it the fall in production) would at least become manageable, that its pace could be kept in check.

The "Chernomyrdin era" began in the economy. The prime minister brought a refreshing note into the atmosphere of market reforms, which in fact continued. It was an accent on reliability, permanence, and stability. Another extremely important aspect of Chernomyrdin's presence on the scene was that political pressure on the government lifted dramatically. The air cleared around people in the government, and it became possible for them to breathe again and work normally.

In the spring of 1992, when Chernomyrdin was appointed prime minister, none of the experts or journalists believed that the inveterate Gaidarite "marketeers" who held key government positions—Andrei Nechayev, Alexander Shokhin,* and others—would be compatible with the hard-line "statists"—Soskovets, Gerashchenko, and Chernomyrdin himself. Nevertheless, they found common ground, and what's more, Gaidar himself returned to government! What had seemed utterly impossible took place: the old and new prime ministers began to work together. In fact, it was at Chernomyrdin's initiative. He repeatedly came to the rescue of Gaidar's ministers, literally fighting for each one of them (for example when a sharp debate over the economy broke out with the appointment of Oleg Lobov, an industrialist.)

In any country in any age, the people who work in government by definition must be cold, pragmatic, and rational in their thinking. They are people of a certain type: willful, hard-working, intelligent, who retreat from the interests of ordinary life. I have noted how the Gaidar government was dragged into a horrible ideological quarrel, into exhausting debates and accusations of "betrayal of Russia's interests," causing us all irreparable damage. In the

*Shokhin was head of the Russian Foreign Ministry's Foreign Economic Department and was appointed economics minister in February 1994. Andrei Nechayev was first deputy minister of economics and finance under Gaidar (1991–92).—Trans.

political sense, for these reasons, the Gaidar government did not have its flanks covered.

With the coming of Chernomyrdin, this state of affairs changed completely. He understood that the prime minister had to be a politician. He was obliged, if you will, to cover for his economic team. He was also obliged to express certain aspirations and sentiments of society.

The prime minister's speech at the Eighth Congress was like a bolt from the blue for the deputies who had positioned themselves for attack. I would say it was a balanced, concise, and even courageous speech. His words—"Let's get down to work," said by a man who had to his credit a lifetime of hard work—managed to shut up for a time even our rambunctious Congress. Chernomyrdin also spoke frankly about the government's mistakes and the dangers the country would face during the reform period.

The appearance of such a figure completely knocked the wind out of Rutskoi's and Khasbulatov's sails and exposed them as purely opportunistic politicians. The hard authoritative prime minister created a bulwark for the president's policy, a second center of power that cemented together all the different government groupings—the strategic group, responsible for the country's security; the economic group that would have to implement destabilizing measures; and the political groups, which pressured the other two as it attempted to put a liberal ideology into effect.

Khasbulatov immediately sensed Chernomyrdin's power and his influence on the public mood. With good reason, Khasbulatov and his team of deputies had spent the summer months formulating a notion of a parliamentary republic with a strong prime minister. They tried to tempt Chernomyrdin into the political struggle on their side, hinting that the parliament was quite happy with him as a figure. But Chernomyrdin did not form an alliance with the "revolutionary" Supreme Soviet.

Chernomyrdin and I also share common values. He doesn't tolerate unscrupulous political intrigue, but neither does he have his head in the clouds. This combination of pragmatic experience and principles honed through the years is common to people of our generation. In all sorts of the most diverse, critical, difficult situations, Chernomyrdin and I had complete mutual understanding. I would like to think that such understanding was not merely from discipline and deliberate necessity, but reached far deeper. In short, the ruckus over the money exchange didn't affect my attitude toward the Chernomyrdin government in the slightest.

On Saturday, May 22, 1993, the Palace Hotel opened its doors on Moscow's Tverskaya Street in the center of town. Many prominent Russian figures—directors, businessmen, and diplomats—were invited to the opening. At the request of Moscow Mayor Yuri Luzhkov, I was in attendance. After all the obligatory formalities (ribbon cutting, Champagne and h'ors-d'oeuvre, ceremonial speeches), I was about to go home. Security Minister Viktor Barannikov, who had also been invited to the reception, asked me to stop and see him for an hour. He really prevailed upon me, saying it was extremely urgent. I suggested we meet in the Kremlin on Monday. He explained that he had hoped to meet me in a more informal setting since a lot of important issues had accumulated.

I don't like such impromptu visits, but Barannikov insisted. It was a rare occasion, I had no good excuses to refuse him, and, reluctantly, I agreed to the meeting. We got into my car together and after we were on our way, I said to the driver and Korzhakov that we weren't going home, but were heading to Barannikov's house. Korzhakov frowned, knitting his eyebrows expressively. He doesn't like such surprise changes in our schedules and routes any more than I do. That's his job.

Soon we arrived at Barannikov's dacha, went into the house, and I said hello to Barannikov's wife. Suddenly, Barannikov was introducing me to an older man, who was smiling and who stretched out his hand, and said, "I'm Boris Birshtein." This was completely against all the rules. Barannikov should definitely have warned me that he had some guests. As I see now, it was so important to Barannikov that Birshtein meet me, he was so dependent upon him, that he was prepared to overstep any bounds of decency and protocol to make this meeting happen. I glared at Barannikov but he only flashed me a guilty smile, and, to cover the awkward moment, cried, "Dinner is served!" He proceeded to pull out a chair for me at the center of the table.

After we had been seated, Barannikov described his guest. Boris Birshtein was a brilliant businessman, a politician, an émigré whose company, Seabeco, was based in Switzerland, but a fellow countryman, who had done an extraordinary amount for Russia. We owe it to him that there is now peace in Moldova instead of war,* because he had served as one of the chief mediators in negotiations with the people in Moldova and had brought a Russian delegation on his private airplane to Chisinav to hold talks. And peace was made. He was also the closest economic adviser of Askar Akayev, the president of Kyrgystan, and had tremendous opportunities to attract investment in Russia from the major financial institutions of the world. On the whole, Barannikov spoke emotionally about Birshtein, eager for me to like his guest. Birshtein listened to his host's praise with the expression of a man who was modest but certainly knew his own worth. He smiled slightly and shook his head when Barannikov complimented him excessively.

I continued to remain silent. Birshtein spoke next, describing his mission to Moldova, then turned to the subject of Russian business and a pitch to me on Russia's great prospects. He showed off his big connections with the businessmen and politicians of the world, dropping the names of presidents, ministers, and heads of corporations. He wanted to make a significant but also pleasant impression, which was quite natural. I didn't hold up my end of the conversation, however. The whole rigmarole lasted about forty minutes. Finally, sensing that he shouldn't push things too far—he'd already done so much for his guest from abroad—Barannikov somehow cued Birshtein that it was time to leave. Birshtein was suddenly in a big hurry, his personal airplane was flying out in half an hour, and, regrettably, he couldn't stay with us longer.

I never saw him again after that. I will note only one detail. When I decided that I'd had quite enough interesting meetings and new acquaintances for one day and was getting ready to leave, I accidentally saw that Birshtein had not left. I pretended that I hadn't seen him.

*When the former Soviet republic of Moldova, originally part of Romania, declared its independence and made Moldovan Rumanian the official state language, the Russian-speaking population in the Trans-Dniester region decided to declare their independence and allegiance to a local neo-Communist government. This prompted break-away elements of the former Soviet Army to join in an armed struggle. The Yeltsin government attempted to intervene to protect the rights of Russian speakers, but did not recognize the Russian-speaking region's declaration of independence or approve the local army involvement.—Trans.

That was how Barannikov introduced me to his friend Boris Birshtein.

That summer, the chief topic, even tabloid cliché, was the charge of corruption among top officials in the government. Rutskoi had laid the groundwork with his talk of "eleven suitcases" of compromising materials that had turned out largely to be empty. To the sheaf of documents about corruption in the provinces, already well known both to the prosecutor and the Kremlin and which were actively being investigated, Rutskoi had added a giant hoax about top officials of the government.

Was there a connection between corruption and the ensuing rebellion in October? Was there any link between politics and crime? Economic reform and the mafia? And what in fact is the Russian mafia?

The meeting with Boris Birshtein had forced me to do some serious thinking. I was to learn much more about him and Seabeco, his ill-reputed firm. At first this somewhat unpleasant introduction to him seemed accidental to me, and I tried to chase away any bad thoughts of a setup. However, these thoughts were to come back to haunt me with a vengeance.

A country can't be rich if it has no rich people in it. There is no real human independence without private property. But money, big money (which is actually a relative concept) is always, under any circumstances, a seduction, a test of morals, a temptation to sin. There's nothing for it. Years will have to pass before a culture of dealing with money, business ethics, will develop in our country. Our society, our people were completely unprepared to accept this phenomenon. The Russian attitude toward the businessmen and tycoons is contradictory—sometimes people curse them, then the next minute they naïvely open their doors wide to them.

There are numerous factors fostering a multibillion dollar "shadow" cash economy in Russia, a black-market dealing in dollars, contraband exports of raw materials, tax dodging, and so on. The mafia appears where normal human ethics are thrown to the devil, where people put themselves up for sale. Soon the simple and logical thought occurs to them, why evade the law all the time? Why not just eliminate it? That is, the person who enforces the law should be bought. Everything is interrelated. The inflationary economy forces our businesspeople to look for ways to make a quick killing and avoid long-term investments and leads to widespread evasion of taxes. As a result, any honest business is always on the brink of collapse. To be more accurate, the line between clean and criminal business is hazy. Any commercial transaction under certain circumstances can become illegal; that's what's so terrible.

The appearance before me of such a magnate as Boris Birshtein was indicative of the severity of the problem. In order to cross that ethical line, in order to run that red stoplight, under Russian conditions you don't necessarily have to peddle pornography, sell drugs, or deal in contraband cheap goods. Why fool around with such nickel-and-dime stuff? It's easier to buy one government official after another. Birshtein tried to get to the very top—and he almost made it. There was just a little ways more to go. An unlimited power of parliament, which Khasbulatov and Rutskoi were attempting to attain by both nonviolent and violent methods; independence for Russia's regions, which a small group of pseudo "subjects of the Federation" began to impose during the coup—this was all the best breeding ground for the mafia. It's always easier and more profitable to bribe deputies who have powers of oversight and allocation, and to buy out local officials.

Gradually, we are discovering who was bought and how, who was approached. What next? A strong, tough government overseen by the parliament, the press, and the courts is the only curb against corruption—another unpleasant aspect of the coup.

Even after the joy of victory over the April referendum and the premature joy at the fact that the constitutional process had finally begun, the overall optimistic mood gradually began to evaporate. Rutskoi's eleven suitcases, regardless of my attitude toward him, kept me awake at night. I felt that something wrong was going on behind my back, and that "something wrong" could easily devalue in the public eye the political results achieved with such difficulty.

A government commission to combat corruption, led by prominent attorney Andrei Makarov, was formed and a probe began. I expected that the powerful forces of the Security Ministry would join in this investigation at any moment. I thought that Barannikov, whose reliability I had not doubted for a second, would help the commission unravel the complicated mystery of forged documents and other evidence of the mafia.

At one of the sessions of the corruption commission, several members, including Makarov and Aleksei Ilyushenko, chairman of the presidential staff oversight administration, expressed the opinion that Dimitry Yakubovsky, a young but talented opportunist widely known in Russia, should be subpoened as a witness in a case of corruption charges against the highest officials in the government. I remained silent.

The first time I had heard Yakubovsky's name was in the following intriguing circumstances. It was the fall of 1992 and an agitated Yuri Skokov came into my office along with Alexander Korzhakov. Skokov is ordinarily such a self-contained person and so rarely flies off the handle that I knew something serious must have happened. Skokov had brought with him a draft of a document carrying initials of approval from many of the country's leaders—Shumeiko, Barannikov, Yerin, Kokoshin (first deputy defense minister), Primakov, Stepankov (the procurator general)—and also a note written by hand, "submitted for Gaidar's approval." The directive, almost ready to be released, stated that a new government position was to be established, government coordinator of the security ministries. Its powers were extremely broad. This coordinator was to be above the security ministries, to oversee them, and was to report only to the prime minister. In the papers that Skokov had brought to me, the person to be appointed to this fairy-tale job carrying a general's rank was none other than the twenty-nine-year-old Dmitry Yakubovsky, who just six months before had been a mere captain.

Naturally I called Gaidar and had a tough, somewhat nasty conversation with him. It turned out that he had been misled. When he had been given the proposal for the new position, he was told that it had also been submitted to the president for approval, that I was completely briefed on the concept of instituting this office and was familiar with the candidate for the post. When I realized that we were dealing with a major scam, I asked Gaidar to immediately rescind all the documents, to get in touch with Shumeiko and the security ministries, investigate the whole affair, and then report back to me. Within three days I received a report that all the instructions had been followed, and that a frightened Yakubovsky had left Russia and flown off to Canada or Switzerland.

Another six months went by and Yakubovsky's name surfaced in the press once again as, one after another, the newspapers began to expose the latest scandal. Yakubovsky had begun to betray his former friends and protectors, and light began to be shed on the original documents he had presented to them. It became obvious what an enormous scandal we would soon witness, and what figures would take part in this spectacle. The problem is that the figures were both black and white. That is, they were people in whose integrity I had long since stopped believing, along with people whose loyalty and honesty I had never doubted. I had met with them, smiled at them, we had discussed problems that were really important for Russia, decided some things, thought up some new ideas, but when they left my office after finishing state business, they went to work pursuing their own private interests.

I formulated this idea for myself and expressed it rather forcefully at a session of the corruption commission. I was not concerned whether a given person was for or against me, whether he was one of "ours" or one of "theirs." If he was dishonest, if he had abused his official position, he should resign and the court should determine his fate.

Ilyushenko and Makarov flew to Switzerland and shortly afterward brought back two sets of documents that Yakubovsky had supplied them. From the receipts, bank statements, and the huge pile of other papers presented to me it was absolutely clear that Russian Security Minister Barannikov, an army general and one of my closest and most trusted colleagues, whom I had always liked because he had a fine mind and was a professional, had been bought in a vulgar and primitive way.

I initially decided not to be too hasty in drawing any conclusions. Documents can be forged, and such a thing is quite possible in Russia. The security minister is a serious enough figure that there could be forces wishing to compromise him. I didn't want to believe the worst, but when the documents were subjected to forensic analysis, they turned out to be authentic.

The story was as banal as they come: the Western firm Seabeco, run by Boris Birshtein, invited the wives of Barannikov and Dunayev, first deputy interior minister, to Switzerland. There the ladies scooped and ladled tons of perfumes, fur coats, watches, and everything else—a total of $350,000 in purchases. The wives took twenty baggage claim checks to Moscow; Seabeco paid $2,000 for the overweight luggage, which was three times as much as the cost of the air ticket from Geneva. I don't think that even in her wildest dreams could the most spoiled foreign millionairess have spent so much money in three days.

What was I to do? What was I to tell Barannikov about all this? My first thought was that the guy had become a victim of a deliberate setup. They sent his wife on a vacation for three days and showered dollars on her and she broke. Barannikov would now be easy to manipulate and just as effortlessly blackmailed. But what should I say to him? Before leaving for my vacation in Valdai, I spoke with Chernomyrdin. Like me, he at first refused to believe that such a thing was possible. He simply waved his arms in dismissal. "Oh, come on, Boris Nikolayevich, you and I both know Viktor Pavlovich. Such a thing couldn't be." When I told him the whole story in more detail, his face clouded. We decided to take the following action: I would without delay sign a decree dismissing Dunayev. Viktor Yerin had for some time had trouble getting along with him, and had raised the issue with me, but Barannikov had insisted that Dunayev be left in that position. I had asked Yerin to be patient but as it turned out, he had been right all along.

We also agreed that I would speak to Barannikov immediately after I got back from vacation. I would ask him to explain the facts that were already out in the open. Obviously, his wife couldn't be invited to Switzerland just like that, so it meant there had to have been some requests, some minor or perhaps major favors. After our conversation, I would ask him to submit his resignation. He could not remain in the office of security minister.

Dunayev's dismissal would of course be a serious blow to Barannikov, and a warning. He would quickly realize that he, too, could very soon be threatened with unpleasantness. I didn't think he would make any kind of abrupt or dangerous moves after that. Although the Security Ministry is fairly powerful—it's not for nothing that the name of its predecessor, the KGB, still gives off a cold blast—but I didn't yet believe in a conspiracy.

I went on vacation, and although my grandchildren, daughters, and wife did everything they could to shield and distract me from affairs in Moscow, my thoughts kept returning to Barannikov. I simply could not get a handle on this ridiculous story.

Soon the first rumors began to reach Barannikov and he tried to get in touch with me. I asked that he not be put through. Approximately a week later, a decree was issued about Dunayev's dismissal.

He was too solid a figure to pension off, but no clear explanation was forthcoming. The next day I received by messenger a thick package from Barannikov with HAND DELIVER PERSONALLY TO YELTSIN written on the envelope. I realized that Barannikov was now trying to save his own skin. The package arrived in the morning, but I couldn't force myself to open it until almost evening. I would pick it up, put it down, then go outside and walk around. I took a shower, saw a film, returned home, sat again in my office, took up the package again, and then set it down again. It was stupid, of course, to put it off, but it was so depressing, and my heart was so heavy . . .

Finally I opened the envelope and read the contents. Barannikov wrote that people were trying to compromise him. Some former agents of the KGB, one of whom (Yakubovsky) was an agent of the KGB's successor, the Russian Security Ministry, had shown Barannikov some information harmful to him. These agents were homosexuals who were quite possibly working in the interests of foreign intelligence agencies and were trying to smear the Russian security minister. Naturally, their information should not be believed. This was a well-orchestrated scheme, and a blow to the country's security.

As I mentioned, I had cut short my vacation because of the furor over the banknote exchange, and I returned to Moscow on Sunday. Barannikov no longer sought a meeting with me; he was waiting for my reaction. We then met on a Tuesday at the regular Security Council meeting, where the issue of the tragedy on the Afghan–Tadzhik border was discussed. A well-armed gang of Afghan extremists had attacked our guard post but the border guards had been unprepared for such a powerful assault. Our soldiers had been killed. Lessons had to be drawn immediately from this grave incident, particularly because groups from the Afghan side were increasingly massing on the border.

The border guards, who had been under the control of the KGB, were then under its successor, the Security Ministry. The troops have their own commander who is a deputy to the security minister. Therefore, ultimately, Barannikov also bore responsibility for the grave negligence that had been discovered when the Afghan–Tadzhik tragedy was investigated. After the reports and speeches from the council members, a decision was taken to dismiss Vladimir Shlyakhtin, commander of the border troops, and to officially reprimand Barannikov for his negligence.

Some of the council members were already briefed about the Barannikov scandal. They were anxiously waiting to see if I'd raise the question of the documents about the wives' shopping spree. It was a very convenient moment. For one thing, I decided it wasn't worth mixing up the two stories. Second, I first had to speak with Barannikov myself. Obviously, he would say one thing in a group; but what would he say in person to me to whom he had sworn allegiance not figuratively, but literally? He and I agreed to meet the next morning. Both during the council meeting and when he asked me to schedule an appointment with him, Barannikov avoided my eyes. That was a bad sign.

Barannikov was on my agenda for the next day at 11:00 A.M. Before his arrival, I asked Yuri Kalmykov, the minister of justice who had worked directly with the corruption commission, to come up to my office. I wanted to hear one thing from him: was there any chance for Barannikov? Perhaps it was necessary to check the authenticity of the documents again. Perhaps some facts had been distorted. Kalmykov could say nothing to reassure me. The materials that he had had the opportunity to examine had led Kalmykov to only one conclusion: it was corruption pure and simple. I excused Kalmykov, and Barannikov came into my office a few minutes later. He was pale. We greeted one another and I asked him to take a seat. A hard conversation immediately ensued. I asked him if it was true that his wife had traveled abroad at the expense of the Swiss firm and if she and Dunayev's wife had spent $350,000 within three days. He lowered his head and muttered yes.

Well, that was it. There's no point in describing the rest of the conversation. He took the blame, saying that it wouldn't happen again, that he had always been loyal only to me, that I had had many opportunities to convince myself of that. He said that it was wrong to ruin his career over some facts brought forward by some homosexuals. I was no longer really listening to him. I kept thinking monotonously that this was what it was like to say good-bye to a person you relied on. When Barannikov was done trying to justify himself, I said that at the upcoming meeting of ministers he would be relieved of his duties as minister.

Barannikov looked miserable but he had only himself to blame, and I had absolutely no desire to pity him. I was just ashamed for him, just terribly ashamed.

At 3:00 P.M., I invited the directors of the Security Ministry to come to the Kremlin.

I briefly informed those present that in connection with the slaying of the Tadzhik border guards and also in violation of ethics, Security Minister Barannikov was dismissed effective immediately; his duties would temporarily be assigned to his deputy, Nikolai Mikhailovich Golushko. Apparently for the majority of those in attendance, my words came as no surprise. When bosses are being removed, the staff usually finds out about it before their chiefs. After I finished speaking, silence fell over the room. I was completely startled to find Barannikov taking the floor. Only three hours previously I had seen him depressed and frightened; he had asked for forgiveness and begged not to be fired. Now he was suddenly speaking rather calmly and firmly, saying that the president of course could dismiss him from his job, but he believed himself to be innocent, and that the conclusions had been drawn on the basis of distorted information. He demanded a real prosecutor's investigation and not the testimony of some "fags."

I looked at him in amazement and said that of course all the facts would be thoroughly checked, by prosecutors as well as others. After that, I said good-bye to everyone. My mood was ruined for a long time after that.

The press was going crazy without hard information on the story. One version after another of the scandal was invented, each one more scathing than the next: that Barannikov had gone over to the side of Khasbulatov, that he had gathered too much compromising material against the president, that his more clever colleagues at the all-powerful Security Council had eaten him alive, and so on.

Barannikov kept mum since he had no interest in telling the press the real reasons for his dismissal. This went on for several days. Eventually, *Nezavisimaya gazeta* carried an open letter from Viktor Barannikov to President B. N. Yeltsin. The gist of the letter was that an honest person close to the president—Barannikov himself—did everything possible not to let the opportunists and extremists surrounding the president manipulate him. But in the end, the extremists prevailed, and the security minister was canned.

This was untrue from start to finish. He knew why I had dismissed him, and he knew perfectly well that the issue wasn't any extremists or opportunists. He decided to have the last word and leave the political arena with the image of a fighter for justice and Russia's interests, but it was a false image. This is why the former Russian Defense Minister Viktor Barannikov was finished for me as a person for the second time. His career was finished in Lefortovo Prison, which until just recently had been under his jurisdiction. He went there because of his role in the October rebellion.

In a while, the October coup will be absorbed into normal life; it will seem a "normal" scandal. I find it difficult to juxtapose these two processes, the criminal investigation and the political developments. When I conceived of a reform of the government, I never expected that it would be used by compromised politicians to save their own hides. That didn't seem possible at the time. But it happened. Barannikov and Dunayev and the other leaders of the October rebellion rushed headlong into a coup. The time bomb planted under the Russian government exploded after all, but in an unexpected fashion. The Russian reform effort became entangled in a crude, disgraceful affair. In that situation, I very much feared creating an atmosphere of a witch-hunt, people informing on each other behind their backs, a rush to find compromising material. Our country had already gone through all that under Stalin. Furthermore, the documents convinced me (and the prosecutor's office concurred with these findings) that many members of the government had been wrongfully accused.

By nature, I cannot tolerate an atmosphere of terror, revenge, third-degree interrogations, and witch-hunts. It's very important for me to feel and see that the people around me are behaving normally. In a word, I wanted to live an ordinary life. To illustrate this thought, I will make a little digression from this depressing topic of crime in politics.

Once when I noticed that Vladimir Shumeiko, a tall and slender man, was starting to get a potbelly, I knew that we couldn't go on living this way. I knew I would have to use the old Bolshevik methods to break this disrespectful attitude toward sports and physical exercise. Everyone would have to be forced to do sports and would be enticed, so to speak, by the personal example of the president himself. In Sverdlovsk, I had dragged practically the whole regional party office staff out on the volleyball court, and then they started liking volleyball so much they couldn't be chased off the courts. I sensed it was time to use the same methods on my Moscow colleagues.

Noticing how Korzhakov was breathing heavily—I don't recall why, but I think he had run from the first floor up to the third in the Kremlin—I said, "Alexander Vasilyevich, what's with you? You're an athlete, a volleyball player. You're supposed to play sports." Korzhakov pulled a long face; evidently, he had been suffering on this account as well. "Yes, I know. I've put on more than ten pounds," he said. "But when am I ever going to have time to play sports? We meet every morning at seven thirty and say good night at ten o'clock at night. The only time I would have is at night." He's right, I thought. The only time we would have would be at night. "All right, Alexander Vasilyevich," I told him. "From seven until eight in the morning the time is yours. At eight thirty, don't come to my house, but be at the Kremlin." He was thrilled, and I could see that he had really missed his physical workout. Now he's in the gym every morning and has long since lost the extra pounds.

It was a lot harder to get the other members of the government moving since they were unaccustomed to sports. I called in Shamil Tarpishchev and told him we would hold a tennis tournament. It would be a presidential tennis tournament. Everyone was to take part: those who were beginners and those who could play well. The main thing was to get everybody out on the court.

Everyone was divided into pairs. The favored pair was Shamil and me. Shamil was number one, of course; I had no illusions on that score, but I was no bit player myself. My serve was very hard to return—I had a powerful punch. That's about how I serve a tennis ball—like a volleyball. My serve to the right isn't bad; to the left it's a little worse as my old back injury gets in the way. When I hit backhand, I have to turn around quite a bit so as to favor my back. But together, Shamil and I fear no one. We were unbeatable.

The outsiders were immediately obvious—Kozyrev and Shumeiko. They lost to everyone. Kozyrev simply couldn't figure out how to serve, and Shumeiko had a hard time hitting the ball backhand. They made an honest and courageous effort to run around the court, trying to catch up with the ball flying ahead of them. I think even losing, they got a great deal of satisfaction just from taking part in the first tennis tournament of their lives.

The leaders were also defined. We won all the matches in two sets, but we had to play a third set against Viktor Ilyushin and Viktoria

Sokolova, a tennis champion and journalist. Viktoria's level of playing was evident, of course. She would serve me some easy ones, but she and Shamil competed like two real champions. Ilyushin, who had played tennis for five years, also looked very decent next to his great partner. Even so, we broke the tie and won with the third set.

I did not drag my comrades onto the court to win prizes or victories. After the tournament, what I had hoped would happen in fact did. Almost all the tournament players fell in love with tennis. Kozyrev began to play practically every day, and only his trips abroad forced him to take breaks. As far as I know, even when he's abroad and travels in a country for only a day, he somehow contrives to play a few sets with the Russian ambassador or someone from the embassy. When he returns to Russia, the first thing he does is head for the gym, not home. He now plays quite decently, keeps the ball in action, moves well, has a steady serve, and you wouldn't even believe that he has not been playing for long.

Viktor Yerin gets out on the court now twice a week. He was always able to move quickly, and now he is honing his technique. He has trained so well that at the Kremlin Cup '93 he played in a special cup tournament of famous people—writers, businessmen, artists, politicians. Yerin even played in doubles with Björn Borg and the great tennis player was very pleased with his partner.

Pavel Grachev began to play tennis regularly, found himself a steady partner, also a general, and trains with him every week. It will be hard to beat the defense minister at the next presidential tournament.

The first presidential tournament gave me another idea. While the tournament was under way, we would meet and talk and it was interesting to be with one another in an informal, human, and relaxed setting. It was then I decided to form the Presidential Club, a place where members could come after work to relax, where they would be expected, where people would be glad to see them. There they could talk, plays sports, and shoot some pool. They could come to the club with their spouses (and only their spouses!) and dance. That would be allowed, too. I proposed that the first members, the founding fathers of the club, so to speak, would be the participants of the first presidential tennis tournament. There would be a charter, membership dues, membership cards, and traditions. Through joint efforts, we proposed incorporating into the charter several fundamental principles, which were vigorously upheld by all the members of the club. Finally, we finished this important document, and although it's not serious and was done for fun, we swore to obey it honestly and unswervingly. Here is an excerpt from the charter of the Presidential Club:

> Any citizen of Russia who has reached the age of majority and certain wisdom may become a member of the Presidential Club.
>
> A citizen of a foreign country who is the president of his country may become a foreign member of the Presidential Club.
>
> The president of the club is the president of Russia.
>
> In order to become a member of the club, a candidate must have the recommendations of three club members, plus the recommendation of the president of the club.
>
> The number of club members cannot exceed 100. Those worthy candidates for club membership waiting in line must wait for the natural departure into the next world of the current members.
>
> The motto of the club is: THINK QUICK!
>
> Since the members of the club are people of the intelligentsia and are intellectual, it is forbidden to use curse words within club bounds. If you really feel like swearing—THINK QUICK!
>
> Any club member may visit the club with his or her spouse. Family togetherness is encouraged and welcomed in the club.
>
> The club and its services will operate 24 hours a day since the club members are busy people and they have irregular schedules.
>
> A club member remains a member for life.
>
> A club member may be expelled from membership for only one reason: treason. Therefore, THINK QUICK! A person is considered expelled if all the members in good standing of the club have voted to expel him.

There are all sorts of other rules in the charter, but the point of this association is now obvious. The people in the Presidential Club are close in spirit, in views, like one another, and want to see one another.

Naturally, the club members are not only people with whom I must work constantly—Prime Minister Chernomyrdin, ministers, other government officials. The club also has scientists, journalists, politicians, businessmen, and cultural figures. True, we have far to go before we reach the critical number of 100, but I think that's as it should be. After all, we were formed only recently. Everything's just getting broken in. We're getting used to the rules.

By the way, the first foreign member has joined our club—Nursultan Nazarbayev, the president of Kazakhstan. He really liked our club. I think he has been so taken with this idea that he wants to start something similar in his own country.

I hope that in one hundred years, the Presidential Club will be as cozy as it is now.

Why is it that I recalled such frivolous things in the context of such serious political events? Not just because I want to destroy the stereotype of the hard-boiled rigid leader. The reader can make what he likes of this stereotype.

I have long noted that before terrible events sometimes an unusually quiet, cloudless patch comes along. When you just don't feel like thinking about bad things. When the soul, even the whole body, craves serenity. Apparently, there is something mysterious in nature that knows everything in advance. It prepares us for harsh experiences, adapts us to reality, and relaxes us. Misfortune, however, always comes unexpectedly.

That was how it was in August 1991. And in August 1993. I knew I would be faced with major decisions and heated politics. There was nothing for it, but I was absolutely calm. I was in a lucid, light mood. Most likely I thought up the Presidential Club for this reason: to prove to myself and others that decent, human, normal life with its sorrows and joys goes on. That we must not only fight, but also talk to one another.

I suspect that approximately the same mood was in the society at large at the time. Yes, there's some squabble going on in Moscow, but so what? Let them fight, as long as they don't bother me. These are roughly the things I would read or hear. I have an ambiguous attitude toward that stance. On the one hand, it's a fairly starkly expressed political apathy. On the other hand, it's time for us to settle down. Isn't this constant overexcitement and tension that the politicians have kept the country in for two years getting to be too much?

I came to the conclusion that in spite of everything, the indifference of Muscovites to the scandals was a positive sign. Society yearns for a quiet life. People are expecting a normal rhythm, even if boring and hard but with a familiar rut, some coordinates by which we can get our bearings and choose a path. I wanted to protect and ensure that tendency toward stability. I have not accepted the thesis that the opposition of branches of government creates this stability. The cloudless, clear sky of August 1993 was deceitful and unreliable.

Soon the Congress will convene, a new furor will break out, and new passions will boil. Once again, people aren't dealing with the economy. Once again, they aren't dealing with current affairs. Once again, we are balancing on the edge, saving the country from a dispersal of power. No one was listening to anyone else. It had grown unbearable.

After Midnight

When I graduated from the institute, I had the rank of lieutenant in the reserves. Now I have the military rank of colonel. As was customary while I was at the institute, we would be sent for training exercises during the summer. I was assigned to command a tank in the armored tank troops.

The hardest part was the night driving and then I would usually sit in the driver's seat, not the commander's seat. That was always a risk. You're going at a high speed, it's dark, and you can't turn on your headlights because the enemy would detect you. You don't see anything ahead of or behind you. You're going about sixty miles an hour across broken terrain and dirt roads.

Once I turned a little bit off course somewhere and in the darkness, the tank ran into a water-filled ditch, landing almost straight up in the air. It bounced several yards more and began to sink into the water. Water in darkness is a great sensation but it was icy. I stepped on the gas. The main thing was somehow to crawl out onto the opposite slope. I pushed the pedal all the way to floor because if we stayed in one place, that would be it; we'd break down, and the tank would sink. Trying to get out would be a real hassle. Again I pressed the pedal, the tank roared and screeched, and I was crooning to it, come on, come on, honey, get some traction, go ahead, go ahead. The sense of that wailing and helpless vehicle is something I will remember my whole life.

Somehow, we all crawled out of there, soaked to the bone. We sat and waited for the brass to come—we were sure to be punished. We thought we'd each get ten days in the brig. But no, they even thanked us for not losing our cool. That's how it was in the army.

9

A HARD AUTUMN

Editor's Note: Yeltsin writes of the October parliamentary rebellion. His decision to disband parliament leads to a confrontation, and Yeltsin reveals how close he came to losing the battle. His generals were slow to come to his support and even misled him. They dispatched troops into Moscow only at the last possible moment. For the first time it is clear that the October crisis was in some ways more ominous than the coup of 1991.

Journal Entry, October 3, 1993

In the morning I went to the Kremlin. All night I had been unable to rid myself of a feeling of anxiety. The White House, although it was surrounded by the police and the OMON, still seemed to be a terrible threat to the stability of Moscow.

When I make some strategic decision, I don't punish myself with ridiculous worries over whether I might have done it differently or whether I could have found another way. Such fulminating is pointless. When I make a choice, there's only one thing left to do—implement it the best possible way, push it, and follow it through to the end. That's how it's always been. I have never tortured myself with postmortems, or why I spoke at the October 1987 central committee plenum. True, I did suffer and agonize, but certainly not because I was racked with doubts, wondering how my life would have turned out if I hadn't mounted the speaker's platform. Once I make a decision, I plunge right into it. I don't know if that is a virtue or a vice.

On that morning as I rode to the Kremlin, for the first time in my life I was tortured by the thought—had I done the right thing? Was there another option? Could it have been done another way? Had I exhausted all the alternatives? Russia was drowning in lawlessness. And here I was, the first popularly elected president breaking the law—albeit bad law, cumbersome law that was pushing the country to the brink of collapse, but the law, all the same. I rolled back the mental tape of all the events in the last month, hour by hour, day by day, trying to see if I had been mistaken . . .

It was early September. I had made a decision to dissolve the parliament. No one knew this, not even my closest aides. Russia simply could not go on with a parliament like this one.

Information leaks should not be tolerated. With the Supreme Soviet so militant in its death throes, news of the president's dissolution of parliament would be like a match to a gunpowder keg. The rebellious parliament leaders would not stop at any bloodshed or spare any casualties to remain in power. For starters, my decree for the parliament's dissolution had to have a legal underpinning. I pushed a button on my intercom and told Viktor Ilyushin that I needed to see him. I had sketched out an outline of a decree, but so far it was all in my head.

When I asked Ilyushin to come upstairs to my office, I set the machinery in motion. Now a crack team of professionals would begin to work. While Ilyushin was on his way, I still had a minute; I could still bring everything to a halt. But the thought did not even enter my mind. Ilyushin arrived and I formulated the assignment for him in a few words, watching him carefully. As usual he was composed, as if he were being assigned to draft a decree about cattle fodder for the coming winter. He asked several questions concerning the number of people who could be brought in on the job, how much they could know of the overall thrust of the document, and the deadline for the draft. I replied that the number of people involved should be kept to a minimum and he should have them work on separate sections so that not one of them would understand the whole gist. The team had a week to complete the draft. Ilyushin nodded and left the room. We were off and running.

Throughout the remainder of September, I reviewed all previously scheduled meetings, negotiations, and trips within the context of this forthcoming decree. Many appointments had been set as far back as June, July, or August. Some items I postponed, others had to be dealt with immediately; but I used these activities to better prepare myself for the coming events. For example, a preliminary schedule had included a visit to the army's Taman and Kantemir divisions. I had long been promising Defense Minister Pavel Grachev to come and take a look at these elite military units. After work on the decree began, this visit took on new meaning for me. When I spoke with the soldiers and reviewed the fine professional work of the divisions, when I met with the officers and commanders after the exercise, I kept thinking of the enormous, worrisome event that loomed ahead. How would these military people behave? How would they react? Naturally, I could tell them nothing of my plans, but I saw unmistakably that they would support me in them. There would be no betrayal.

A week later the draft of the decree was ready. During the last stage I had permitted Ilyushin to involve Yuri Baturin, the presidential legal aide. I had some doubts as to whether this was worth doing. It was not that I didn't trust Baturin completely; I just wanted as few people as possible to be burdened with excess information. Especially information of this nature. As far as I know, computers have a special system to protect excess, unnecessary information from cluttering and overloading their systems. That is why people have heartache and insomnia—from an overload of negative information. Some serious legal nuances had emerged that required a highly professional legal opinion, and there was nothing else for it. I had to bring Baturin up to speed. As always, he performed his part of the job correctly and professionally.

I also had some questions regarding the constitutional court as well, and its role after the declaration of the decree. When I first outlined the future decree's main premises to Ilyushin, I phrased the point about the constitutional court as follows: the court was not to hold sessions until after elections to the new Federal Assembly. Then, after long reflection, I realized it would be much more appropriate if I did not prohibit the members of the court from convening, but if I recommended that the court not hold sessions until the election of the new legislative body. The formulation was softened; I did not offend the constitutional body in any way but I still expressed my opinion in no uncertain terms. It was now on the conscience of the judges whether they would refrain from political infighting or take an active part in it by taking the side of the Supreme Soviet.

Journal Entry, September 12, 1993

Sunday, 12:00 noon. This was perhaps the most crucial moment in overcoming the crisis, so I brought my closest comrades in on the plan. I invited Grachev, defense minister; Viktor Yerin, interior minister; Nikolai Golushko, acting security minister; and Andrei Kozyrev, foreign minister, to come to a government dacha in the Moscow suburb of Staroogaryovo. Essentially, the entire strategic leadership of the country except for the prime minister would be gathered together here. Viktor Chernomyrdin was still on an official visit to the United States, but I planned to meet him the next morning at 11:00 A.M.

Would they support me or not? And if any of them would not support me, what next? There was no turning back. I was dissolving the parliament not because I was sick of it but because this Supreme Soviet had become a powerful, destructive force, a threat to Russia's security. The step *had* to be taken, but what would be the price? Much depended on the positions taken by the people who convened that Sunday afternoon.

Viktor Yerin. I trusted him as much as I trusted myself. I knew that for him, as head of one of the law-enforcement ministries, the crisis of dual authority between the parliament and the executive branch had become intolerable. The police were being pulled in different directions. In addition, the soviets* were trying to bring law enforcement under their control, especially in the areas where they were powerful.

I had seen Yerin in a number of different situations—both in cheerful moments (for example, when he had shown off his troops

*Local representative bodies of government, in some cases allied with the conservative policies of the Supreme Soviet, or standing parliament.—Trans.

to me during their exercises) and in difficult times (as when on Skokov's and Rutskoi's initiative and with Barannikov's active support, the matter of Yerin's resignation had been placed on the Security Council's agenda). At that time I had spoken adamantly against removing Yerin; he had only been working for four months, and it was not his fault alone that crime had soared. At the very least it was unfair to dump all the blame on solely one minister. Yerin was instead given a strict reprimand. Later, when I got to know him better, I found him to be a serious, intelligent, and very conscientious person. He is respected among policemen and has many other professional attributes. He is a great person.

Pavel Grachev. Over recent months he and I often discussed the country's deadlock. Grachev was convinced that this Supreme Soviet should have been closed down long ago. More than once during our conversations he had tried to persuade me to be tougher, complaining that I was dragging my heels. I replied that it was not a question of firmness, but of the price that must be paid if I sent the parliament into retirement. So when I made the decision, I had no doubts of the defense minister's full support. Furthermore, I sensed from his taut, combative demeanor that he had figured out why we were meeting and was glad that I had taken action.

Andrei Kozyrev. Another man whom I had not regretted choosing. Perhaps like no other government official, he had observed the enormous damage being inflicted on Russia's international image by its militant, chauvinistic parliament. The Supreme Soviet was not even pretending to pass itself off as peaceloving, as its predecessor in the era of Communist stagnation had done, feigning advocacy for disarmament, peace throughout the world, etc. The rebel parliament deputies were openly opposed to the international community on most issues, like the Yugoslav conflict and Russia's relations with the Baltic countries. In addition, there was the parliament's provocative declaration claiming control over the Black Sea Fleet. It is terrible to imagine even for a second what would happen to the world if the neo-Communists circa 1990 from the Supreme Soviet were to come to power in Russia.

Nikolai Golushko. I had my doubts about him. I did not know him very well. He had every moral right to reject the proposed option for solving the crisis. We had never worked together; more, Golushko was still only acting minister of security. We had drawn him into this unusual operation and it was quite possible that the decision to disband parliament would go against his political and human principles. I did not know how he would react. At the same time, perhaps it was a good thing I was getting the opportunity to test him in an extremely grave situation. Soon it would be clear to me if we had a new security minister or whether I would have to look for another candidate.

These were the thoughts flitting through my mind as we greeted one another and took our seats. Finally, an anxious silence fell on the room.

"I have invited you all here, today, gentlemen, to inform you . . ." I began. The situation was sufficiently analogous to Gogol's as to quote the classic remarks.* But would my news be highly unpleasant or, on the contrary, long-awaited and perceived as helpful in untangling the current complexities? Most likely it would be distasteful and difficult, but there was nothing for it.

I talked without a preamble; everyone knew what was going on in the country without me having to tell him. I informed my colleagues of the decision to dissolve the Supreme Soviet because its actions were constituting a threat to Russia's security. I asked those present to listen to a draft decree. Since there was only one copy, I read it aloud. I read slowly and carefully and finished it in about ten minutes. There was a brief pause, then each person said that he was completely in agreement with my proposed measures. Golushko also concurred. Andrei Kozyrev broke the tension when he pronounced solemnly in his soft voice, "I have a serious comment. I am not in agreement with one fundamental point, Boris Nikolayevich." Everyone looked at him in surprise. He continued: "Such a decree should have been passed long, long ago." We all smiled, although, in the larger scheme of things, he was absolutely right.

I named a date for the declaration of the decree—September 19, a Sunday. I outlined the following plan of action. At 8:00 P.M., there would be a televised broadcast of my appeal to the people. Units of the Dzerzhinsky Division, which by that time would be in Moscow, would take control of the White House. On Sundays, the building is empty, and no problems should arise. Khasbulatov and Rutskoi were likely to make their own statements, and would call press conferences in their apartments, but what was important was that they

*The rest of the quote is "of some highly unpleasant news. The Inspector General is paying us a visit." Nikolai Gogol was a nineteenth-century Russian satirist.—Trans.

would have no place to meet. The danger to the city was emanating from the White House. Mountains of weapons were stockpiled there. By occupying the White House, we would resolve several problems at once: we would deprive the dissolved Supreme Soviet of a headquarters from which to coordinate all the opposition's moves, and we would prevent it from reconvening. Without the White House, the rebel deputies would turn into a handful of loud-mouths. What were six hundred people compared to the whole population of Moscow? No one would listen to them.

This was a very preliminary outline that my ministers were supposed to flesh out in the coming days. If there were any alterations, we agreed that the same group, plus the prime minister, would deal with questions as they arose.

That same day I spoke with Mikhail Barsukov, chief of the main security directorate, and Alexander Korzhakov, the head of my own security. These two men were to play key roles in the upcoming operation.

The preliminary stage was now complete. Some bleak days began, perhaps the bleakest of my entire life.

Many times afterward, reporters and all sorts of people, acquaintances as well as strangers, would ask me the same questions I'd asked myself: could Russia's "Black October" have been avoided? Could a peaceful compromise have been found that would have led us out of the impasse?

In theory, yes. I do want to point out, however, all the many "peaceful" options we'd exhausted by that time. We'd changed the head of government (Chernomyrdin was elected by the Congress) and formed a reconciliation commission to bring parliament and government back together. The opposition had made an aborted attempt to impeach me, only proving the futility of their confrontational stance. Then there was the April referendum, where the people gave a clear sign of their support for me. Finally, there was the constitutional conference, involving many of the deputies, where it had been moved to pass a new Constitution at the next Congress.

Not to be outdone, Khasbulatov gave the command to sabotage the constitutional process. Several of his statements were vivid indications that further aggravation could be expected at the next Congress.

My priorities had been constant: political stability, clarity, definition. Enough of this pulling the blanket back and forth like an old couple. Enough of this fiddling with the legislation. The law should be applied the same way for everyone, and there should be one government for everyone. Russia would no longer tolerate our squabbling at the Congress. If this kept up, a new Russian Stalin would emerge who would crush this intellectual fussing with democracy with his little finger. I therefore chose my option for stabilization.

The next morning at 11:00 A.M. I met with Chernomyrdin at the Kremlin. He had just returned from the United States and gave me an account of his official visit. I did not interrupt him, although, understandably, I was entirely absorbed with other thoughts. When he finished his report, I quickly brought him back to planet earth. I told him of the decision to disband parliament and the discussion that had taken place in Staroogoryovo and gave him the draft of the decree already signed by four ministers. Chernomyrdin read it and signed it with a bold flourish. I had had no doubt that he would stand shoulder to shoulder with me at the crucial moment. Even so, I could not help admiring the calm assurance with which he took the news of the coming events, in which he was to play a major role. I had a real strong, sturdy man aboard.

Chernomyrdin left and my usual day at the Kremlin resumed. At noon I met with Sergei Filatov (I had decided to wait until closer to the events to brief him; the main work would be after the decree was issued; so for the time being I could allow myself to leave him in blissful ignorance). We discussed the upcoming session of the Soviet Federation* on Saturday. At 1:00 P.M., a scheduled telephone conversation took place with Finnish President Mauno Koivisto. Next, Academician Yuri Osipov;† then Academician Yevgeny Primakov, head of foreign intelligence; and after him came Ramazan Abdulatipov, deputy chairman of the Supreme Soviet. It was a brutal schedule with one meeting after another and the constant switching of topics so unavoidable in my position. A typical, full, busy day.

*A special body created by Yeltsin in September 1993 as a counterweight to the parliament.

†Chairman of the Russian Academy of Sciences. "Academician" is a Russian scholarly title granted to academics by election of their peers.—Trans.

The following afternoon, a Tuesday, the Presidential Council* met at 3:00 P.M. I had deliberately scheduled it for this week. It was important for me to run my plan to dissolve the parliament by these powerful intellects. Naturally, I told them nothing of the actual decision taken. But since this option had been floating around for a while, I could with a clear conscience suggest that the members of the council mull it over. I asked them to tell me all the pros and cons and attempt to simulate a future scenario of events in the country. It is hard for me to recall now exactly how I felt during this discussion. I was probably dissatisfied. For one, I had expected greater support from these leading public figures. Second, I thought they would be able to more thoroughly analyze society's possible state after parliament was closed down. Nevertheless, the exchange was extremely useful for me. I was confirmed on some points and some of their comments forced me to pay attention to details that had seemed less important until then.

Later, I met again several times with the key players of the upcoming operation. There were numerous questions, starting with the actual scenario and ending with larger issues—for example, the mechanism for enforcing the decree's statutes. The worst thing would be to pass such an act and then have it ignored. We had to decide how to respond to those regional soviets that would refuse to acknowledge the president's decree; how to react to a decision from the constitutional court (none of us had any doubts that there would be a ruling against us); and so forth and so on.

On Wednesday, September 15, there was yet another session of the Security Council. One more set of top officials were briefed about my plans and they, too, joined the preparation for zero hour. The meeting was closed and I asked that minutes not be taken. All the council members who were hearing my proposals for the first time supported the decision. The machinery of the operation set in motion began to accelerate.

On Friday, however, everything almost ground to a halt. On September 17, I had scheduled a final meeting where we were supposed to work out the last details. I asked the security ministries (defense, interior, and security) to give me their situation analyses. Suddenly, one after another, they began to suggest that my address

*Special advisory body formed by Yeltsin in 1991, whose members include a number of prominent figures.—Trans.

to the people set for Sunday should be postponed and hence the decree on the dissolution of parliament. A new date was proposed—the end of the following week. Several major reasons were cited. On September 24, a meeting of CIS heads of state had been scheduled in Moscow. During a state of emergency this could be canceled and the heads of the republics would not travel to Moscow, which would greatly undermine the president's authority.

Second, there had been an obvious leak of information. Khasbulatov and Rutskoi knew the most important thing—that a decree had been drafted to dissolve parliament and on Sunday it would be announced and then go into effect. They didn't know the details, but they knew the main thrust of the decree and were in a panic. The plan calling for an occupation of an empty, inactive White House on a Sunday when no deputies or workers would be there had to be altered. On Sunday, Khasbulatov would bring all of his supporters there and the White House would turn into a fortified center of resistance. He must not be given this opportunity. We had to put the rebels into an awkward position. They might gather to resist and fight, but there'd be nothing to resist or fight against.

At this same meeting someone raised the idea that the September 19 was really not the best day for such a declaration; the parallels to August 19, the day of the coup in 1991, would be too obvious. It would be better to do it, say, on September 26, at the least. Then there wouldn't be so many unhealthy associations.

I agreed to postpone the date, but just for two days, not for a week. On September 21 at 8:00 P.M. I would speak on television. This was my fundamental position: there could be no more postponements. In the next few hours we had to think how to neutralize the influence of the White House. Exactly what we had so wanted to avoid had now become inevitable: the White House would be a center of opposition to the decree. I asked Yerin, Grachev, and Golushko to find a way to occupy the White House given the new turn of events. I established the chief condition: we would not allow any casualties. If that was not possible, then we would change our tactics—let them sit in the White House, and we will simply ignore the sessions and congresses of the nonexistent parliament. I noticed that all the participants in this emergency meeting left my office in agitation. Sergei Filatov, my chief of staff, who had just now learned of the decree and our tactics, was quite shaken.

On Monday, that is, after the emotions had apparently died down, he met with me. Filatov was usually a calm self-contained person but this time he began heatedly and emotionally to try to persuade me to back down from my plans. He said no one would support the decree and that we would doom ourselves to confrontation with all the regions of Russia. Such an antidemocratic method of resolving a conflict of powers would not be supported by the countries of the West, and we would find ourselves completely isolated.

I let him talk. Furthermore, I was even glad he was telling me all this. It is always important to hear the con arguments, especially from a close comrade. It was wonderful that he wasn't afraid of expressing his reservations to me. Filatov is an intelligent, honest, conscientious man and I like him very much but I realized he did not have a feeling for the current political situation. He was living in the past, in that world of compromises and concessions that I had been dwelling in until recently. I thanked him for all his comments, and once again confirmed that on September 21, I would begin to act. I asked him to assist in implementing the decree in spite of his position. With that we parted.

But to come back to our strategy. I had to think how to act next. Where had that leak come from? As zero hour approached, because the decisions were of such import, the number of people involved in the whole plan or in some of its details was constantly growing. Golushko briefed some of his deputies and Yerin and Kozyrev had to do the same. We had to keep in mind that Barannikov, former security minister, and Dunayev, former deputy interior minister, both recently dismissed, had naturally retained informal ties to their former subordinates. Most likely it was from these two ministries that information had been leaked to Rutskoi and Khasbulatov. It was pointless to speculate; a plan of action had to be outlined, a political plan.

In the event that the White House would remain in the hands of the dissolved parliament, I saw our tactic as follows: yes, they would convene a congress and apparently would announce my impeachment and President Rutskoi would therefore make his debut in the world. Most likely they would immediately announce their government, with the fascist Iona Andronov as foreign minister and perhaps Sazhi Umalatov as security minister who promised everyone that she would hang President Yeltsin upside down. Their government would consist of a president of the White House and a cabinet of ministers of the White House, but such a political dinosaur would not gain support in Russia.

That meant that we had to throw our weight behind the election process. After September 21, preparations for the new December elections would pick up speed. The deputies sitting in the White House would be faced with an alternative—either leave their bunker and join the election campaign or remain inside, thereby falling out of Russia's political life forever. They had become so accustomed to the word *deputy,* they liked legislating so much, living well and never answering for anything, traveling without charge on public transportation, that they would not endure more than two weeks of confinement. They would flee. They would sign up at the electoral commission, garner votes, and do everything to become deputies again. There was another important tactical element I intended to exploit to remove the tension that would naturally arise after dissolving the legislative branch of government. I decided to announce that presidential elections would be held ahead of schedule.*

I kept repeating to myself and everyone who was actively involved in our implementation of the future decree that only nonviolent methods could be used. There were to be no violent clashes. All possible options were to be weighed in advance so there would be no casualties, and not a single life would have to pay for the measures I was compelled to take.

At the end of the week after the meeting of the Soviet Federation at the Kremlin, I went to a government dacha called Rus'† outside Moscow to escape, even for one night, the tension that I had been living under. Before my departure, Interior Minister Yerin and I agreed that the troops being brought into Moscow for the Sunday operation would make an anticrime sweep in the city on Saturday and Sunday. Policemen held surprise raids at all the train stations, airports, and hot spots of the capital and caught a large number of criminals.

I left for Rus' along with Grachev, Barsukov, and Korzhakov. I felt like relaxing, as much as was possible before the difficult days ahead, to take some walks in the woods and to breathe the fresh autumn air outside the city.

*Originally, elections were scheduled for 1996.—Trans.

†The ancient name for Russia.—Trans.

That night, after dinner, a heated argument suddenly broke out between Pavel Grachev and Mikhail Barsukov. Barsukov, whom I knew to be a cool, self-possessed, even mild-mannered fellow suddenly began to fiercely try to persuade Grachev that the security ministries had turned out to be unprepared to implement the decree. Everyone was proceeding from the premise, he said, that we did not need harsh measures, that everything would go peacefully and smoothly. That was great—if we managed to occupy the White House on the first day. We had to make sure we occupied that building immediately after the decree was announced. But, asked Barsukov, furious, what if we don't? Had anyone made a realistic assessment of what a threat the White House could become within a few days? Where was the plan of operation drafted by military experts? I am not speaking of the political plan, he said—that was the bailiwick of the president and his administration. What if some army division took the side of the parliament? What if the police could not maintain order? Anything could happen when the decree was announced. The actions of the military had not been thought through. A simulation should be conducted and all the alternatives worked out to coordinate ways and means among the ministries of security, defense, interior, and the chief security directorate. We should take every possibility into account now. As a military man, Barsukov concluded vehemently, I believe that we are not prepared to implement the decree!

Grachev was barely able to restrain himself. He attacked Barsukov, charging that he just didn't believe in success and that it would be better not to get involved in such a great matter if he had an attitude like that. Everyone was absolutely prepared for this step by the president, and the army had long been impatiently waiting for it. There was nothing to be frightened of here. The White House would be ours, and the victory would be ours.

Only my presence cooled these outbursts and even then with difficulty. I respect both generals but I, too, could not restrain myself and almost shouted at them to stop their senseless talk. I understood that everyone's nerves were on edge yet I, too, was angered by Barsukov's position. Why was he saying all of this now, two days before the decree was to be declared? Grachev was right; it was better not to begin anything at all with that kind of attitude.

I said to Barsukov: Mikhail Ivanovich, perhaps you really should take a vacation now, and when it's all over, then you can come back and get down to work.

Barsukov looked at me with a hurt expression. He replied that it would be better if he remained in the Kremlin and if I would permit it, he would like to continue the work assigned to him. I nodded my consent.

Everyone left displeased with one another, apprehensive, and nervous.

Many episodes of those days appear different to me in hindsight. Barsukov's "mutiny," for example. At the time I saw it as a display of weakness. Now I see he had instinctively sensed the danger. As a seasoned security officer, he had a hunch that events would become unmanageable. Indeed, by the fall of 1993, the country was fraught with anarchy, sabotage, and large-scale terrorism. There was divisiveness in the army, society at large, and the regions.

My youth and manhood and those of my generation had passed in an era of peace; war had become a kind of phantom, a childhood nightmare. Our whole lives had been lived under the reliable but terrible nuclear shield, and the belief that while the two confrontational systems of capitalism and socialism may clash, they would not come to war. Unpreparedness for war was already deeply ingrained in our subconscious. For some reason I believed that the most terrible events of our history were somewhere in the remote past and could not come again. On one hand, this was incorrigible Soviet optimism. And on the other, it was an attitude that said: hey, come on, how many civil wars, dictatorships, revolutions, and terrorist acts can Russia endure? Optimism aside, however, one always had to prepare for the worst. That was a kind of law. There were plenty of examples—Chernobyl, the ethnic clashes in Armenia and Moldova, the internecine wars of the Caucasus and Yugoslavia, the August 19 coup. These were ominous warnings to those of us who lived in this country technically not at war that we should be on our guard.

Yet another problematic area had led to tragedy. That was a fear and unwillingness to use force. We had no clearly formulated plan of action in the event of a rebellion, a state of emergency, or a local conflict, and we had to admit that. Such a plan could only be based on experience but there was no precedent of a major state of emergency as such throughout Russia. Because we had no plan—the only model for us of a free-for-all situation involving the entire government was the August coup—we had become obsessed with a fear of demonstrations and a concern that we could not cope with spontaneous street rallies. As a result, we ordered the police to stand unarmed near the demonstrators, pitting their rubber truncheons and shields against the rebels' machine guns, Molotov cocktails, sawed-off shotguns, and jackknives. On top of this, there was the tangled web of political contradictions.

Formally, the president was violating the Constitution, going the route of antidemocratic measures, and dispersing the parliament—all for the sake of establishing democracy and the rule of law in the country. The parliament was defending the Constitution—in order to overthrow the lawfully elected president and establish total Soviet rule. How had we found ourselves in such a fix? Why was Rutskoi able to get away with telephoning military districts and large defense plants and unleashing a civil war? Why were gunmen and terrorists given the green light to battle the lawful authorities? Why was the country subjected to such a terrible risk?

On Monday, there was yet another stressful conversation, again with Filatov. I sensed that the closer we came to the moment of action, the greater the tension in the Kremlin, on Old Square,* and in the Defense Ministry.

The array of forces was as follows: the White House leadership was awaiting the issue of the decree at any moment. On Saturday, Khasbulatov had held a meeting at the parliamentary center with representatives of local as well as regional and national soviets. It was a real Soviet-style extravaganza at the height of which Khasbulatov made a rather obscene gesture. While standing at the podium, he said something to the effect that not much could be expected of our president; after all, he's a Russian muzhik, and when he's "had a few," he'll sign anything—whereupon Khasbulatov snapped his fingers against his throat.† This insult did not touch me deeply—how can you be hurt by a doomed man?—but it really outraged the media and the public. He had crossed a certain line that he'd been afraid to cross in the past, whether out of desperation or on the contrary, in a bravado attempt to brandish his power.

*Russian government office buildings are located on Old Square (Staraya ploshchad'), the former seat of the Soviet Communist party's central committee.—Trans.

†A crude gesture universally understood among Russians as referring to a drink of alcohol.—Trans.

On Sunday, at Khasbulatov's urging, the entire convention of representatives from the local soviets moved from the parliamentary center building to the White House. Khasbulatov and Rutskoi had made the decision to turn the regional deputies into a living shield. On Sunday afternoon, the White House, which was supposed to have been empty according to our initial plans, was in fact packed to the gills. On Monday, panic-stricken activity continued. More and more people were summoned to the White House, and just what I had wished to avoid began to happen. The White House was turning into an organized headquarters for resistance to my decree.

On Tuesday morning, I spoke on the direct line with Chernomyrdin, Golushko, Grachev, and Yerin. I asked my security ministers one crucial question: how should we handle the White House now? Was there still some way of smoking those deputies out of there? Come on, come on, I pressed them—*think*. Perhaps a lightning-quick shock-troop assault with SWAT teams, perhaps other options that we hadn't managed to review? It would be a terrible mistake to leave such an explosive hotbed in the center of Moscow. Each one of the ministers spoke his opinion in turn. Their reports were brief and to the point but didn't make me feel any better. The picture was starkly clear with no ambiguities: the White House could not be taken. Proceeding from that fact, we had to plan our future tactics. This was, of course, a heavy blow. I frigidly asked all the ministers to come to the Kremlin at noon. They sensed my state, but could do nothing to help.

To reiterate, it was not the building itself that concerned me. Now I had an almost physical sense of what a messy, complicated, and dangerous situation we had entangled ourselves in. I could see in my mind's eye the crowd surrounding the White House, from which death, destruction, and war would be unleashed. To avoid this, we would have to walk the razor's edge, and obviously compromise, discuss some matters, and make a few concessions to the Supreme Soviet leaders. Or rather, the *former* Supreme Soviet, which is what it was by that time. I was willing to meet them halfway. The main thing was not to allow bloodshed and casualties under any circumstances.

To be sure, these would be the last compromises in Russian history with the form of government known as the soviets. Within several hours, I would announce the dissolution of the parliament—the Supreme Soviet. With that, I was absolutely certain that soviet rule would be ended forever in our country.

At noon, all the key players reconvened. Everyone was tense. When I gave Pavel Grachev the floor, he was so agitated that he asked permission to read his terse report. He had never done that before, but now in a loud, firm voice he read from his notes. Chernomyrdin, Yerin, and Golushko, who had been appointed the new security minister on Saturday, also gave their briefings.

Due to the turn of events, we made some adjustments in our plan, primarily concerning the White House. We decided to turn off all the city and government communication lines to the building in order to weaken the parliament's influence with Russia's provincial regions. I recalled my experience in August 1991, when the government telephones were cut, hampering our efforts considerably. (At the time, a telephone the coup plotters forgot to turn off in Viktor Ilyushin's office helped a great deal.) I requested General Starovoitov, head of the Federal Agency for Government Communications and Information,* who was in charge of our communications, to meet with me as soon as possible. As of 8:01 P.M., immediately after the broadcast of my address, all the telephones in the White House must fall silent.

After a brief discussion, we decided not to place any heavy army or police cordons around the parliament building. Such a show of force could incite unnecessary aggression from the people inside the White House. In the same vein, we decided not to bring in any army divisions to Moscow. I saw our tactics as follows: yes, we were taking severe, resolute, and appropriate measures but only in response to the unlawful actions of the White House leadership. I believed that we should not aggravate the situation.

The meeting broke up and I began to prepare my television address. The taping was scheduled for 5:00 P.M. The camera crew did not know exactly what they would be filming. Only after they arrived at the Kremlin were they told about my address. They were professionals not ruffled by anything, and went about setting up their equipment, cameras, and microphones in room 4 of the Kremlin. They obviously sensed that this would not be an ordinary message to the people.

As always in these situations, after the text of my speech had been loaded into the computer and was supposed to appear on the

*The new agency in charge of the special telephone lines used in government communications, created after the coup, previously under the jurisdiction of the KGB.—Trans.

TelePrompTer, the machine broke down. The text refused to come up on the screen, and when it finally did reappear, instead of scrolling slowly across the screen line by line, the words flew by at top speed. The engineers fiddled with it, but curiously this little incident somehow helped to allay my tension. It was classically mundane: the equipment always breaks down in front of the bosses at the most crucial moment. Eventually, everything was fixed. People who were not immediately involved in the taping were asked to leave. Complete silence fell on the room. I looked squarely into the camera and began, "Citizens of Russia!"

I finished reading the text, stood, and thanked everyone. The television crew passed the videotape of my speech to my aides. Within a few minutes, a car with an armed guard raced off to Ostankino Television, where the chief executive, Vyacheslav Bragin, who had already been notified, was to take the cassette and air it at 8:00 P.M. Another detail: my press secretary, Vyacheslav Kostikov, asked the TV crew not to leave the Kremlin until 8:00 P.M. They were fed dinner and entertained so that they would not feel uncomfortable. These security measures might seem superfluous now, but at the time they were necessary.

In the office, copies of the decree were being sealed into envelopes. Now the decree finally had a number and a date—it happened to be number 1400. In fact I had signed it a week earlier. It went into effect on September 21 at 8:00 P.M. At precisely 8:00 P.M., a courier was to deliver copies to everyone who would be immediately affected: Khasbulatov, Rutskoi, and Zorkin, the head of the Supreme Court. I knew what their reaction would be, but the formalities had to be observed.

I decided not to wait at the Kremlin until 8:00 P.M., so at approximately 7:00 P.M. I went home and watched my address on television. There were minor rough spots that only I would notice, but as much as I tried to be objective, it seemed to be a good speech.

Russia was entering a new epoch. We were shrugging off and cleansing the remains of the filth, lies, and falsity accumulated for seventy-odd years. Just a few more shakes and we would all start to breathe more easily and purely. If I hadn't firmly believed this, it would not have been worth starting any of my efforts in the first place.

Once again I plunged headlong into events.

Meeting after meeting, conference after conference. The sense of alarm was snowballing. Then came the crushing news that the White

House was already in control of the deputies. This was all bad, very bad. It would have been the easiest thing of all—as I was being advised—to keep delaying any decision by a week, then another, and yet another, thereby never making a decision at all in the end.

If I had hesitated, people would have lost trust in me forever. I don't mean the political consequences and the legal chaos that would be unleashed in the country after the next Congress. There was also the human element. My people were not an unthinking team of executors. They would not forgive me for such insane vacillations and such sharp turnarounds. I had to follow through to the end. The exercise of power does not always look pretty. I had already understood that from the example of economic reform. But it was also true of some political situations.

The moral vacuum forming around the White House was not accidental.

The myth that Russians admire strong authority needs some refinements. Russians really love defenders, people who are protecting something. They don't like those who are attacking, aggressors. Strong, lawful authority is well perceived everywhere but in our country, people have not become accustomed to a legitimate government. In our history, it has been all or nothing. Either revolutionary anarchy or a ruthless regime. That is why, when a democratic president came on the scene, a leader who took determined action, it didn't make sense. People didn't get it. Some were irritated; how can this be?

Rutskoi, Khasbulatov, and General Albert Makashov hastened to fill that moral vacuum. They hurried to pursue a clear order—*storm! attack!*—and thus signed their own arrest warrants.

The next day did not bring any unexpected news, although it was already a whole new ball game. Almost everything we had calculated in advance did happen. Khasbulatov and Rutskoi announced they were convening the Congress. From the first hours of the crisis, the White House became the armed headquarters of resistance to my decree. The constitutional court held a night session and predictably pronounced decree number 1400 unconstitutional. As was usual with the court's deliberations, four judges produced dissenting opinions.

That morning I met with Viktor Chernomyrdin at the Kremlin on a number of matters. First, there was the dismissal of Viktor Gerashchenko, chairman of Central Bank of Russia, and the appointment of Boris Fyodorov, the current finance minister, in his place. Chernomyrdin put up quite a strong resistance to my suggestion that Gerashchenko step down, saying that he was completely happy with relations as they stood now between the government and Central Bank. Gerashchenko was a professional and knew the banking business inside and out. With the Supreme Soviet out of the way, dealings with Central Bank would be qualitatively different. Meanwhile, Fyodorov had quite enough to do at his current job. Surely such a tough, almost aggressive minister who would guard the country's finances like a watchdog was just what we needed now; why look for a new one?

I demurred, but not for the reasons he cited, well argued though they were. The prime minister had to work both with Central Bank and the finance minister. If I were to interfere in these matters, it would mean that I did not trust my prime minister and I would merely be getting in his way.

The second matter I discussed with Chernomyrdin concerned the figure of the procurator general. The whole country knew that Valentin Stepankov, the current procurator general, was utterly under Khasbulatov's spell. Stepankov did not even try to conceal either his political or personal allegiance to the speaker. Their relations had almost become friendly; they helped one another and gave each other awards. Stepankov presented Khasbulatov, his ultimate boss,* with an identification card from the procurator's office labeled NUMBER 1. It was almost like the old Brezhnev days—true, they usually bestowed people with party cards back then, but the fashion had merely changed.

It was Stepankov, at Khasbulatov's urging, who had delayed an objective procurator's inquiry into mass disorders during the celebration of the May 1 holiday earlier in 1993. When the group working on the case concluded beyond doubt that the neofascist demonstrators were to blame for the melee and police had acted in self-defense, Khasbulatov demanded that the investigation's findings be revised and that the case officers be replaced. There was one other factor compelling me to seriously assess the figure of the procurator general—his connection to an émigré businessman

*Technically, at this time the procurator general was supposed to report to the Supreme Soviet.—Trans.

named Dmitry Yakubovsky and a firm called Seabeco. It was a mystery what services the procurator was performing for businessmen of this type. Why would a young fellow like Yakubovsky speak to the procurator general like a petty thug, swearing and behaving so brash and rude? (There were transcripts of their conversations in the newspapers.) The fact was, Dima Yakubovsky had some kind of hold over Stepankov and Stepankov seemed unable to avoid contacts with Yakubovsky, although they were unpleasant for him. There was no covering it up.

Chernomyrdin's suggestion came as a surprise. He proposed leaving Stepankov in place. Frankly speaking, I wasn't comfortable with the idea. Still, I could not insist on replacing the procurator because I had no other candidate at hand. It would have been unforgivably stupid at this juncture to appoint some temporary figure to this strategically important position. Upon reflection, I conceded that Chernomyrdin was right. We agreed that if Stepankov began to play ball with Khasbulatov and abet the nonexisting Supreme Soviet, he would immediately be removed from his job. To be sure, I knew the press would kick up a fuss and I would have some hard talks with the democrats—they would accuse me of betrayal and say I had made unworthy compromises for the sake of political advantage. But the decision was made and time would soon tell whether it had been correct.

On September 22, the chiefs of the security ministries gathered in the reception hall at 1:30 P.M. I noted with satisfaction that all the ministers had shrugged off that apprehension and excessive anxiety that had clung to them all week. Now something concrete had been started, and as professionals, they had a job to do.

Once again I emphasized that we would stick to an unvarying tactic—we would not respond to provocations and would push very hard for elections. In that way we would leave the White House in political isolation. We would maintain order in Moscow with the help of the Interior Ministry's troops, so the chief burden lay on Yerin. If the situation required a tougher response, the army should be ready to enter the capital at any moment.

After we said good-bye, on the way to the Kremlin I decided, as was my old custom, to stop where there were a lot of people. The motorcade came to a halt on Tverskaya Street. I got out of the car and was surrounded by a crowd of Muscovites. "Well, what do you think? Do you support the decree?" Without their backing, nothing else made sense. There were shouts, cheers, and encouraging smiles. It was extremely important to see and hear all this. It was a breath of fresh air.

I know that some people are skeptical of my walk-abouts among the people. They find them pretentious, a pose, and the wrong way to find out public opinion. I know quite well myself this is not the best way to learn what people are thinking. For that there are several independent sources from which information reaches me immediately through direct channels. But something entirely different happens at these encounters. I see the eyes of many people. I sense their emotions, their states, their pain and hope. This is not something you can find in memos, coded intelligence reports, or news digests.

By then almost all the leaders and governments of the major Western countries, the nations of Eastern Europe, Asia, North America, and the third world had spoken in favor of my proposed resolution of the political crisis in the September 21 decree. I think such a tough, unequivocal position from the world community was a heavy blow to the White House occupiers. A second, and I believe no less heavy blow, was leveled against the defenders of the dissolved parliament on Thursday, September 24. Without exception, all the leaders of CIS countries came to Moscow for the scheduled meeting. Khasbulatov and Rutskoi were forced to express their barely concealed displeasure at this news.

On Wednesday and Thursday, when my staff kept reporting to me the arrivals of various CIS leaders, I recalled how harshly I had debated some of my ministers who were convinced that with such an unstable situation in Moscow, the meeting in the Great Kremlin Palace would not take place. I, on the contrary, was absolutely certain that it would take place. Furthermore, by holding the meeting calmly without fuss and apprehension, we would supply one more weighty argument in favor of the course I had taken.

I believe this CIS meeting was one of the most effective ever. There were both objective and subjective reasons for this. I suppose the main factor was that in the two years we had been torn apart, everyone had become so fed up with sovereignty, that is, ill-conceived sovereignty (poorly envisaged or unfounded economically) that we simply met each other halfway. The heads of state spoke in official support of my course. And there were many informal tête-à-têtes. Virtually every one of the presidents considered it his duty to tell me his position on my decision to dissolve parliament; moreover, their assessments of the former Supreme Soviet were hardly expressed in diplomatic terms. They would never have said such things in an official document. I saw that every single leader of a republic of the former Soviet Union sincerely took an interest in Russia's destiny. Each one gave me his confidential advice; some suggested that I impose presidential rule without any December elections; others firmly advocated that all the White House conspirators be arrested. Some of their ideas were radical, even revolutionary. Their advice was highly unlikely to be heeded, but I could not help but be touched by their concern, especially in such distressing circumstances.

By the conclusion of the CIS meeting, the White House crisis was about to explode. On September 23 at about 9:10 P.M., a group of gunmen attempted to seize the soldier on duty at the former headquarters of the CIS joint armed forces on Leningradsky Prospect. Eight outlaws armed with machine guns managed to disarm the guard. An OMON squad was sent out in response to the soldier's call for help, and they soon forced the intruders out of the building. Two people were killed in the gunfire, Captain Sviridenko of the police force and Vera Malysheva, a sixty-year-old woman who lived in the building across the street. Hearing shots, she had come to her window and was hit by a stray bullet.

These were the first casualties in the undeclared civil war unleashed by the White House. After this senseless—from both a political and a military tactical point of view—act, the confrontation with the former parliament took on an altered significance. Though the people occupying the White House were certain political forces that did not wish to submit to my decree and had an armed guard and well-equipped gunmen, they nonetheless tried to conduct a civilized dialogue with the authorities. They convened congresses, appointed new ministers, sent telegrams to the regions, and received help from the constitutional court. After the deaths at the former CIS building, all talk about constitutionality, legality, and deputies' concern for the Russian people seemed a cynical farce.

The White House's ordering of an attack on a military building meant that either the leadership of the former parliament was no longer in control of the situation and real power was in the hands of armed extremists or that after Khasbulatov and Rutskoi saw we were acting so delicately, they decided to test the government's reaction to the first blood. How would they respond at the Kremlin? In fact, it was possible that both of these poorly controlled processes were happening simultaneously.

That night Pavel Grachev issued an order to reinforce security at all Defense Ministry buildings. He and I and Chernomyrdin as well as the other law-enforcement ministers continued to consult over the telephone. We had an agreed-upon position: army troops should not interfere in the establishment of order in Moscow. The brunt of the crisis therefore fell on Interior Minister Yerin.

Up until that point the encirclement of the White House was purely symbolic. Anyone who wished to do so could get inside the building and if he grew tired of hanging around and protesting, he could leave and go home or go to work. Starting on September 24, Yerin ordered a strict blockade of the building using policemen. Now it was possible only to leave the White House; no one could enter. Electricity, hot water, and heat were turned off. It became impossible for the people of Moscow to tolerate such a site bristling with weapons and politicians ferocious over their loss of power in the middle of a city with a population of millions. However, there could be no talk of any storming or occupying of the White House at that moment. In the meantime, large crowds of people began to gather around the White House.

At first I was very concerned about this, then I realized what was happening. Aside from the professional demonstrators turned out by Anpilov, leader of Working Moscow, others had been drawn by either curiosity, sympathy, or simple outrage. They were indignant at the sight of such an unprecedented political show in Moscow. Some people came to the White House simply to stare at the huge lines of policemen in helmets; others came to express their outrage and displeasure. The same was repeated later during the storming, but in an even more hideous and confounding way. When we were forced to order the storming of the White House, at enormous risk to life and limb, the crowd stood near tanks on the embankment* in a cross-fire zone within the sights of snipers on rooftops. Why? I was plagued by this question for a long time. I think psychologically it was understandable. People were in a terrible state of nervous apprehension, emotionally distraught, and were simply unaware of what they were

*The White House is located on the bank of the Moscow River.—Trans.

doing. Only later would the horror and the shock of what they had seen register, but at first the mood was even gay.

Carrying a megaphone and some flags, Rutskoi performed a few loud theatrical gestures near the White House. He called on the police to think twice and come over to the side of the Supreme Soviet. They had decided, apparently, that a spontaneous popular rebellion had finally begun. That was their fatal error.

The events took an unexpected turn. For one, I could not account for why the people milling around the White House were not at all affected by the deaths of Captain Sviridenko and Vera Malysheva. Those people had been victims of a criminal operation. Yet much more was said and written about the fact that the government was using wrongful methods against its political opponents and putting too much pressure on them. The poor things had nothing to eat or drink. It was beastly.

There was one other unexpected reaction involving the guarantee of benefits for the deputies.* Of course there was a hidden agenda here—we wanted to cool the hotheads somewhat and bring them down to planet earth. But in fact, no fraudulent buyout was being perpetrated here. Perhaps it was too late, perhaps it should have been announced earlier and explained as part of the decree: we simply wanted to give people, many of whom had worked in the parliament without incident, some confidence in the future. After all, not all the people in the White House were extremists. Actually, the deputies could have picked up their government aid and returned to the White House.

The number of tactical errors grew. Insignificant when taken separately, together they created an impression of chaos, even though there was no hysteria. We thought we were doing the right thing. In hindsight I see the reasons for all these mistakes: we were not ready to fight. There was no battle plan. Internally, I simply could not accept the possibility that a constitutional dispute could lead to shooting people.

There was more. The decree was perhaps the most difficult decision of my life. I was undergoing an agonizing process of decision making, and that is why our vehicle of state did not roll along the

*The government had promised the deputies that if they left the White House by a certain deadline they could receive severance pay and retain their government apartments.—Trans.

highway in a straight line, but knocked down telephone poles and ran into a ditch.

The direct threat to state security brought everything into perspective but, at first, each step came hard. I realized there was only one way out of the constitutional deadlock where virtually any action could be declared illegal. But, oh, how I didn't want to break the law in order to extricate us from this tar baby!

Once again I realized what democracy means. Above all it is a heavy, terrible responsibility. That is, if you are a decent human being.

I have always relied on common sense and was certain it would prevail once again, especially because with each passing day the plight of the White House occupiers was growing more apparent. The support they had expected was nowhere to be found. Not the army, the trade unions, or the coal miners were backing the former deputies. Only the local and regional soviets were sending telegrams of acknowledgment to their old comrades, but pieces of paper aren't very effective. In desperation, Rutskoi called on the working class to declare a general strike. His appeal sparked no activity whatsoever. Khasbulatov energetically negotiated with provincial leaders, hoping that the Novosibirsk comrades, who had promised to block the Trans-Siberian Railroad, would come through. If they could paralyze such a strategic artery, that would mean serious business; the authorities might be frightened into negotiating. No one wanted to cut the rail line, though Khasbulatov and the others talked until they were blue in the face.

Rutskoi telephoned the military districts and demanded they pledge allegiance to the new president and defense minister. He of course had some friendly relations among military people. There was Rutskoi's personal friendship, for example, with General Pyotr Deinekin, commander of the air force. He begged, demanded, and shouted at his friend to get him to come to his aid. The general replied, using Rutskoi's nickname, Sasha, don't be a fool. I have one president, Yeltsin, and one defense minister, Grachev. You had better surrender quickly.

Most important, the White House leadership remained in both a political and information vacuum. I believe this was a terrible shock for Khasbulatov, Rutskoi, and company. All along they had had a false sense that all they had to do was give one push and everyone in the entire country would dash after the Communist Bolshevik parliament as it retreated into the past; but the people never came running. They left the rebels alone, albeit back in the past where everything was great, everything was understandable. There was the great powerful Soviet Union, bread for a mere sixteen kopecks, a job, even if it was a dead-end one, free housing, five square meters of housing per person, and the hope that if they behaved nicely after many years the government would give them a whole nine meters. They could read *Pravda,* watch the news program *Vremya,* and be happy with special television programming three times a year on the holidays. The funny thing was, though, people didn't want such a predictable life. Funny, instead of a well-fed slavery, they preferred an uncertain, difficult freedom.

On the day of the decree, Mstislav Rostropovich arrived in Moscow. As he had in August 1991, he landed smack in the center of revolutionary events in Russia. He made some wry remarks about this and the press noted it as well. On September 26, he gave a concert for Muscovites on Red Square with a symphony orchestra from the United States. It was a cold and windy day in Moscow. Rostropovich waved his conductor's baton and the music swelled. I could not look at this amazing scene without some emotion. Against the backdrop of St. Basil's Cathedral, there was a man in a black tuxedo, his gray hair blown about by the wind, his hands and face transfigured.

Galina Vishnevskaya (Rostropovich's wife) and the Rostropoviches' daughter attended the concert with me. Afterward I invited them to my home, where we had a family meal all together. Mstislav and Galina told us humorous stories from their musical life. It was pleasant having them with us. I love them. Each time Mstislav comes to Russia, he and I always make sure to see each other. I become infected with his enthusiasm, his energy, his bright, pure openness. He is easygoing and straightforward and it doesn't matter to him whether he is dealing with a boss, a worker, or a member of the nobility. He finds everyone interesting and, in the same way, people find him interesting.

I was fascinated to watch how he and his wife got along. Galina is an emotional woman, sometimes severe, but she is elegant and delightful. When she told her husband something in her well-modulated voice, he gazed at her with unconcealed admiration. I had the impression that he was truly enjoying the fact that he was being obedient and that she was put out with him. I was sorry to see them go; people were waiting for them and they had to leave (Mstislav was meeting with the intelligentsia). We agreed that the next time he came there would be no coups or revolutions. Without any special reason we would just see each other and enjoy one another's company.

The start of the next week brought nothing new in the confrontation between forces. Interior Ministry police officers continued to maintain a tight ring around the White House. The information coming out of the White House revealed that with each passing day, its defenders were growing more distraught and hysterical. Armed people had already seized power inside and army commanders were dictating their will to the deputies. Their combat formations were composed of the special assignment battalions Dniestr and Delta from the breakaway Trans-Dniestr region of Moldova; OMON troops from Vilnius and Riga; several hundred officers from the Supreme Soviet's security department; and combat troops from the fascist parties. Altogether, they made up a pretty serious army. Many officers had seen action; some were mercenaries, some young combatants. All told, these people in the White House were quite "qualified," able, and willing to kill.

Practically every night, the "defenders of the Constitution and democracy" worked themselves up to a hysterical pitch when information "from reliable sources" came in claiming that the White House would imminently be stormed. By the next morning, when the rumor had failed to be confirmed, the fighters, who had not slept all night, would get drunk and fall asleep. Deputies coming out of the White House later recounted the night of September 28–29 in particular, when Khasbulatov, expecting a storming, gathered everyone together in the Hall of the Soviet of Nationalities.* He himself was wearing a bullet-proof vest and a stunned expression on his face. He said the White House would be stormed by the Alpha group. The opposition's putative defense minister, Vladislav Achalov, enthusiastically told the frightened deputies that the defense of the White House would hold strong. They sat up all night in the hall until 4:00

*The Russian Supreme Soviet was made up of the Soviet of the Republic and the Soviet of Nationalities.—Trans.

A.M. This was all part of their paranoia: no one intended to storm the White House. They had whipped themselves up to scare everyone, so that they could sustain the militant hysterical mood.

During these days we never considered even a theoretical plan to take the building. I was firmly convinced that by using political methods and leaving the leadership of the White House in complete isolation, we could force them to surrender their arms. In general, our chief objective was to confiscate their weapons. After conferring with Chernomyrdin, Grachev, Yerin, and Golushko, we made a decision to give the conspirators a deadline to turn in their guns—October 4. If they did not fulfill our demand, then we would look at harsher ways of putting pressure on them.

I want to reiterate that the police surrounding the White House had no assault weapons. Our plans, ideas, and calculations were based on the desire to do everything to avoid accidental casualties. I understood how psychologically difficult it was for the Interior Ministry officers, equipped only with rubber truncheons, when a dozen yards away from them bandits were swaggering around ready to use machine guns and grenade launchers.

I later exhausted myself trying to understand whether I'd done the right thing, believing that we shouldn't let ourselves be provoked, and that our restraint would force the outlaws to stop their armed resistance. Now that the bloody events are over, it can probably be said we were tragically mistaken. If the police had been armed, if the Interior Ministry officers had had the chance from the start to react properly to the armed attack, the ferocious barbarism of the night of October 3–4 in Moscow would have been avoided. The rebels were drunk with their own impunity. Yet if the police had been armed, an even greater tragedy might have occurred. All told, I don't know, and to this day I cannot be sure. I know only one thing: from the moment I announced the dissolving of parliament, I tried through every means to avoid any casualties. Whether these were theirs or ours was not important—it would be the same tragedy for all of us.

The Russian Orthodox Church made some attempts during the second half of that week to alleviate the situation. On Thursday, I met at the Kremlin with Aleksy II, the patriarch of the Church. As always, our conversation was very frank and serious. I am always impressed with his holiness's calm self-possession and profound wisdom. He did not talk politics and tried as much as possible to remain impartial and was not overly anxious about the details of the decree. He asked that we accept any help the church offered to ensure a peaceful outcome be accepted—anything to avoid a tragic ending to the clash between brothers and sisters. I accepted this assistance with great relief and joy. We agreed that representatives of mine and the government would meet with authorized emissaries from the White House at St. Daniel Monastery, and the patriarch would mediate. Aleksy did not limit himself to only this mediation. He also appealed to Russians in a public statement in which he, with great concern, warned people to refrain from violent clashes.

That's how the negotiations at St. Daniel Monastery began. Before the talks could start, the White House leadership demanded that the electricity be turned back on. I felt we shouldn't even be discussing any preliminary conditions while arms were being handed out left and right from the White House to anyone at all, even psychotics and criminals. First give up your arms, I told them, then we'll talk terms. But then Sergei Filatov persuaded me that this was a material rather than a political condition because they had begun to freeze. I relented, although perhaps that was yet another mistake. The fact that their very first demand—turn on the electricity in the White House—was fulfilled gave them the false sensation that the way to keep talking was to use ultimatums. When the lights came on, people whooped and hollered and almost shot their rifles into the air from joy. They saw our concession as an important victory.

Within a few hours, the negotiations at St. Daniel broke down, proving once again that the situation had spiraled out of the politicians' control. Everything hammered out by our representatives and theirs was denounced by the White House leadership. Their most radical group had completely taken power into its own hands and apparently had at that moment decided to move to an armed struggle with the authorities. With one hand they drafted a plan to seize the television center, the Kremlin, ITAR-TASS,* the telegraph agency, and military installations, and with the other, Rutskoi wrote these penetrating words to Aleksy II: "As a religious believer and as

*ITAR is the Russian acronym for Foreign Telegraph Agency of Russia, which merged with TASS (former Soviet Telegraph Agency) after the coup.—Trans.

a citizen of Russia invested with high authority, I assure you that I will do everything possible to overcome the crisis by peaceful means." And later: "You will find me an unconditional advocate of your efforts to arrange mediation at St. Daniel Monastery."

That was how we came to a black day, Sunday, October 3, 1993. A black day indeed in Russia's new history.

That morning, I went to work at the Kremlin. Although it was a Sunday, at 10:00 A.M., I convened a meeting with the leaders of the Council of Ministers to discuss current events. Although the deadline for the ultimatum was October 4, we did not discuss forceful options to resolve the conflict. As before, we were hoping for a renewal of the talks moderated by the patriarch. We were also hoping that since the election process had accelerated, it had become absolutely clear that elections to Russia's new representative body would take place December 12. In order to participate in them, in order to stay in politics, the deputies would have to come out of the building and become actively involved in the election campaign. Otherwise, it would be too late.

After the meeting, I worked on some papers and then went home. Riding along a quiet Novy Arbat, I looked up at the windows of the White House. Who would have guessed that I would be seeing that building white for the last time? The next day it would be black.

The only day that I can spend a few hours with my family is Sunday. Following our tradition, we gathered together for a midday meal. I was apprehensive but, as I have said, I make a point of stopping all conversations about political and current events when I'm at home. If only for a few hours, I try to be husband, father, and grandfather. This time I failed. Mikhail Barsukov called me on a special line to report that the situation at the White House had worsened. He related the details: people were breaking through the police cordons, the mayor's office was being stormed right that moment, and the blockade had fallen apart so that all the opposition's armed formations were threatening to descend on the city in large detachments. I listened to him, my heart heaving in my chest, thinking to myself, Oh Lord, is it really starting? . . .

They had done what we had kept believing to the end they would not do. They had crossed the line that the Russian people should never cross. They had started a war, the most terrible kind of war—a civil war.

Later, many people commented that I had become flustered, that I had lost the reins of government, that no one heeded me. I hate to justify myself and it is ridiculous at the very least to be offended by such criticism. People need a comprehensible explanation for government inaction. I was all the more responsible for the fact that for several terrible hours, Muscovites did not know whether someone was defending them from armed bandits or whether they would be left to face the machine-gun-toting fascists all by themselves.

I was not panicked. There wasn't a second of agitation or uncertainty. Immediately after Barsukov's phone call, I contacted my aides to prepare an immediate decree imposing a state of emergency in the city of Moscow. At 6:00 P.M., the decree was signed, granting the law-enforcement agencies additional powers to put a stop to the rebellion and bloodshed in the city. I called Yerin and Grachev. I was concerned that though they were prepared for such a development in theory, when they actually encountered it they, too, would become agitated. But their initial reports were calm, and I did not sense any panic. Yerin briefly described how an organized attack had been made on his people, how the police had been forced to step back when the armed crowd surged forward, and some officers were forced to flee. With his voice shaking slightly, he reported how his policemen, who had been strictly reminded each day not to react to provocations and who had come on duty without assault weapons, had been taunted, had had their uniforms and overcoats torn from them, had been beaten and some even killed. We agreed that from now on, the police would be tough and if necessary would use assault weapons. There could be no compromises or negotiations. All the outlaws had to be apprehended and all the organizers of the armed rebellion arrested. Grachev reported that army troops were ready to come to the assistance of the police at any moment, they had already spoken to a number of the regiment and division commanders, and combat-ready formations were prepared to enter Moscow to defend the legitimate government.

I spoke once again with Barsukov on the phone and asked him to send a helicopter to Barvikh to pick me up. The ride in was only fifteen minutes by car, but if the rebels closed off the center of town and the entrances to the Kremlin, I did not want to be cut off from the real levers of government. Within half an hour, I heard the roar of helicopters arriving from Vnukovo Airport. I telephoned Chernomyrdin, Yerin, and Grachev and then Barsukov and Korzhakov, who were already at the Kremlin. The latest news was depressing: gunmen had attacked Ostankino Television Center. A battle was under way there. At any moment they could pull the plug on the broadcasts. I discussed with Korzhakov the best way for me to travel and we decided that the helicopter would be faster. At that hour the Kremlin could be reached only by making a long detour since Novy Arbat was completely blocked by the rebels. I climbed into the helicopter, and Naina and my daughters saw me off as if I were going to war. In fact, I was. I was flying into a civil war.

We made a little U-turn so that the rebels wouldn't give us a good whack with a Stinger or something and landed on the square inside the Kremlin at 7:15 P.M. There were talks with the prime minister and the law-enforcement ministers. Grachev informed me that he had given the order for the army units to march on Moscow.

At 8:00 P.M., I witnessed the same awful scene as the entire nation. Channels 1, 3, and 4 of Ostankino Television were cut off. An agitated anchorman, Viktor Vinogradov, appeared on the screen to report that *Vesti* was broadcasting out of a backup studio outside of Ostankino; meanwhile, the battle still raged in back of the studios on Korelev Street.

For the third time in the last hour, I telephoned Grachev, who told me that the troops were entering Moscow and would be sent to defend strategically important buildings and also to help defend Ostankino Television. I asked how soon they would arrive. He replied adamantly that they would enter Moscow any minute.

I phoned Yerin and told him that his men had to hang on just a little longer because help was soon on the way. At that moment, the Vityaz unit of the Dzerzhinsky Division was defending Ostankino's technical center. The rebel gunmen, whose arsenal included grenade launchers and APCs, had already seized the first floor of the building and were racing toward the studios. They were planning to go on the air.

At the White House, Khasbulatov reported to the people's deputies, now frenzied by the bloodshed, that Ostankino was already taken and that the Kremlin would be taken very soon. His news was greeted by applause, roars, and shouts of "*Hurray!*" Their illusory fantasy of becoming masters of the Kremlin, which had always been just over the horizon, was suddenly within reach. It seemed to them that they only needed a little more effort, and Moscow would be at their feet.

At approximately this time another group armed to the teeth entered the ITAR-TASS building. The gunmen said that they were supporters of the new president, Rutskoi, and demanded that the entire world be informed of the change of government in Moscow and Russia over TASS wires. Nevertheless, the board of ITAR-TASS, all the employees, and its general director, Vitaly Ignatenko, behaved courageously. Although they were looking down the barrel of a gun, they refused to obey the thugs' demands.

I was receiving this information from many sources and realized that the country was truly hanging by a thread. The army had not yet entered Moscow, either because it did not want to or had not been able to, and the police, who had been ordered not to react to provocations or to use weapons, were in no condition to display sufficient resistance to citizens who were not just merely noisy, shouting, or intimidating, but who were real professional killers, combat officers skilled in fighting and enjoying it.

I had by then already internally realized that a storming of the White House could not be avoided. Once again I telephoned everyone who could be mobilized—Yerin, Grachev, Barsukov—and asked them to prepare their forces for a possible storming.

Dmitry Ryurik, my foreign affairs aide, reported that he was receiving information from all over the world. Within a matter of minutes, the governments of most of the civilized countries had managed to take a position and gave their firm and clear support of lawful presidential authority in Russia.

I telephoned Grachev, who reported that the troops were now in Moscow, moving along Leninsky Avenue, Yaroslavsky Avenue, and other major Moscow thoroughfares. The Defense Ministry building was completely blockaded by APCs and powerful army units had gone to Ostankino. The television station would now be completely liberated.

I asked Grachev to speak to the duty officers at GAI, the state traffic control, so that they could report exactly at what mile post the combat units were located on their way to Ostankino. Within a few minutes, General Fyodorov, chief of GAI, telephoned to say there were no troops in Moscow. They had remained beyond Moscow Ring Road, the highway surrounding the city. I wanted to bang my fist on the table and shout at him—how could they have stopped?

They were supposed to be right next to the television station! But what did the head of GAI have to do with it?

Periodically, I went into a back room where a television had been turned on. The Russian channel,* the only one that stayed on the air, was what saved Moscow and Russia. Politicians, artists, businessmen, writers, and everyone who valued their country managed to find out where Channel 2 was broadcasting from and went to the studio to appeal to the Russian audience to stand up in defense of democracy and freedom. For the rest of my life I will remember the anxious but resolute and courageous expression of Liya Akhedzhakova, the anchorwoman. I see her image before me now; her hoarse cracking voice remains in my memory. Yegor Gaidar also appealed to his fellow citizens, calling on all Muscovites to come out to the Moscow city council building. He was later criticized for this. People questioned why unarmed, defenseless people should be sent against armed rebels. Nevertheless, his call was a deciding factor. Viktor Chernomyrdin made a tough statement that democracy and the lawful government in the country would be defended.

I saw that the confusion caused by the hourlong break in the broadcasts had been allayed. The shutting down of four channels, especially Channel 1, had come as a shock. I don't know whether the management of Ostankino was right to make the decision to stop broadcasting. Some specialists say there was a danger that rebels would seize the airwaves; others said that the existing degree of security made it technically impossible for the rebels to go on the air even over the functioning channels. But that was not the point. When state television went dead, a large portion of the population perceived it as a disaster. Even I felt as if I'd been knocked out of the ring. After the Russian channel was restored with vigorous, active, tough, but very emotional and human anchors (it would have been impossible to fake that), everything changed drastically. Most people were greatly relieved. It was a significant turning point.

Many of those who appeared on television asked why I was remaining silent and they demanded that I address the country.

At that moment, however, I had a far more important job to do, and speeches were the last thing on my mind. I was trying to bring

*As distinct from channels broadcast throughout the former Soviet Union.—Trans.

my combat generals out of their state of stress and paralysis. I saw that the army, despite all the assurances of the defense minister, for some reason was not able to come quickly to Moscow's defense and fight the rebels. The forces of the interior minister turned out to be insufficient for waging combat in the capital against such heavily armed rebels.

I spoke with Vyacheslav Bragin, Ostankino's director; the battle was still raging at Ostankino. Once again I contacted Chernomyrdin, Grachev, and Yerin. Grachev reported that a meeting of the collegium was under way at the Defense Ministry, and I asked Chernomyrdin to chair the meeting. I would get there as soon as possible.

By 2:30 A.M., I had the following update: the fighting was continuing at Ostankino, right in the television station. The police, who had been told not to become involved in clashes, had withdrawn after the first one, leaving the city to be torn to pieces by armed bandits. Meanwhile, the army, numbering two and a half million people, could not produce even a thousand soldiers; not even one regiment could be found to come to Moscow and defend the city.

To put it mildly, the picture was dismal. Strangely enough, I remained confident that both the police and, in the coming hours, the army would eventually take complete control over the armed groups of thugs roaming the city. Several people met with me throughout the wee hours of that night. Perhaps in time they will write their memoirs of these trepidacious moments. They can confirm that I was calm and collected and absolutely certain that October 4 was the last day of civil war in the history of Russia.

I called for my car, put on my coat, and rode to the Defense Ministry. It is a five-minute drive from the Kremlin to the Defense Ministry headquarters near the Arbat. It wasn't much time, but it was quite enough for me to understand what had really happened with Grachev, and why it was that the troops had not even entered Moscow, although according to him they were supposed to have liberated Ostankino almost two hours before and blockaded the White House in preparation for seizing it.

All of us—me, the defense minister, the government, and our society—have been hostages to the idea that the army is outside politics. We were proud of this deeply democratic slogan. But now, when the army had been called to defend society from bandits, fascists, and criminals, we were surprised: why is the army finding it so difficult to react? Why is it so poorly obeying orders? Because the army had been pulled into pieces and everyone was jerking on his part. How fortunate that no mad colonel had popped up with a squadron of bombers and flown over Moscow to defend his friend Rutskoi. So now there was no reason to shout and demand something or cause hysterics. On the contrary, the military had to be supported now; they had to see that the president was calm and sure of himself and the army.

At that point, the APCs blocking the entrance to the Defense Ministry building rolled away from the doorways, giving my ZIL a chance to glide into the inner courtyard. When I entered the meeting room, everyone fell silent. I sat a little to the side and asked them to please continue the discussion. One of the commanders was reporting that some troops stationed outside Moscow had been doing farm work. After September 21, they had consulted with Mayor Luzhkov and had decided not to remove the soldiers from the fields. Overall, I must say the generals' expressions were grim, and many had lowered their heads. They obviously understood the awkwardness of the situation: the lawful government hung by a thread but the army couldn't defend it—some soldiers were picking potatoes and others didn't feel like fighting. A discussion began about the taking of the White House. Everyone realized that the headquarters of the incitement of war must be isolated. But Chernomyrdin's call for suggestions was received by a heavy, morose silence.

I was surprised then to hear Korzhakov request the floor. Since he and some of his colleagues had been deeply involved in the defense of the White House in August 1991, his people had naturally reviewed all the options for assaulting the building. It could be attacked through underground tunnels, from roofs, and so on. He asked that his colleague from the chief security directorate be permitted to speak since he had an actual plan for seizing the building.

Chernomyrdin asked if there were any objections and Korzhakov invited into the conference room a gray-haired wiry military man who introduced himself as First Captain Zakharov. Zakharov was initially intimidated by such a collection of brass, but in the end spoke confidently. He proposed using tanks at first, ten vehicles that would approach the White House from two sides. Five would be placed near the Pavlik Morozov Children's Park and another five would move from the direction of the Novy Arbat Bridge. Several salvos would deal a paralyzing blow to the gunmen in the White House. Then strike forces should be sent in to create cover for the special assault teams. The operation inside the White House by the elite Alpha and Vympel units would be the final strike. For each stage of the attack, Captain Zakharov had an explanation that took into consideration the peculiarities of the building and the possibilities of defending it. He believed that the plan he put forth would cause the least number of casualties among the defenders. The centerpiece of his plan was the tank strike. Several shots into the windows of the upper floors of the White House where there were probably few people would have enormous shock value against occupiers of the building.

After Zakharov finished, I observed how the generals came alive and Chernomyrdin began to visibly cheer. Having a real plan, while it could be disputed, countered, or refined, at least gave us a point of departure. I suppose from this moment (and the clock was already showing after 3:00 A.M.) the military men's morale took a turn for the better. The commander of the ground troops and the chief of staff of the armed forces immediately contacted the division commanders and within a few minutes they reported to their colleagues that by 7:00 A.M. the tanks could be in place.

Chernomyrdin asked, "Well, now, does anyone have any fundamental objections? Is the plan acceptable?" Everyone nodded his approval. Grachev raised his hand and addressed me, slowly squeezing out the words: "Boris Nikolayevich, are you giving me sanction to use tanks in Moscow?" I looked at him in silence. At first he stared me right in the eye, then dropped his gaze. Chernomyrdin, unable to contain himself, turned to Grachev. "Pavel Sergeyevich, what are you saying now? You've been assigned to command an operation. Why should the president decide what precise means you require for it!" Grachev mumbled in a hurt voice something to the effect that, of course, he could make the decision independently, but it was important to verify . . .

I rose from my seat, asked everyone to work out the rest of the details without me, and said to Grachev, "I'll send you a written order." With that I left for the Kremlin.

My first order of business was to call in Ilyushin and ask him to draft a directive from me to Grachev assigning him command of the operation to liberate the White House from the armed fighters occupying it. Ilyushin brought me the paper within a few minutes. I signed it and asked that it be sent by messenger immediately and handed to Grachev in person.

It's true: I never gave these advisers an opportunity to start doubting, never allowed them to slacken, or to let weakness and uncertainty creep in. We had already paid a heavy price for having vacillated for several hours. We had nearly sent the entire country into a state of shock. I acted tough and pushed people and apparently offended many of them, but I had no time for subtleties.

Now that I had returned from the Defense Ministry and the machinery for managing the crisis had been set in motion and I was absolutely certain it would continue to operate, I could speak publicly to Muscovites and the citizens of Russia. Alexander Kuznetsov, our Kremlin video operator, taped my message since we decided not to invite any television crews. With the attack on Ostankino, everyone was needed over there. The tape was not more than ten minutes long. Soon the news agencies reported that my address would be televised shortly, and a car with an armed guard and a courier carrying the videocassette sped toward the television station.

As for how the parliament building was seized, I can hardly add anything to the story. CNN carried live coverage of the storming of the White House for the entire world to see, and it doesn't make sense to reiterate what everyone saw with his own eyes. There were tanks, there were shots, automatic-weapon fire, there were rubberneckers who came to gawk at the spectacle of people being killed. There were many deaths, and our grief was shared without dividing the victims into "ours" and "theirs." Everyone was "ours."

That evening I invited Chernomyrdin, Yerin, Grachev, and Filatov to the Kremlin. It was public knowledge by 4:30 P.M. that virtually the entire leadership of the White House had been arrested. Now Korzhakov and the security people were escorting them all to Lefortovo Prison in APCs and armored assault vehicles. For some reason I thought of Barannikov, the former security minister. I imagined the horror with which he would enter the cell block. Only two months ago, he had been a general, the boss of this establishment and others like it. Then I brushed away the thought. He had made his own bed and had personally signed the warrant that was taking him to Lefortovo Prison. I did not even want to think about the other prisoners.*

The "October Revolution" of 1993 had come to an unsuccessful conclusion.

Now we were mourning the dead.

It is amazing how the events of August 1991 coincided with the details of the "defense" of the White House in October 1993. I don't want to look into that "mirror," but I must.

There were women in the White House during the October rebellion as well; although they did not leave. There was also the homemade "defense"—the barricades made out of furniture, the round-the-clock guard posts, civilians with assault rifles, the attempts to bring the army over to their side, the plans to use the underground tunnels.

Rutskoi desperately tried to get in touch with the foreign embassies so that the world community would take him under its wing. I refused to go to the American Embassy, although I was offered such protection, and the leaders of Western countries contacted me themselves. But if we take a broader look at the typology, as the scientists would say, both the August 1991 and the October 1993 crises had in common this hope for help from outside.

In October we made every effort to avoid a violent clash. In order to do that we took a very dangerous step, as I now understand it: we disarmed the entire police, the Interior Ministry forces mobilized for the operation. Carrying only plastic shields, the police faced a crowd armed with stones, metal pipes, and Molotov cocktails.

The effect of our excessive caution was immediately obvious. As soon as people were injured or killed, the Moscow police left their posts. They did not want to lose their unarmed officers and soldiers for no reason. Meanwhile, the most strategic government

*In February 1994, Alexander Rutskoi, Ruslan Khasbulatov, Gen. Albert Makashev, and at least a dozen other leaders of the rebellion were amnestied before trial by parliament and released from prison. A disagreement with Yeltsin over the legality of the amnesty led to the resignation of Procurator General Aleksei Kazannik and the dismissal of Security Minister Nikolai Golushko. The case of the August coup plotters remained open and in March 1994, the military procuracy announced they would pursue prosecution. Ultimately, the president denounced the amnesty of the leaders of the violent parliamentary rebellion but conceded its necessity for social peace.—Trans.

buildings were left unguarded, not for long, but without security nonetheless.

No, the "mirror" lies, even so. During the August coup, Moscow was packed with troops, the streets were bristling with tanks and armored vehicles. During the rebellion, there were no troops throughout the days of resistance in September until they were deployed at 4:00 A.M. on the night of October 3–4. Recalling the bitter lessons of August, when the army was used to intimidate the public, the military very much feared being exploited in the same fashion. What if suddenly the people *did* rise up against an antipopular regime, as Rutskoi and Khasbulatov were urging in their revolutionary manifestos? (No doubt those manifestos quickly found their way into army barracks.) What if this really was a popular revolution?

In October, the military tried not to do any shooting until the very last moment. In August, they were forced to shoot, but cautiously.

In October, all of us on both sides of the conflict were under the spell of the August 1991 "coup syndrome." Subconsciously, we recalled the experience of those terrible hours and days, the sensation of hanging over an abyss, when the situation could go either way, when force of circumstances first elevated politicians, then plunged them to the very depths.

In October, the people in the White House tried their hardest to reproduce the scenario of two years earlier, and were confident that the success of that revolution would be repeated. They launched a rebellion not grounded in any common sense.

The people in the Kremlin—me among them—feared ending up in the role of the August coup plotters. That accounted for our terrible clumsiness and indecisiveness and our lurch almost to the brink of the abyss, which cost a great deal of bloodshed.

As I see it, there exists a very peculiar attitude toward power in Russia. The government has always been perceived as the incarnation of some kind of incredibly all-pervasive force, so terrifying and invincible that even the thought of attempting an overthrow, a coup, a rebellion seems quite absurd.

A government can collapse only by itself, as it did in 1917, as it did in August 1991, and as it almost did in October 1993—owing to a certain inability to not only reinforce itself but also to protect itself as the heart of national security, as the key to the control panel governing the country. The government—with its actual corridors, offices, and floors.

The rebels occupied the White House. They took the mayor's office. They seized two floors of the Ostankino Television Center. They seized ITAR-TASS. The gunmen seized the customs committee (from which they issued a command to blockade all the airports and train stations and prevent any members of the government, democratic journalists, or public figures from leaving Moscow). They seized the radio station on Kachalov Street, and tried to take the CIS joint armed forces headquarters. The taking of all these buildings was executed according to a detailed, elaborate plan.

The October rebellion really was a mirror of the August coup. And as in a mirror, everything reflected seems to be the same, but, in fact, it is just the opposite. A mirror image is in reverse, after all.

Our passive, virtually unarmed resistance to the state of emergency in August 1991 ended with the withdrawal of troops. The "defense" of the White House in September and October 1993, when hundreds of people were issued guns, when the inventory of firearms was in the thousands, when the rebels broke the skulls of policemen, when they launched grenades as they attacked Ostankino, when they deliberately led people into the storming, when they seized government buildings—that defense ended in the defeat of the rebellion.

Absolutely nonviolent people, a crowd of many thousands defending the White House, saving the country from enormous bloodshed and preventing the return of totalitarianism. That was August.

Hysterical demonstrators inflamed with anger, hurling themselves at unarmed policemen, provoking a horrible massacre. That was October.

An army that was immediately brought to Moscow in an enormous show of force which refused to storm the White House because it saw that thousands of people were willing to place themselves in front of the tanks. They disobeyed orders. That was August.

An army that was not brought into Moscow for quite some time, a very long time indeed, until the very last moment—and when soldiers received the order, they fired hard on the rebels because they sensed that Muscovites backed their determined actions completely. Moreover, the soldiers understood the point of their orders. That was October.

Alpha, the special KGB division, refused to storm the White House in August. The same Alpha, having overcome that same White House syndrome hanging over all of us, having lost one soldier who was shot in the back while performing his military duty, occupied the White House in October.

It was like an absurd film with the reel run in reverse. Why did it have to happen? Perhaps it was once again a testing of will, a probing of our new government. It might have been avoided if the politicians had behaved more intelligently. If they had not tried to repeat the role they had already played. As for the ordinary people, the Muscovites who came out on both an August and an October night to protect democracy, the journalists, the doctors, and the young teenage soldiers—all of them proved to be staunch defenders who knew exactly what they were risking and why.

10

PREMATURE CONCLUSIONS

The former empire will not disappear just like that. It has even more cataclysms in store for us. It will produce new fighters, fanatics, and leaders, with or without epaulets. The empire is exacting its revenge for having been dissolved. How can we protect ourselves from this political Chernobyl? Above all, I think we must frankly and objectively analyze events, not succumbing to euphoria or depression—which, I'll admit, seized me after the traumatic events of October. Everyone threw himself into concocting fantastic theories of intricate provocations—a conspiracy against the White House. I have described how it all was in reality but I would also like to evaluate the reasons for what happened.

Politics is a hard thing, sometimes a terrible thing, yet human all the same. The same laws operate in politics as in the rest of life. A politician must have some scruples, a certain decency; he cannot smear himself in the mud for the sake of a high ideal.

No one compelled Rutskoi, the battle officer, or Khasbulatov, the professor, to accept help from neo-Nazis, bandits, and outright fascists (although they consider themselves profoundly moral politicians). Idolizing Hitler and his ideas, the Russian fascists received their baptism by fire at the walls of the White House. The impulses that pushed people into committing the most terrible acts—arson, murder, and mayhem—emanated from the White House. It was there that this senseless and ruthless Russian rebellion was instigated. There it was thoroughly prepared and planned, all under cover of the high-sounding name of the "political opposition."

I believe that the main reason for the fall of my opponents was their lack of discrimination, their moral blindness, their state of arousal, a kind of intoxication from the ongoing drama.

On October 3, Rutskoi and Khasbulatov made an appeal to the people at the moment the mayor's office was seized. They decided that an authentic popular uprising was under way, and called on the public:

> Dear Friends! The victory is not yet final, armed units under the leadership of commanders who have sold out may still be flung at you. They are supported by Yeltsin's underlings and stooges. Be vigilant and stand firm. We appeal to all collectives, to all citizens of our motherland: do not obey the criminal decrees and orders of the Yeltsinites. Unite around the lawfully elected government bodies—the soviets of people's deputies.
>
> We call on soldiers of the Russian Army and Navy: display civic courage, preserve your military honor in loyalty to the Constitution, support the concrete deeds of popular power and the law. Russia will be grateful to you and will give genuine patriots their deserved appreciation.

Those were their words. I understand the profound upheaval and devastation that the citizens of Russia experienced after the October events. It is a terrible thing when tanks shoot in your own capital. When people die. And there is an immediate desire to blame the central government for everything. Imagine the rivers of blood that would have been shed if the authors of this appeal had implemented their plans. If the army had fought against the army. If soldier had gone against soldier, crowd against crowd. No negotiations can be tolerated with individuals who incite the people to a fratricidal war. I remind you that their appeal was made even before the storming of the Ostankino television station.

What great historical decisions was the congress in session at the White House supposed to make? To restore in an instant our motherland's "bygone glory"? To annex the Crimea to Russia? To declare Moldova, Georgia, Ukraine, Central Asia, and the Baltic States a zone of primordial Russian interests? And say that everyone who disagrees will be looking down the barrel of a Russian gun? That would have been only the beginning. Far more "brave and resolute" people were awaiting their moment. People gripped by a thirst for global warfare with Western civilization. And that conflagration would begin with a conflict inside Russia, with local enemies—with everyone who thinks differently, with those who "served the Yeltsinites," with those who decided to open their own business. In October 1993, we were on the threshold of war and terror, although we did not want it.

We're experts at keeping all of Russia in suspense. No wonder such "romantic, noble" people streamed to the White House from all the ends of the country (one of them wrote on the wall of a church bell tower from which he had been sniping at people with a machine gun, "I killed five people and I'm very glad of it."

I recall Grachev's look. It was a hard look because the decision was a hard one for him. To use weapons of battle in peacetime is a most arduous test for soldiers and officers. We understood this during the August 1991 coup; no one wanted to kill anybody then, either.

The White House was a time bomb with the switch pulled, ticking under Russia. Minutes, seconds remained. An explosion was inevitable. Yes, you must shoot, General Grachev! Shoot in order to save Russia. To save civilians, to save millions from civil war, where there is no right or wrong, where brother is set against brother, son against father. After all, we have already experienced civil war in our country. When it was permitted to happen. When an armed crowd was let through to the Winter Palace in Leningrad in 1917. It was the same kind of crowd, pumped up with slogans, led by fighters and commissars. History repeated itself. Only this time, Russia turned out to be smarter.

I am now trying to accept criticism calmly. An unhealed wound aches in the heart of everyone writing about these events. A normal person finds it hard to forget, to escape from this madness. People are now criticizing me more often and more relentlessly than they have ever criticized a leader of Russia during his lifetime. Cursing the bosses has ceased to be something in Russia that could cost you your life. *Finally!*

Fear is disappearing in Russia. The fear, secrecy, and gloominess that were always features of Russian society are dissipating. An unprecedented situation is emerging. Government is becoming a kind of continuation of private life. The life of a citizen. The president is a citizen and not some kind of exceptional being sitting somewhere on high, intimidating and inaccessible. The very foundation on which Russian history was always constructed is changing. An end is coming to the period of usurpation of power by unpopular rulers.

The values of private family life are moving to the forefront in Russia as elsewhere. "Government service," of course, remains a sphere of effort for a great many people but we are ceasing to ascribe to it some kind of sacred significance. Not the service of citizens, but citizens themselves are now important to the government.

It is easy to tell the future of Russia by looking at the treatment of children. People are fervently concerned now about children in our country. They are feeding them better, dressing them more fashionably, finding better schools for them.

There is an elusive irrational reason for a strange paradox: people are criticizing the president for no good cause, but for some reason are voting for him. The number-one man in the government no longer possesses the magic of mystical, untouchable other-worldliness. And, oh, how they lambast me! I'm an Aquarius, which explains this, that, and the other thing. I don't know how to work with people. I can only feel alive in a crisis. That's the refined criticism. There are primitive attacks as well—he drinks. After a few too many, he doesn't think clearly. He does whatever they tell him to do, etc.

There is one reason for people's vexation. They can now imagine anyone in my place. The seemingly endless gulf between society and the government in Russia has now been bridged. It is obvious that the framework of "us" and "them" in which the Russian person has always existed is finally gone. In this scheme, there were "us," the normal, simple, ordinary people with ordinary joys and sorrows, and there were "them," the powers-that-be, the rich. They can get away with everything; they have everything. Between "us" and "them" there was a wall. The impenetrable wall of power.

We lived for a very long time with this slavelike mentality. Then it suddenly became clear that there was no wall. There, sitting in the Kremlin, were the same kind of "us."

Something important has happened in Russia in these last years. People no longer want an abstract government in the Kremlin. The person who has taken upon himself the title of "leader" must be comprehensible, controllable, and dependent upon public opinion. He must listen.

I really love to give presents. It's a wonderful feeling on New Year's Eve* when the gloomy cold blazes up like a fairyland with a tree, lights, and fireworks—everything sparkles. Only we Russians, I think, experience the full delight of this New Year's radiance, contrasting so with the terrible frosts, snow drifts, and blizzards. This eternal expectation of the new is somehow mystically, inexplicably connected to our naïve faith in changes for the better—just as Russia's people believed in the revolutionaries, in the revolution, the bright paradise that would come any day. Everyone was under the spell of this "music of the revolution." Like children at a New Year's celebration. The whole country.

As far as I can tell, this eternal expectation of a miracle is what is boosting Russian reforms right now. People are not merely patient; they believe. They believe in the very word *reform*. The "irreconcilable opposition" takes advantage of this faith. We'll overthrow the Yeltsin clique, they say, and with a wave of our magic wand, the Soviet Union will reappear with a comfortably safe, familiar life. Rivers of milk will flow. But no matter which way Russian history turns, these rivers never flow. Reform is a wrenching, agonizing separation with birth traumas and severe congenital defects. By itself, reform cannot bring anything except pain.

When reform is completed, people will have to rely only on themselves, on their own mental and physical strengths. The time has ended when people can only hope the old social order will change.

The very existence in the world of the enormous Russian state has left a peculiar mark upon us. We have grown very dependent on this wide unbounded space; we are steeped in it to the very marrow of our bones.

Nations and cultures are intermingled. Our Russian society is no exception. Still, the perennial comparing, the perennial glance at one's neighbors will continue to be a feature of the Russian mindset—I don't know for how many years. Nature itself gave us the psychological complex of a country turned inward; human history allotted Russia precisely this predicament. We are surrounded by the very diverse and very conflicting interests of other countries.

*In Russia, New Year's Eve has traditionally been celebrated with all the elements of Christmas Day in the United States—a decorated tree, Father Frost bringing presents to children, etc.—Trans.

Russia has always surrounded itself with a controlled stretch of territory, expanding all the while. Strained to the limit, it kept seizing more and more territory and eventually clashed with all of Western civilization. As a result it became overtaxed spiritually, not materially. Such a degree of self-isolation is not possible.

But it does not follow that Russia should become eroded or dissipate its mighty energy. The interim, unfixed expanse of the Commonwealth of Independent States surrounds us now. No one wants to be dependent upon Russia but at the same time, no one wants to lose Russia. Because of this ambiguity and the disorder and instability in the independent states, we simply cannot define a concept of our own national security.

Responsibility for peace around us is not just a strategic but a moral agenda, even a family one. Our peoples—all the peoples of the USSR without exception—are intermingled. There are thousands of blood ties. There is a common memory, a common culture, common victims from the war and Stalinist terror. It is impossible to forget this; it cannot be escaped. Intermingling is a great thing—it obliges us to look around with completely different eyes.

In fact, this "Russian complex" will afflict us until we recognize our place in the new world. In the past we were tormented with an entirely understandable shame: the Soviet Union potentially threatened the community of civilized nations. Now there is no Soviet Union and Russia does not threaten anyone. But we seem to be embarrassed by the fact that we are so large and incoherent and don't know what to do with ourselves. We are plagued with a certain sense of emptiness. In point of fact, Russia has only one way—to be a guarantor of peace. That is, to be a "big man" who must not harm people by colliding with them on the street, but who must also look over their heads to protect those walking beside him.

It is completely unrealistic to predict who will be the next president of Russia. Clearly, he will be a different kind of person, born after World War II, most likely with a different upbringing and life story. The leaders who ran the show back in the Communist or post-Communist era are leaving the scene one after another.

We must finally admit that Russia comprehends democracy poorly—not merely for global, historical reasons but for rather prosaic ones: the new generation simply cannot break its way into power. The Socialist mode of thinking has left its imprint on all of us. I am not speaking of myself; I'm an obvious example. I am painfully ridding myself of my party complexes. But the entire midlevel bureaucratic class in Russia came out of the party and government offices.

The Russian intelligentsia, the middle class, shuns power and avoids politics or any active social stance. They have more than enough willingness to sacrifice, and readiness for spiritual exploits and creativity but I don't see a willingness to work. People come into politics from the intelligentsia with an exaggerated degree of vanity, and sometimes an inflated opinion of themselves.

Russian political life still awaits new leaders, decent young people with a head on their shoulders, with good education and common sense. The new generation must come to the forefront as quickly as possible. The leaders of the era of stagnation knew how to "keep good form," which is important. However, their thinking is completely inflexible, their decision making too slow. We will not get very far that way.

Sooner or later, I will leave political life. I will exit according to the rules, the Constitution, and the law. I would definitely like to make that contribution to the history of Russia, to set the precedent of a normal, civilized, orderly departure from politics.

Leaders have never voluntarily parted with power in Russia. Two revolutions were associated with the abdication of Nicholas II. No Communist leader left by his own good will. I am trying to comprehend this phenomenon of Russian rule. What explains it? Why has this medieval principle enthralled us for so long? Is it merely because of the stagnant, undemocratic nature of society? It's as if leaders were told: you have been given power, so hang on to it. Don't let it go for anything. Whoever is on top must step on those below. It is better in Moscow than in the region. It is better in the region than in the country. It is better in the city than in the village. That is the vertical structure of society. Russia is one and indivisible. Everyone strives upward, to the very top. Higher and higher still. Once you have scrambled to the top, the altitude is so dizzying, you cannot back down.

At the end of the millennium, however, even this fundamental trait in us will change. Not all at once. Russia's strength is in its cities, its provinces, and its culture. It is there that the standard of living will rise rapidly. Otherwise, we will live from one coup to another.

I clearly realize that this book will have a different destiny than my autobiography, *Against the Grain,* published in 1990. The reader will come to it with a completely different feeling. Perhaps a chillier one, perhaps more hostile.

After all, the dominant theme of the first book was the struggle with the Communist regime. The Russian reader sought in it the answer to the question of how the struggle would end. Could he pin his hopes for the defeat of communism on this man? How soon would it happen?

Now it has happened.

Since the first book was written, not only communism has collapsed but much else has happened as well. Within a short period—only two or three years—Russia has made a giant leap into the unknown.

Now the Russian reader wants to know the answer to a completely different and far more mundane question: when will they stop jolting us all? For they have been shaking us very hard for a very long time. Our strength is running out. Another question comes hard on the heels of this one: could we have avoided all of this? Could we have dismantled communism in some easier, gentler way? Without psychological stress, without a protracted political battle, without risk? And was it necessary to dismantle it in the first place?

I understand where these questions are coming from. The value of stability, firmness, consistency, conservatism (in the good sense of this word) in our lives is growing by the day. There is not a trace of the euphoria, illusions, and romantic elation that reigned in society sometime between 1989–1991, in the last period of Gorbachev's era.

It is hard to leave the world of rosy hopes and return to the world of real life, but we must.

I repeat: I have a clear and sober view of society's great expectations of stability and consistency in politics and the economy. I also understand the syndrome of irritation provoked by the sight of any familiar politician, including the first president of Russia. Such a shift of opinion is inevitable; it cannot be avoided. I would like to believe, however, that the majority of Russians realize something else: the only definite guarantor of calm is the president himself. That is, if they elected him, they should stick to their choice. If the country is gradually, though very slowly, coming out of the crisis, if the day of judgment promised by both the left and the right is not coming, then that means it is possible to live—and live with that president right up to the next elections.

So whether people like it or not, they must figure out who this Yeltsin is—what kind of person is he, what does he think, where is he taking us?

The last question is particularly interesting. Where is this Yeltsin taking us?

I think the answer will intrigue many people. I am not presenting people with a global strategic goal. I am not setting my sights on some shining peak that must be scaled. Nor am I trying to wipe out the entire path traversed until now.

No. The chief goal of this restless president is Russia's tranquillity.

APPENDIX A

PRINCIPAL FIGURES IN *THE VIEW FROM THE KREMLIN*

Aleksy II (Aleksei Mikhailovich Ridiger). Since 1990, Russian Orthodox Church Patriarch of Moscow and All Russia, the chief spiritual leader of the Russian Orthodox Church.

Iona Ionovich Andronov. Former foreign correspondent for *Literaturnaya gazeta.* Deputy chairman of Russian parliament's Committee on Foreign Affairs and Foreign Economic Relations (1991–93).

Viktor Ivanovich Anpilov. Correspondent for Soviet television (1978–85). Secretary of Russian Communist Workers' Party; leader of neo-Communist Working Russia movement. Arrested for October 1993 rebellion and amnestied in February 1994.

Yury Nikolayevich Afansyev. Rector of Russian State University for the Humanities. Member of Soviet parliament; one of the leaders of Interregional Deputies' Group, the liberal opposition. Co-chairman of Democratic Russia movement (1991–92).

Pyotr Olegovich Aven. Russian minister of foreign economic relations (1992). President of Alpha Bank. Member of State Duma.

Vadim Viktorovich Bakatin. USSR interior minister (1988–90); chairman of KGB (1991); presidential candidate. Since 1992, vice president of Reform Foundation.

Oleg Dmitrievich Baklanov. Minister of general machine-building (1983–88). Central Committee secretary (1988–91) in charge of military-industrial complex. Deputy chairman of Soviet Defense Council (1991). August coup plotter arrested for treason and amnestied in February 1994.

Viktor Pavlovich Barannikov. Army general. September 1990–August 1991, Russian minister of internal affairs. Subsequently held various top posts in security ministries during reform of these agencies in 1991–92. Security minister of Russia (January 1992–July 1993). Dismissed in July 1993 for ethical violations and negligence. Appointed acting minister of security by rebel parliament leader Alexander Rutskoi in September 1993. Arrested during suppression of the White House rebellion in October 1993, amnestied by state duma in February 1994, and released from prison in March 1994.

Mikhail Ivanovich Barsukov. Lieutenant general. Since 1992, head of the Chief Security Directorate of the Russian Federation, responsible for guarding the president and the Kremlin.

Yury Mikhailovich Baturin. Legal aide to President Yeltsin (1993); national security aide (1994).

Alexander Alexandrovich Bessmertnykh. Soviet ambassador to U.S. (1990–91); Soviet foreign minister (1991). Resigned after August 1991 coup. President Russian Foreign Policy Association (1992–93). Chairman of World Council of Ex-Foreign Ministers.

Boris Iosifovich Birshtein. Emigrated from USSR to Israel in 1979 and started two firms, Silon Ltd. and BODA Trading. Emigrated to Canada in 1982 and became a Canadian citizen. Currently resides in Switzerland, where he has registered a large group of firms under the title Siabeco, formed from the first letters of his children's names, Simon and Alex, and his last name. (The name also appears as "Seabeco" in English.) In 1988, he registered his company with the Soviet Ministry of Foreign Trade and in 1991 signed an agreement in Kyrgystan to form Seabeco-Kirghizia.

Valery Ivanovich Boldin. Head of Central Committee's General Department (1987–91). Member of Soviet Presidential Council (1990). President Gorbachev's chief of staff. Arrested for participation in the August 1991 coup; released in December 1991, amnestied in 1994.

Vyacheslav Ivanovich Bragin. Chairman of Russian parliamentary committee on mass media, liaison with public organizations, mass civic movements and public opinion polling. Head of Ostankino, Russian state television, from January 1993 until his dismissal in December 1993.

Gennady Eduardovich Burbulis. Special representative of speaker of Russian parliament (1990–91); state secretary to President Yeltsin (1992); head of advisors' group to President Yeltsin; resigned from government in 1993 to head nongovernmental Strategy Center. Elected member of state duma in December 1993.

Viktor Stepanovich Chernomyrdin. Soviet minister of gas industry (1985–89). Chairman of board of Gazprom, state gas concern (1989–92). Chairman of Russian Federation government (prime minister) since December 1992.

Eduard Dmitrievich Dneprov. Russian education minister (1990–92).

Sergei Aleksandrovich Filatov. First deputy chairman of the Russian parliament (November 1991–December 1992). President Yeltsin's chief of administration since 1993. Elected to state duma in 1993.

Boris Aleksandrovich Fyodorov. Russian finance minister (1992–February 1994).

Yegor Timurovich Gaidar. Director of Institute for Economic Policy (1990–91); minister of economics and finance (1991–92); acting prime minister of Russian Federation (June–December 1992); first deputy prime minister of Russia (September 1993–January 1994). Chairman of Russia's Choice party; member of state duma.

Viktor Vladimirovich Gerashchenko. Chairman of USSR State Bank (1989–91); chairman of the Central Bank of Russia (1992 to present). Member of Russian Council of Ministers.

Mikhail Sergeyevich Gorbachev. General secretary of the Communist party (1985–1991); president of the USSR (1990–91). Resigned in 1991 after collapse of the Soviet Union. Chairman of the Foundation for Social Political Research (Gorbachev Foundation).

Nikolai Mikhailovich Golushko. Russian security minister and director of Federal Counterintelligence Agency (1993); member of Russian Security Council. Dismissed in March 1994 for refusing to stop the amnesty of the August 1991 coup plotters and leader of October 1993 rebellion.

Pavel Sergeyevich Grachev. General who served in Afghanistan. Commander of Soviet air force (December 1990–August 1991). Soviet deputy defense minister (1991). Russian defense minister since May 1992.

Boris Vsyevolodovich Gromov. General who served in Afghanistan. Soviet first deputy interior minister (1990–91). Russian deputy defense minister (since 1992).

Vladimir Ivashko. Deputy general secretary of the Communist party (1990–91).

Vitaly Nikitich Ignatenko. Gorbachev's press secretary. General director of ITAR-TASS news agency (since 1993).

Viktor Vasilyevich Ilyushin. Aide to Yeltsin in Central Committee and Moscow Party Committee. Chief aide to President Yeltsin (since 1992).

Aleksei Nikolayevich Ilyushenko. Chief of oversight directorate in President Yeltsin's administration. Acting Russian procurator general (since February 1994).

Viktor Fyodorovich Karpukhin. Head of KGB's anti-terrorist Alpha group. Dismissed in 1991 in connection with the coup.

Ruslan Imranovich Khasbulatov. Professor of law and corresponding member of Russian Academy of Science. First deputy chairman of the Russian parliament (1990–91). Chairman (Speaker) of Russian parliament (October 1991–October 1993). Arrested for organizing the October rebellion and amnestied in February 1994.

Konstantin Ivanovich Kobets. Russian deputy defense minister (since 1993).

Aleksandr Vasilyevich Korzhakov. Officer of KGB's ninth directorate (1970–91). Head of security service for President Yeltsin since 1991.

Andrei Vladimirovich Kozyrev. Russian foreign minister (since 1990). Member of state duma.

Vitaly Alekseyevich Korotich. Editor in chief of *Ogonyok* (1986–91). Member of Soviet parliament. Visiting professor at Boston University.

Vyacheslav Vasilyevich Kostikov. President Yeltsin's press secretary (since 1992).

Leonid Petrovich Kravchenko. Head of Soviet state television (1990–91). First deputy to editor in chief of *Rossiyskaya gazeta*.

Leonid Markovich Kravchuk. President of Ukraine since December 1991.

Vladimir Aleksandrovich Kryuchkov. Chairman of the Soviet KGB (1988–91) until arrest for the August 1991 coup. Amnestied in February 1994.

Alexander Ivanovich Lebed. Lieutenant general. Commander of Tula Airborne Division (1989–91). Member of Russian Communist party central committee (1990–91). Commander of 14th Army, stationed in Transdniestr region of Moldova (since June 1992).

Oleg Ivanovich Lobov. Secretary of Sverdlovsk Region party committee (1982–85). First deputy prime minister, minister of economics (1993). Secretary of Russian Federation Security Council (since 1993).

Vladimir Mikhailovich Lopukhin. Russian minister of fuel and energy (1991–92).

Yury Mikhailovich Luzhkov. Chairman of Moscow Soviet Executive Committee (1990–91). Mayor of Moscow (since June 1992).

Anatoly Ivanovich Lukyanov. Speaker of Soviet parliament (1990–91). Arrested in connection with August 1991 coup. Elected deputy of state duma. Amnestied in February 1994.

Andrei Mikhailovich Makarov. Attorney. Head of Anti-Crime and Corruption Commission of the Russian Federation Security Council (since 1993). Member of state duma.

Albert Mikhailovich Makashov. Retired general. Chairman of Committee for National Salvation (1993). Arrested as one of the leaders of the October 1993 parliamentary rebellion. Amnestied in February 1994.

Mikhail Alekseyevich Moiseyev. Chief of general staff of soviet armed forces (1988–August 1991). Acting defense minister (August 1991).

Nursultan Abishevich Nazarbayev. First secretary of the Kazakhstan Communist party (1989–91). President of Kazakhstan since 1991.

Valentin Sergeyevich Pavlov. Soviet prime minister (1991). Arrested for participation in the August coup and amnestied in February 1994.

Yury Vladimirovich Petrov. President Yeltsin's chief of administration (August 1991–January 1993). Head of State Investment Corporation since 1993.

Yury Sergeyevich Plekhanov. Chief of KGB's ninth directorate (security of government leaders) (1983–91). Arrested in August 1991 in connection with the coup. Amnestied in February 1994.

Ivan Kuzmich Polozkov. First secretary of the Russian Communist party (1990–91). Arrested as one of the leaders of the October rebellion and amnestied in February 1994.

Mikhail Nikiforovich Poltoranin. Russian minister of press and information (1990–92). Head of Russian Federal Information Center (1992–93). Chairman of state duma committee on information policy and communications (1994).

Gavriil Kharitonovich Popov. Dean of Moscow University Faculty of Economics (1977–80). Mayor of Moscow (1991–92). Chairman of Russian Democratic Reform Movement. Member of Russian Presidential Council since 1992.

Yevgeny Maksimovich Primakov. Director Institute of World Economy and International Relations (1985–89). Member Soviet Presidential Council (1990–91). First deputy chairman of KGB, then director of Soviet Central Intelligence Service (1991). Director Russian Foreign Intelligence Service since December 1991.

Boris Karlovich Pugo. General. Chairman of Latvian KGB (1980–84). First secretary of the Latvian Communist party (1984–88). Soviet interior minister (1990–91). Participated in August 1991 coup, during which he committed suicide.

Mstislav Leopoldovich Rostropovich. Russian émigré conductor. Head of American National Symphony Orchestra since 1977. Stripped of his Soviet citizenship in 1978. Citizenship restored by Soviet parliament in 1990.

Alexander Vladimirovich Rutskoi. Major general who fought in Afghanistan and was awarded the title Hero of the Soviet Union. Vice president of the Russian Federation (1991–93). Active in Civic Union bloc in parliament. Dismissed from office in Septeber 1993. Arrested as one of the organizers and leaders of the October 1993 parliamentary rebellion. Amnestied in February 1994.

Nikolai Ivanovich Ryzhkov. Communist Party central committee secretary (1982–85). Chairman of Soviet Council of Ministers (1985–91). Retired 1991. Advisor to Military Industrial Investment Company.

Yury Alekseyevich Ryzhov. Russian ambassador to France and member of Russian Presidential Council since 1992.

Oleg Semyonovich Shenin. Communist party central committee secretary (1990–91). Arrested for participation in August 1991 coup; amnestied in February 1994.

Eduard Amvrosievich Shevardnadze. Soviet foreign minister (1985–91) who resigned in protest of the impending coup. Co-chairman of Democratic Reform Movement (1991–92). Head of state and chairman of parliament of Georgia since 1992.

Vladimir Filippovich Shumeiko. First deputy chairman of Council of Ministers (1992–94). Chairman of the Soviet of the Federation of the Russian Federation Federal Assembly (parliament) since February 1994.

Stanislav Stanislavovich Shushkevich. President of Belarussian State University (1986–90). Chairman of the Supreme Soviet of Belarus (1991–94).

Ivan Stepanovich Silayev. Chairman of the Russian Council of Ministers (1990–91). Russian permanent representative to the European Community (1991–94).

Yury Vladimirovich Skokov. General director of Quantum, a defense plant (1986–90). First deputy prime minister of Russian Council of Ministers (1990–91). Secretary of Russian Security Council (1992–93). President of Federation of Commodities Producers since 1993.

Anatoly Aleksandrovich Sobchak. Mayor of St. Petersburg (Leningrad) since 1991. Co-chairman of Democratic Reform Movement (1991–92). Member of Russian Presidential Council since 1992.

Vasily Aleksandrovich Starodubtsev. Chairman of the Soviet Peasants' Union (1990–91). Arrested for participation in the August coup, released in 1992, and amnestied in February 1994. Elected to Soviet of the Federation of the Russian Federal Assembly (parliament) in 1994.

Valentin Georgievich Stepankov. Russian procurator general (1991–93), responsible for investigating the August 1991 coup.

Lev Yevgenyevich Sukhanov. Aide to President Yeltsin since 1990.

Shamil Tarpishchev. Adviser to President Yeltsin on sports since 1992.

Aleksandr Ivanovich Tizyakov. Vice president of Soviet Scientific and Industrial Union (1990–91) and president of Association of State Enterprises and Industrial Associations (1991). Arrested for role in the August coup and amnestied in February 1994.

Amangeldy Moldagazyyevich Tuleyev. Elected to Russian parliament in 1990, and nominated for president in 1991. Elected to state duma in 1994.

Valentin Ivanovich Varennikov. Commander of soviet ground forces.

Arkady Ivanovich Volsky. Aide to general secretary of the Communist party (Andropov, Chernenko) (1983–85). Emergency administrator of Nagorno-Karabakh (1989–90). President of Russian Union of Industrialists and Entrepreneurs (since 1992). Co-chairman of Democratic Reform Movement and leader of Civic Union bloc in parliament.

Yury Mikhailovich Voronin. Chairman of Russian parliamentary commission on the budget, plans, taxes and prices (1990–91). Russian first deputy prime minister (1993). Member of Communists of Russia parliamentary faction.

Vitaly Ivanovich Vorotnikov. Chairman of the Russian Supreme Soviet (1988–90).

Alexander Nikolayevich Yakovlev. Soviet ambassador to Canada (1973–83). Head of Central Committee Propaganda Department (1985–86). Central Committee secretary (1986–90). Politburo member (1987–90). Senior advisor to President Gorbachev (1991). Member of Presidential Council (1990–91). Vice president of Gorbachev Foundation. Since 1993, director of Russian Federal Television and Radio Service and acting chairman of Ostankino Russian State Television Company.

Yegor Vladimirovich Yakovlev. Editor in chief of *Moscow News* (1990–91). Chairman of Soviet State Television and Radio Company (1991). Member of Gorbachev's Political Advisory Council (1991). Chairman of Ostankino Russian State Television Company (1991–92). Since 1992, general director of RTV Press, a state media programming company, and editor in chief of weekly *Obshchaya gazeta* [Common Newspaper].

Dmitry Olegovich Yakubovsky. Attorney, secretary of the board of the Soviet Union of Lawyers. Representative of law-enforcement agencies and security services to Russian Federation government. Deputy head of Federal Agency for Government Communications and Information (1992).

Gennady Ivanovich Yanayev. Deputy chairman, Soviet Union of Friendship Societies (1980–86). Chairman of All-Union Council of Trade Unions (1990). Soviet vice president (December 1990–

September 1991). Member of Soviet Security Council (March 1991–August 1991). Arrested for participation in the August 1991 coup and imprisoned until January 1993. Amnestied by the state duma in February 1994.

Viktor Nikolayevich Yaroshenko. Russian minister of foreign economic relations (1990–92).

Grigory Alekseyevich Yavlinsky. Co-author of 500-Day Plan for transition to a market economy. Chairman of nongovernmental Center for Economic and Political Research. Elected to State Duma December 1993.

Viktor Fyodorovich Yerin. Army general. First deputy Soviet interior minister (September 1991–December 1991). Russian interior minister since January 1992. Awarded title of Hero of Russian Federation for his part in the suppression of the October 1993 parliamentary rebellion.

Valery Dmitrievich Zorkin. Chairman of Russian constitutional court (1991–93).

APPENDIX B

FROM THE ARCHIVES OF THE GENERAL SECRETARY

The materials published here are only one thousandth of the most secret of all secret documents. These documents were preserved under lock and key for many years, and were passed on by inheritance from *gensek* to *gensek,* as we called our party's general secretaries for short. Each time the current boss would depart, new folders stamped SECRET, TOP SECRET, or TOP PRIORITY would land in the safe.

Perhaps many people will be disappointed. Why out of all the Kremlin secrets that have fallen into my hands have I selected for publication precisely these relatively old and not especially hot documents so to speak?

Of course there are far more sensational materials in the archive that Gorbachev turned over to me during our last meeting in December 1991. In seventy-odd years, the Soviet leaders accumulated so many terrible secrets that newspaper editors would have more than enough to keep themselves busy publishing documents for years. The time will come when all these documents will be carefully studied by archivists, and anyone who wishes to may obtain access to them. Then, if they like, journalists can put out one sensation after another.

But my book has another purpose. I selected for publication the most ordinary documents, materials that give a sense of the everyday, routine, bureaucratic side of the KGB's activity. I must say that what impressed me personally about these documents was precisely their ordinary, mundane tone.

In a letter dated November 23, 1963, addressed to the central committee of the party, KGB Chairman Vladimir Semichastny reports what the KGB knows about Lee Harvey Oswald, the man who assassinated U.S. President John F. Kennedy:

> Having come to the USSR as a tourist in October 1959, he [Oswald] appealed to the Praesidium of the USSR Supreme Soviet to be granted Soviet citizenship and the opportunity for permanent residence in the USSR. . . .
>
> In connection with the fact that Oswald was denied this request, he tried to commit suicide by slashing the veins of his wrist.
>
> Oswald was denied citizenship, "because the Americans who have been accepted for Soviet citizenship in the past lived for a time in the USSR and then left our country." However, Oswald was issued permission for temporary residence in the USSR for a period of one year.
>
> In accordance with a directive from the USSR Council of Ministers dated December 1, 1959, Oswald was sent to Minsk, where he was provided an apartment of his own, and in consideration of his wish, was given employment at the Minsk radio factory. Through the Red Cross, Oswald was given material assistance in the amount of 70 rubles per month.

Despite this, within several months Oswald followed the example of his American predecessors in the Soviet Union and, as the document stated, "began to persistently seek permission to leave the USSR and, in connection with this, established an official correspondence with the U.S. Embassy in Moscow."

In June 1962, Oswald, who by that time had managed to marry a "Soviet citizen, Marina Nikolayevna Prusakovina, born 1941," was able to depart for the United States with his wife. Within a year, the couple was once again asking to come back into the USSR.

> In October 1963, Oswald visited the Soviet consulate in Mexico and once again appealed for political asylum in the USSR on the grounds that as a secretary of a pro-Cuban organization, he was being persecuted by the FBI.

His petition was turned down. At the end of the memo, Semichastny recommends

> publishing in a progressive paper in one of the Western countries an article "exposing the attempt by reactionary circles in the USA to remove the responsibility for the murder of Kennedy from the real criminals, the racists and ultraright elements guilty of the spread and growth of violence and terror in the United States." The article should illustrate the intent of "crazy men" related to the "provocateurs and murderers among counterrevolutionary Cuban émigrés to alter the foreign and domestic policies of the USA."

A memo from Semichastny to the central committee's international department dated December 10, 1963, states that in the words of Brooks (a well-known American Communist figure and KGB agent):

> Upon his return from the USSR, Oswald appealed in a letter to figures in the U.S. Communist party offering his services to organize underground work on behalf of the Communist party and Cuba. His appeal was viewed as an FBI provocation and a reply to his letter was made stating that America is a free country, any underground activity is ruled out, and that the U.S. CP has no need of his services . . . in the opinion of Gus Hall, the official representative of the Soviet Embassy in the USA, [we] would find it expedient to visit the widow of Oswald, since interesting information about the events in Dallas can be obtained from her, as a Russian and a citizen of the USSR . . . [However], in the opinion of the New York *rezident** of the Committee for State Security [KGB] of the USSR Council of Ministers in New York, a trip from a Soviet Embassy officer to Oswald's wife was not expedient, since this trip could be exploited by right-wing elements in the USA for anti-Soviet propaganda and also Oswald's wife was under increased police surveillance.

Semichastny's deputy, Zakharov, sent a memo to the central committee's international department outlining "some intelligence data on the political purposes and short-term consequences of the murder of U.S. President J. Kennedy."

> According to some information, the ultimate organizer of the murder of President Kennedy was a group of Texas oil magnates who wield major economic and political power not only in the state of Texas but in other southern states of the USA. A reliable source of the Polish friends,† an American entrepreneur and owner of a number of firms closely connected to the petroleum circles of the South, reported in late November [1963] that the real instigators of this criminal deed were three leading oil magnates from the South of the USA—Richardson, Murchison, and Hunt, all owners of major petroleum reserves in

*That is, the KGB agent in charge of intelligence operations in the foreign country of residence.—Trans.

†That is, Polish intelligence services.—Trans.

> the southern states who have long been connected to pro-fascist and racist organizations in the South.
>
> Ward, a reporter for the *Baltimore Sun* who covers foreign diplomacy, said in a private conversation in early December that on assignment from a group of Texas financiers and industrialists headed by millionaire Hunt, Jack Ruby, who is now under arrest, proposed a large sum of money to Oswald for the murder of Kennedy.

Oswald was the most suitable figure for executing a terrorist act against Kennedy because his past allowed for the organization of a widespread propaganda campaign accusing the Soviet Union, Cuba, and the U.S. Communist party of involvement in the assassination. But as Ward emphasized, Ruby and the real instigators of Kennedy's murder did not take into account the fact that Oswald suffered from psychiatric illness. When Ruby realized that after a prolonged interrogation Oswald was capable of confessing everything, Ruby immediately liquidated Oswald.

A KGB memo to the central committee dated December 12, 1963, stated:

> On December 6, 1963, Colonel G. N. Bolshakov, an officer of the GRU* working in the Novosti [News] Press Agency, met the artist William Walton, a friend of the assassinated U.S. President J. Kennedy at an exhibit of American graphic art.
>
> Comrade Bolshakov became acquainted with William Walton at the home of Robert Kennedy in 1951 and has met with him several times in Washington.
>
> On December 9, 1963, W. Walton telephoned Comrade Bolshakov and invited him to dinner . . .
>
> Keeping in mind the opportunity of using Comrade Bolshakov's contacts with R. Kennedy in the future, it would be expedient to organize a meeting between W. Walton and Comrade A. I. Adzhubei,† with the participation of Comrade Bolshakov.
>
> A transcript of the conversation between Comrade Bolshakov and W. Walton is attached.
>
> Attachment: transcript of conversation with Comrade Bolshakov and W. Walton—five pages.

Transcript of that conversation in Bolshakov's retelling:

> Walton has analyzed the political situation after the Kennedy assassination in detail, devoting attention to the possible candidates for the

**Glavnoye razvedyvatel'noye upravleniye,* the chief intelligence directorate of the Defense Ministry, or military intelligence.—Trans.

†Khrushchev's son-in-law, who was editor in chief of *Izvestia* for many years and frequently traveled to America.—Trans.

office of president. He gives a profile of Johnson, expresses the reservation that "as a result of Johnson's accession representatives of big business may penetrate into the government." He sends a "big hello" to Khrushchev from Robert and Jacqueline Kennedy and recommends sending through him "small Christmas presents to Robert Kennedy and his family. That would be very nice for Robert Kennedy, who considers you his friend."

President Kennedy's assassination has shown us that the vice president must be one of ours. The selection of Johnson was a mistake on J. Kennedy's part. I still don't understand why he chose that Texan. When J. Kennedy was choosing candidates for vice president, there were always two candidates, Senators [Stuart] Symington and Johnson. R. Kennedy wrote their names down on pieces of paper and threw them into a hat. J. Kennedy picked the piece of paper with Symington's name written on it. Why he changed his opinion isn't clear. This is a bitter lesson for us all. Walton asked Bolshakov to help him organize a meeting with Adzhubei and said he didn't want people to know about this meeting at the consulate. He said that when he got back to Washington he would only report to R. Kennedy about the meeting.

Both the preceding document and the following, concerning our role in the conflict in Ulster, deal with the topic of the "Soviet threat," a popular subject in years past. But they are interesting from another perspective. The future assassin of Kennedy—whether acting on his own or as an agent of someone else—offered his services to the KGB himself, and came to our country on his own initiative. The KGB feared making use of this service. The extreme leftist Irish also approached us, begging us for arms year in and year out.

Europe in the 1960s was undergoing great upheavals, and the world as a whole was on fire with crises breaking out everywhere. A number of assassination attempts were made on Charles de Gaulle; there was the French student revolution and the division in society over the Algerian crisis. The severe Northern Ireland conflict erupted in Great Britain. There was the war between Egypt and Israel. The end of the decade was marked by the war in Vietnam, the Cultural Revolution in China, and our invasion of Czechoslovakia.

In short, although a major war seemed to be brewing on the planet, something saved humankind from that disaster. I don't think it is right to paint this era black and white, to say that there was supposedly a "good" Western world and a "bad" Communist world. It was far more complicated than that. After splitting up into camps for some mysterious reason, the world managed to come back together again. Contacts between people and countries were far more extensive than what we now believe. Civilizations—both Western and Communist—began to interpenetrate. The real poles of opposition, despite the logic of the military conflicts, were not West–East but stability versus aggression. Imagine what the USSR would have done in the 1930s if the Irish Communists had come to them begging for weapons; firearms would have been sent within a week. I think there would have been a fantastic display of enthusiasm in the process.

It's nothing like that in the new era. A decision grinds slowly through the bureaucracy. The central committee has a long and tedious discussion of a request from the terrorists. The years pass, and we're still trying to decide how to send the damned weapons to the Irish, because we really don't feel like it.

The USSR did not at all try to form a bloc with China, which was leftist at the time, or with leftist terrorists around the world. The Soviet government would pass a whole range of resolutions in support of Communist regimes in the world, but our policy was to spite the Americans. Two enormous powers played on the contradictions and tragedies of the third world. The lethal decision to send troops into Czechoslovakia was made. Still, on the whole, the values of stability prevailed, despite the evident realities of the cold war.

To reiterate, the situation on the planet was far more explosive than it is now. Even so, the desire of people not to endure a new war forced the politicians to make responsible decisions.

Today there is no great political polarity on the planet, but the situation has changed drastically. The generation that fought the last war has aged, and the subconscious fear of a nuclear disaster has receded into the past. Now the main threat emanates not from the superpowers but from small localized wars, from conflicts among different nationalities, where ethnic antipathies flare. Such conflicts are the nuclear bomb of the new century as is the arms trade. And just as in the 1960s, people of various civilizations extended their hands to one another in order to unite against war, and just as government representatives from different countries tried to understand each other through the barriers, today we must all unite as well against the threat of a new war.

If a system of collective security is not developed to prevent small wars, to combat the unchecked arms trade, and to stop political terrorism and the violation of international law, we will not see peace in the next century.

People have always wanted to fight, and at the same time have always wanted to live in peace. Such ambiguity is peculiar to human nature. Unfortunately, such a thing as a totally peaceful era does not exist, despite all our treaties. That means that peace must be defended. At any time.

This threat is particularly aggravated now because of the new political reality. Ethnic wars in the Balkans and Caucasus are spreading to Turkey on both sides, and Turkey is hardly indifferent to the fate of its fellow countrymen in Europe. Meanwhile, race riots have begun in Germany. The treatment of immigrants has grown more harsh in other European countries. Something similar is happening in Russia, and it must not be tolerated. It is wrong to retreat into selfish nationalist interests.

If we permit the escalation of racial, ethnic, and religious dissension, once again as in the 1960s the world will reach the brink of a global war. What saved us then was civilization, the expansion of civilized living standards, an understanding of the immorality of war that alleviated the suffering of millions of people. Today we need to search for this path again and not spare any effort to achieve peace.

Letter from M. O'Riordan to the central committee of the party:

> Moscow, November 6, 1969
> Dear Comrades,
> 1. I would like to outline in written form a request for assistance in acquiring the following types of arms:
> 2000 assault rifles (7.62 mm) and 500 rounds of ammunition for each; 150 hand-held machine guns (9 mm) and 1,000 rounds of ammunition for each . . .

The letter details the history of the founding of the IRA and notes that

> there has always existed more or less good relations between the IRA and the Irish Communists. We not only conduct a number of public and antiimperialist activities together, but for more than a year a secret mechanism for consultations between the leadership of the IRA and the Joint Council of the Irish Workers' Party and the Communist party

of Northern Ireland has existed and is operating. They unfailingly accept our advice with regard to tactical methods used in the joint struggle for civil rights and national independence for Ireland.*

O'Riordan writes that during the "August crackdown" in Belfast the IRA "didn't play the role of an armed defender since its combat potential was weakened by the fact that it had previously concentrated its efforts on social protests and educational activity."

O'Riordan did not rule out the possibility of civil war in Northern Ireland in the future and clashes between the Catholic minority and British troops:

> The request for supplying of weapons is made in the light of just such a very possible development.
>
> Two leading figures of the IRA (Catal Goulding and Seamus Costello) officially appealed to me with this request.
>
> The weapons may be delivered to Ireland on a tugboat, which will be run by a small select and reliable crew consisting of IRA members.

A memo to the central committee dated November 18, 1969:

> The leadership of the IRA promises to keep in strictest confidence the fact that the Soviet Union is supplying it with arms and will guarantee the complete secrecy of their shipment to Ireland.
>
> In conversation with Comrade M. O'Riordan, the inexpediency of supplying Soviet-made arms was pointed out, since that would create an excuse to accuse the IRA of action "on orders from Moscow."
>
> It was deemed possible to assign the Committee for State Security of the USSR Council of Ministers and the USSR Defense Ministry to review the request of Comrade M. O'Riordan, to study the possibility of providing assistance to the IRA with weapons of foreign make and to set a two-week deadline for proposals to the central committee.
>
> A draft resolution of the central committee is attached.

The draft was as follows:

> To assign the international department of the central committee of the CPSU, the Committee for State Security of the USSR Council of Ministers and the USSR Defense Ministry to review the request of Comrade M. O'Riordan, the general secretary of the Irish Workers' party, and to submit their proposals to the central committee of the CPSU within a two-week period.
>
> /Signature/ Secretary of the Central Committee

*This letter and subsequent communications from the IRA are back translations of the Russian translation of the original documents in the English language in the KGB's archives.—Trans.

Next there followed eight memos from Yuri Andropov to the central committee on this issue, the first dated January 8, 1970, and the last August 21, 1972. The text of the January memo is as follows:

> Taking into consideration the great complexity of ensuring the necessary secrecy in shipping the weapons and ammunition to the territory of Northern Ireland and also that recently in the Irish and British bourgeois press (*The Irish Press* and *The Times*) provocative reports have appeared on the Soviet shipment of weapons to extreme right-wing Protestant elements in Northern Ireland that allegedly took place, we believe it is expedient before making a final resolution on the issue of granting the request of Comrade M. O'Riordan to establish contact with him and determine his real capabilities to guarantee the necessary conspiracy in shipping the weapons and preserving the secrecy of the source of their supply.

April 7, 1970:

> Comrade O'Riordan was told that before deciding such an issue, a thorough study of all the aspects was necessary. In particular, the question must be seriously weighed as to what the likely advantage of the shipment of weapons and what would be the disadvantage in the event that the operation failed.
>
> Moreover, Comrade O'Riordan's attention was directed to the serious technical difficulties that would have to be encountered in conducting the operation and the great risk of the possibility of its exposure. This made a noticeable impression on Comrade O'Riordan.
>
> Comrade O'Riordan understood the caution with which we were approaching the decision of this matter.

October 21, 1970:

> Considering the persistent requests of Comrade O'Riordan and his assurances that the necessary measures of conspiracy and security will be taken by his friends in delivering the weapons to the appointed place, the committee for state security has drafted a basic plan for delivering in neutral waters to the Irish friends 100 captured assault rifles, 9 machine guns, and 20 pistols with ammunition.
>
> We do not have grenade launchers, grenades, rifles, and other small arms of foreign make.

March 21, 1972:

> Comrade O'Riordan has spent more than two years trying to obtain a positive decision on the question of the illegal delivery of quantity of arms to Northern Ireland . . .

The submerged weapons will be retrieved only by representatives of the Irish Republican Army. The Communist party of Ireland will not have any direct participation in either the retrieval of the weapons or their use. All the details of the operation conducted are known only to Comrade O'Riordan.

Resolution: File in the archive—directive of Comrade K. U. [Konstantin Ustinovich] Chernenko.

May 25, 1972:

On May 22, Comrade O'Riordan made a special trip to Moscow in order to accelerate the resolution of this matter . . .

Considering that the Soviet Union is the only source for the clandestine supply of weapons, Comrade O'Riordan stated that he will continue to persistently seek a positive resolution of the matter.

In this connection it would be expedient to return to a review of the request of Comrade O'Riordan once again regarding the illegal transfer to the Irish friends of a small shipment of captured weapons.

A letter from O'Riordan to the central committee of the CPSU dated July 3, 1972:

Dear Comrades,

In November 1969, I appealed to you for help in the form of war material.

The fact that there has not been the slightest leak of information for two and a half years proves, in my opinion, a high level of responsibility with regard to preserving the secret, so to speak.

As soon as you have made a political decision, I will take absolutely no part in the transport operation, and my role will only involve transferring the technical information about this to Seamus Costello. The shipment and all other operations will be carried out by members of the official IRA, who will not know anything about how this military material appeared or where it was obtained.

Postscript:

1. In the course of two and a half years since November 1969, I have had many substantive discussions with your technical specialists on the matter of shipment of military material to Ireland.

I do not see a more effective, more secure, or more reliable means than what was suggested by your specialists.

The only other possible alternative is as follows:

—the CPSU appeals to the Cuban comrades;

—the promised military material must be shipped to Cuba; from there they must be redirected on a Cuban ship to a meeting place somewhere in the ocean and transferred to an Irish ship that belongs to fishermen who are members of the official IRA . . .

Thus, neither the CPSU nor I will figure in and then the question will be decided by direct negotiations between Costello and the Cubans.

A memo from Andropov to the central committee dated August 21, 1972:

The KGB may organize and conduct such an operation. . . .
A plan for conducting the operation is attached.

Andropov

Plan for the Operation of a Secret Shipment of Weapons to the Irish Friends (the working name for the operation is SPLASH):

The illegal shipment of arms to the Irish friends will be carried out by submerging them at night to a depth of 40–42 meters in neutral waters near the shoals of Stanton 90 kilometers from the shore of Northern Ireland.

A reconnaissance ship, *Reduktor,* has at our request already been to the intended site of the operation and has conducted preliminary surveillance of the area and sounded the depths.

Weapons packed for submerging will be delivered by KGB officers to Murmansk by the time the regular navy intelligence ship leaves the base, will be loaded onto the ship, and be accompanied by KGB officers who will organize and conduct OPERATION SPLASH according to the confirmed plan.

At a time to be fixed by us, the intelligence ship will sail out to the area of the shoals of Stanton and after visual and instrumental inspection of the area, they will lower the load at the location stipulated and immediately leave the area.

The friends' fishing vessel will sail to the fixed point after about 2–3 hours and will find the marker (a buoy of the type ordinarily used by fishermen of all countries to indicate nets below; in this case of Japanese or Finnish make), will raise the submerged load, and deliver it to an Irish port where, according to Comrade O'Riordan's statement, a clandestine removal from the vessel and delivery to secret hiding places will be assured.

This method of conducting the operation prevents direct contact of our ship with the Irish vessel, and the latter's crew will not know what is in the load.

The captured German weapons including 2 machine guns, 70 automatic rifles, and 10 Walther pistols lubricated with oil of West German manufacture, and 41,600 cartridges will be packed into 14 bundles, each weighing 81.5 kilograms.

The packing materials and other items used in the operation will be acquired through the offices of the KGB residencies abroad.

The preparation of the captured weapons available to the KGB to be shipped to the friends will be conducted at a special KGB laboratory.

One of the bundles will be subjected to a comprehensive analysis at a special scientific research institute in order to determine any possible Soviet provenance of the load and the packing materials.

> No one will know of the nature of the load on the intelligence ship. Before the ship sets off, the load will be marked as experimental underwater exploration equipment that is to be submerged at a certain point in the Atlantic and then allowed to self-destruct.
>
> In order to work out the details of the organizational matters connected with OPERATION SPLASH, a meeting has been planned with Comrade O'Riordan outside the territory of the Soviet Union.

This was the last document in the folder, and the story of the weapons transfer breaks off. It is not known whether O'Riordan was finally able to extract even a few captured grenades and machine guns from the central committee for our "Irish friends." Quite possibly, his persistence was rewarded and the "friends" once again made themselves known with their trademark explosions and murders, causing the whole world to shudder.